The TransAtlantic reconsidered

MANCHESTER
1824

Manchester University Press

Key Studies in Diplomacy

Series Editors: J. Simon Rofe, Giles Scott-Smith

Emeritus Editor: Lorna Lloyd

This innovative series of books examines the procedures and processes of diplomacy, focusing on the interaction between states through their accredited representatives, that is, diplomats. Volumes in the series focus on factors affecting foreign policy and the ways in which it is implemented through the diplomatic system in both bilateral and multilateral contexts. They examine how diplomats can shape not just the presentation, but the substance of their state's foreign policy. Since the diplomatic system is global, each book aims to contribute to an understanding of the nature of diplomacy. Authors comprise both scholarly experts and former diplomats, able to emphasize the actual practice of diplomacy and to analyse it in a clear and accessible manner. The series offers essential primary reading for beginning practitioners and advanced level university students.

Previously published by Bloomsbury:

21st Century Diplomacy: A Practitioner's Guide by Kishan S. Rana
A Cornerstone of Modern Diplomacy: Britain and the Negotiation of the 1961 Vienna Convention on Diplomatic Relations by Kai Bruns
David Bruce and Diplomatic Practice: An American Ambassador in London, 1961–9 by John W. Young
Embassies in Armed Conflict by G.R. Berridge

Published by Manchester University Press:

Reasserting America in the 1970s edited by Hallvard Notaker, Giles Scott-Smith, and David J. Snyder
The diplomacy of decolonisation: America, Britain and the United Nations during the Congo crisis 1960–64 by Alanna O'Malley
Sport and diplomacy: Games within games edited by J. Simon Rofe

The TransAtlantic reconsidered

The Atlantic world in crisis

Edited by Charlotte A. Lerg, Susanne Lachenicht, and Michael Kimmage

Manchester University Press

Published by Manchester University Press
Altrincham Street, Manchester M1 7JA
www.manchesteruniversitypress.co.uk

British Library Cataloguing-in-Publication Data is available

ISBN 978 1 5261 1937 7   hardback
ISBN 978 1 5261 1939 1   paperback

First published by Manchester University Press in hardback 2018

This edition first published 2020

Typeset by Out of House Publishing

Contents

Contributors

Thomas Adam (PhD University of Leipzig 1998) is Professor of Transnational History at the University of Texas at Arlington. He is the author of *Intercultural Transfers and the Making of the Modern World, 1800–2000*, *Transnational Philanthropy: The Mond Family's Support for Public Institutions in Western Europe from 1890 to 1938*, and *Buying Respectability: Philanthropy and Urban Society in Transnational Perspective, 1840s to 1930s*. He is also the founding editor of the *Yearbook of Transnational History*.

Bernard Bailyn is Adams University Professor and James Duncan Phillips Professor of Early American History, emeritus, Harvard University. He founded and directed Harvard's International Seminar on the History of the Atlantic World, 1500–1825 (1995–2015).

Nicholas Canny is Emeritus Professor of History at the National University of Ireland, Galway. An expert on early modern history broadly defined, he edited the first volume of *The Oxford History of the British Empire* (1998) and, with Philip D. Morgan, *The Oxford Handbook of the Atlantic World, c.1450–c.1850* (2011). His major book is *Making Ireland British, 1580–1650* (Oxford, 2001). He remains an active publishing scholar on Atlantic History and is also completing a book entitled *Writing Ireland's History: From the Sixteenth Century to Yesterday* for Oxford University Press.

Giuliana Chamedes is an Assistant Professor of European International History at the University of Wisconsin, Madison. Her articles have appeared in the *Journal of Contemporary History*, the *Historical Journal*, and *French Culture, Politics, and Society*. Her first book, *Catholic Internationalism: The Vatican and the European Order, 1918–1958*, is under contract.

Konrad H. Jarausch is Lurcy Professor of European Civilization at the University of North Carolina in Chapel Hill as well as Senior Fellow of the Zentrum für Zeithistorische Forschung in Potsdam. He has written or edited more than forty books on German and European History, most recently *Out of Ashes: A New History of Europe in the Twentieth Century* as well as *Different Germans, Many Germanys* and *The Cold War: Historiography, Memory and Representation*.

Michael Kimmage is Professor of History at the Catholic University of America. He is the author of two books, *The Conservative Turn: Lionel Trilling, Whittaker Chambers and the Lessons of Anti-Communism* (Harvard, 2009) and *In History's Grip: Philip Roth's Newark Trilogy* (Stanford, 2012). He is the translator of Wolfgang Koeppen's *Journey to America* (Berghahn, 2012). His next book, *The Decline of the West: An American Story*, is forthcoming with Basic Books.

Susanne Lachenicht is Professor of Early Modern History at Bayreuth University, Germany. Her publications include *Information und Propaganda: Die Presse deutscher Jakobiner im Elsaß* (Munich, 2004), *Hugenotten in Europa und Nordamerika: Migration und Integration in der Frühen Neuzeit* (Frankfurt am Main, New York, and Chicago, 2010), *Religious Refugees in Europa, Asia and North America* (Hamburg, 2007), *Diaspora Identities: Exile, Nationalism and Cosmopolitanism in Past and Present* (Frankfurt am Main, New York, and Chicago, 2009), *Die Französische Revolution* (Darmstadt, 2012), *Europeans Engaging the Atlantic: Knowledge and Trade* (Frankfurt am Main and New York, 2014) and, as editor with Dagmar Freist, *Connecting Worlds and People: Early Modern Diasporas* (London, 2016).

Ariane Leendertz is a senior researcher at the Max Planck Institute for the Study of Societies in Cologne. Previously she has held positions at the Amerika Institut of the Ludwig-Maximilians Universität, Munich, and at the Department of History at the University of Tübingen. Moreover she was granted visiting fellowships at Princeton University, and by the German Historical Institute in Washington, DC. Her research focuses on German and US history of the twentieth century, the United States in the world, intellectual history, and the history of science. Recent publications include 'US-Außenminister John Kerry und der Krieg. Essay über biographische Kontinuität und amerikanische Politik' (Zeitgeschichte online 2016/17) and *Die neue Wirklichkeit: Semantische Neuvermessungen und Politik seit den 1970er-Jahren* (Frankfurt/Main, 2016, ed. with Wencke Meteling).

Charlotte A. Lerg teaches American Cultural History at Ludwig-Maximilians-Universität Munich, where she is also managing director of the Lasky Center for Transatlantic Studies. Furthermore, she has taught at the University of Münster and has held fellowships at the John W. Kluge Center (Library of Congress) and at the German-Historical-Institute in Washington, DC. Recent publications include: 'Off Campus: German Propaganda Professors in America 1914–1917' in *The Academic World in the Era of the Great War*, ed. Marie-Eve Chagnon and Tomás Irish (London, 2017) and (with Heike Bungert) *Transnationale Universitätsgeschichte* (Stuttgart, 2017).

Charles S. Maier is Leverett Saltonstall Professor of History at Harvard and served as director of CES from 1994 to 2001 and in the fall of 2006. He was distinguished fellow at the Woodrow Wilson Center for Scholars in Washington during the spring of 2011, taught at the École des Hautes Études en Sciences Sociales in spring 2007, and was a Humboldt Prize fellow in Berlin in 2003. Maier's 'Leviathan 2.0: Inventing Modern State' was published in autumn 2012 as a contribution to *A World Connecting*, vol. 5, edited by A. Iriye and J. Osterhammel. Other books include *Among Empires: American Ascendancy and its Predecessors* (2006); *Dissolution: The Crisis of Communism and the End of East Germany* (1997); *The Unmasterable Past: History, Holocaust, and German National Identity* (1988); *In Search of Stability: Explorations in Historical Political Economy* (1987); and *Recasting Bourgeois Europe* (1975, 1988). He directs the Weatherhead Center's Initiative in Global History (WIGH) with Sven Beckert.

Philip D. Morgan is Harry C. Black Professor at Johns Hopkins University. He has co-edited *Atlantic History: A Critical Appraisal* (Oxford, 2009) and *The Oxford Handbook of the Atlantic World* (Oxford, 2011). Other reflections on the Atlantic can be found in Neil Safier, 'Thinking Atlantically: A Conversation with Philip D. Morgan', *Atlantic Studies* 10:4 (2013), pp. 431–42; and 'A Concluding Comment', in Susanne Lachenicht, ed., *Europeans Engaging the Atlantic: Knowledge and Trade, 1500–1800* (Frankfurt/Main and Chicago: Campus Verlag, The University of Chicago Press, 2014), pp. 151–60.

Giles Scott-Smith holds the Ernst van der Beugel Chair in the Diplomatic History of Transatlantic Relations since WW II at Leiden University, and is the academic director of the Roosevelt Institute for American Studies. From 2013 to 2016 he was Chair of the Transatlantic Studies Association. His most recent publication (with Charlotte Lerg) is *Campaigning Culture and the Global Cold War: The Journals of the Congress for Cultural Freedom* (Palgrave, 2017).

Introduction

Susanne Lachenicht, Charlotte A. Lerg, and Michael Kimmage

The end of the transatlantic era?

In the eyes of political commentators the Atlantic Community is crumbling. With the election of a US president who, it appears, no longer feels committed to international cooperation – including the role of the United States in NATO – certain assumptions about transatlantic relationships are being called into question. In Europe, too, populist nationalism(s) further fracture(s) the union. Great Britain, in particular, is struggling to reposition itself along European, Atlantic, and global parameters. Established beliefs about shared values and common goals seem to fade. The alarm and disbelief this rupture causes among numerous observers on both sides of the Atlantic, and the fact that so few of them saw it coming, reminds us of how powerful the idea of the Atlantic World had become. Arguably, already with the end of the Cold War, with the global war on terror and with the redirection of US foreign policies towards the Pacific under President Barack Obama, the end of a transatlantic era beckoned (e.g. chapters 2, 5, and 9 in this volume). All these developments 'marked a watershed in transatlantic relations'.[1] Some scholars have since argued for 'a new and constructive Transatlantic Bargain for the twenty-first-century'.[2]

Against this background and as we consign the twentieth century to history (chapter 2),[3] while major shifts ripple through global politics, how do we as academics assess the Atlantic World? It is time to critically reconsider the concept of the Atlantic World and the field of Transatlantic Studies.

The birth of a concept

Walter Lippmann coined the concept of the Atlantic World in 1917. He envisioned states and societies on both sides of this ocean sharing a common history and common values, such as freedom and democracy. As he wrote in *The New Republic* (February

1917:60) the United States of America had to 'fight for … the common interest of the western world, for the integrity of the Atlantic Powers'. During the Great War, Germany obviously did not belong to this early alliance of the 'West'.[4] As much as the United States, Germany was promoting a specific pathway to 'modernity' – fighting the war for a specific notion of *Kultur* – which clearly opposed American ideologies and ways of life. As G. Scott-Smith explains in his contribution to this volume, Lippmann was to revive and strengthen the narrative of the Atlantic Community to secure American national interest following the German *blitzkrieg* and continental dominance in 1940/1. He did so with American security interests in mind but at the same time his views were firmly grounded in an ideological framework.[5]

The Cold War and its legacies

The Cold War restructured the Atlantic World. A powerful transatlantic narrative came into focus, and this time it included West Germany.[6] It would shape political relations, economies, societies, and cultures far beyond the Atlantic World itself. The key narrative cast the 'Democratic Revolutions' (R. R. Palmer) of the late eighteenth century as the beginning of an Atlantic World reigned by freedom and democracy. Such a powerful presumed legacy came with the perceived need to preserve, protect, and eventually spread it in defence against any kind of totalitarianism, directed particularly against communism.[7] This narrative (re-)created, corroborated, and historicized the 'West', a concept soon established in intellectual discourse, which has since been modified, mediated, and repeatedly challenged.[8] Yet it remains a powerful trope for political and popular debate.

Out of this historical context and political undercurrent grew a number of related research fields: Transatlantic Relations, European–American Relations, and Atlantic History. The heyday of the traditional approach to transatlantic relations was as such simultaneous with the Cold War; this research field thus had close connections to a normative brand of political science and policy-making that spanned the public and private sectors. Post-Second World War 'Atlanticisim' or transatlantic relations were meant to 'privilege relations between the United States and Europe within the broader foreign policy frameworks of both sides, emphasizing that Europe and the U.S. share a host of common interests and values, and that they are historically and culturally connected in a way that makes them ideal partners', as Ariane Leendertz writes in her contribution to this volume.

Changing paradigms

Methodologically the study of transatlantic relations traditionally focused on the political and diplomatic history of the twentieth century. However, with the dawn of the twenty-first century the research area transformed into the more encompassing field of Transatlantic Studies. The latter include political theory as well as a new emphasis on cultural, social, and transnational history.[9] Furthermore, in recent years scholars have uncovered the global nature of the Cold War, altering the analytical framework by incorporating new angles of vision, from post-colonialism to populist nationalism.[10]

As the field has been acquiring a wider geographic and theoretical purview, it is beginning to change. Now, the Atlantic World comes across as both a powerful political discourse and a heuristic method that brings together the Humanities, the Social and Political Sciences, Economics, and Cultural Theory. Through these changes, Transatlantic Studies as updated *area studies* are experiencing a revival and shed new light on diplomatic, cultural, and intellectual history – far beyond the research that the Transatlantic Studies Association traditionally promotes on its website. In recent years, however, some TSA members have opted for a more open approach with promising new perspectives.[11]

Can these new Transatlantic Studies further historicize and theorize the underlying powerful historical narrative and its products, the narrative of transatlantic relations in terms of diplomacy, economies, education, the exchange and transfer of ideas, goods, and people that more often than not solely includes the United States, Canada, Europe, and Britain?

Atlantic History

Atlantic History – as the contributions by Bernard Bailyn, Nicholas Canny, Philip D. Morgan, and Thomas Adam in this volume show – have as much as Transatlantic Studies evolved since the Cold War era. As Bailyn writes: the 'intersection of academic proliferation and developments in world affairs created a general sense of a regional world' (p. 13). From its beginnings, however, as Bailyn and Canny both point out, Atlantic History has challenged the national and imperial approach to the history of the Atlantic World and the master narrative that posits freedom and democracy as the foundational assumptions of a coherent 'West'.

The traditional focus on the early modern period in Atlantic History accelerated a critical reassessment of the foundational narrative early on. Key steps included for example extending the realm of the 'Atlantic' beyond the Northern Hemisphere and taking seriously the history of colonial conquest.[12] The making of the Atlantic World between the fifteenth and the eighteenth centuries was 'based on slavery rather than on liberty and [was] one [world] that encompassed Africa as well as Europe and the Americas' (Canny, p. 37). Furthermore, Atlantic History, especially in Bernard Bailyn's words, is hostile to determinism and against conceptualizing the Atlantic World as a closed space. Its practitioners conceptualize the Atlantic World as an open space. Research on the Atlantic World has grown to include intercultural, interethnic, and transnational complexities.[13] The scope has also geographically and chronologically widened to include intercontinental, hemispheric as well as South–South entanglements,[14] reaching far into the nineteenth century and occasionally into the late medieval period.[15]

Conceptualizing the TransAtlantic

With a series of crisis experiences in transatlantic relations from the 1970s onward,[16] as well as challenges posed by the changing agendas in Atlantic History and the need to tackle the ideological burden of the Cold War, the discourse on the Atlantic World saw numerous transformations. The Atlantic World is no longer seen as the teleological function of a long history of freedom and democracy. Borrowing from Sociology, International Relations (Human) Geography, Cultural Studies, and Anthropology new approaches are opening up new vistas.

As historians of the Atlantic World now argue, the latter has 'never been wholly discrete, self-enclosed or isolated from the rest of the globe'.[17] Traditionally, studies of transatlantic relations in the nineteenth and twentieth centuries posited empires and nation states at their core. Historians of the early-modern period were among the first to productively apply approaches of transnational history, which more recently we are also seeing in Transatlantic Studies. More recent studies from both fields highlight the degree to which relations between the 'Old' and the 'New World' have always crossed the borders between empires and nation states, connecting and fostering exchange between nations on the one hand and leading to all manners of conflict on the other; in addition, recent scholarship has emphasized the structural power of networks in the Atlantic World.[18] As historians have shifted their attention towards transnational brokers with mobile biographies, intellectual milieus, protest movements, or humanitarian issues that crossed borders, the old framework has expanded considerably.[19] Thus, the TransAtlantic has to be conceptualized as hybrid, and entangled.[20] Arguably, the once highly problematic and ideologically charged construct of the Atlantic World has successfully made the transition from being a politically motivated heuristic concept, to offering a more up-to-date framework for inquiry. Transnational approaches and notions of entanglement promise innovative new insights into the field, whether we conceive of the TransAtlantic as a sphere of intellectual discourse, as a common ground of transfer and exchange, or as a potential field of discord.

Moreover, in emphasizing this transnational framework at a time of growing nationalist isolation the volume highlights that political ideology and structural configurations do not necessarily converge. Unlike earlier uses of the transnational approach, more recent studies – not few of them on transatlantic phenomena – have shown that transnationalism is not (necessarily) about open borders and free proliferation of people, ideas, and goods in a somewhat post-national sphere. Instead, the concept refers to discourses, mentalities, and social currents like populism, racism, and, indeed, even nationalism itself that transcend national contexts. Moreover transnationalism allows us to focus on systems of governances not tied to state actors, which opens up new ways of conceptualizing global spaces – including the Atlantic.

The concept of this volume

The TransAtlantic reconsidered brings together established experts from Atlantic History and Transatlantic Studies – two fields that are closely connected in their historical and disciplinary development as well as with regard to the geographical area of their interest. However, generally there is little to no dialogue as questions of methodology and boundaries of periodization tend to separate them. The scholars represented in this volume have helped to shape, re-shape, and challenge the narrative(s) of the Atlantic World and can thus (re-)evaluate its conceptual basis in view of historiographical developments and contemporary challenges. The chapters of this volume thus document and reflect on the changes within Transatlantic Studies during the last decades. New perspectives on research reconceptualize how we think about the Atlantic World. At a time when many political observers perceive a crisis in transatlantic relations, critical evaluation of past narratives and frameworks will provide an academic foundation to move forward.

The first part of this volume deals with the current state of research in Atlantic History *and* Transatlantic Studies. It opens with an interview with Bernard Bailyn, founder of the Harvard Atlantic History Seminar which has been *the* center for Atlantic History for the past two decades. Bailyn understands the Atlantic World as a 'great regional entity linking four continents and stretching over three centuries'. According to Bailyn, 'this region's history helped lay the foundations of the modern world'.

We continue with Charles Maier's plea for global history. He uses the lens of political passion to present a transatlantic comparison and particularly emphasizes as much as Canny and Morgan later in this volume that the Atlantic World has never been as unified as some of the historiographies have us believe. Maier identifies four major fields that have given rise to conflict and political passion: religious authority, self-government, defining the (national) community, and the distribution of wealth and goods. However, as the analysis zooms in on Europe and the United States it becomes evident that these transnational themes may and should also be explored from a global perspective. European history has always had a global dimension, from colonialism to the divisions of the Cold War.

Nicholas Canny writes on the evolution of Atlantic History from the Cold War era onward. From the 1960s historians such as Jack P. Greene and Edmund S. Morgan challenged Robert Palmer's Liberal-consensus narrative of the Democratic Revolutions in the Atlantic World. With more research on the Black Atlantic it became clear that the rise of an Atlantic Community had heavily relied on slavery and violence. Economic history further strengthened insights into how the Atlantic empires evolved out of the exploitation of Africans and indigenous peoples in the Americas. Moreover, from the mid-1990s the concept of multiple Atlantics made Atlantic History more transnational in its scope.[21]

Building on Bailyn and Canny, Philip D. Morgan shows in his chapter how, in recent years, studies on the early-modern Atlantic World have become global and multi-faceted, giving rise to comparative and entangled histories. Atlantic History tackles themes that are prevalent in twenty-first-century history at large: ecology, port towns and cities, multinational and religious societies, networks, scientific revolutions, families and the individual.

The second part of the volume assesses the challenges faced by scholars of transatlantic relations and focuses on the late nineteenth century and twentieth century. The contributors re-develop theoretical parameters like governances, religion, and policy discourse, while others are concerned with practical dimensions such as research cooperation and teaching.

Defining the transatlantic era as a specific moment in twentieth-century history provides the starting point for Giles Scott-Smith in his analysis of the Transnational Transatlantic from a Foucauldian perspective. He posits the 'overflow of the state's role into new spaces of politics' as a key development in this period: the Cold War Atlantic Community was much more than a structure described by the rationalist theory of political scientists, he argues. With the Anglo-American bond at its core, it was indeed a transnational public sphere that spanned the Atlantic. Scott-Smith suggests a combination of the history of mentalities and (new) governmentality.

Konrad Jarausch analyses the transatlantic cooperation of historians dealing with National Socialism, the Holocaust, and the Second World War. He examines historiography as well as infrastructure, like the building of new institutions and the founding of periodicals. He also traces the way sources were handled and made accessible, from the collection of data for the Nuremberg Trials to digitization projects of the recent decade. How did this affect the writing of history both in Central Europe and in the Anglo-American world? He points out that the historical writing which emerged in this particular framework was at once collaborative, implicitly comparative, and decidedly distinctive.

In her contribution, Ariane Leendertz investigates changing perceptions of transatlantic relations in the United States since the late 1960s. Looking into the complex relationships of decision-making at the political level and how they are being informed by changing epistemics, discourses, and perceptions, she concludes that the United States were emerging from a moment of crisis (war in Vietnam, increasing economic competition with Europe, and the loss of credibility in Europe) with a growing awareness of global interdependencies. This resulted in a rather pessimistic approach to transatlantic relations that have since the 1970s informed US politics towards Europe.

Giuliana Chamedes identifies two distinct visions that characterized the ideological construct of the 'Atlantic order' for the post-war world: a liberal-democratic American and British narrative that helped the United States strengthen its political and economic ties with Europe so as to protect a shared democratic worldview; and another vision, advanced by the Holy See, a handful of European Christian Democratic leaders, and certain key American Catholic opinion-makers, which did not have 'democracy' as its endgame. Rather, it proposed to build a peaceful transnational post-war order through the reconstitution of the 'Christian West', an early-modern concept of the 'Old and the New World' which was defined as an imagined community built on a shared commitment to Christian principles. This move enabled them to embrace the 'Atlantic Community', all the while remaining wedded to a conservative, anti-liberal, and anti-communist worldview.

Teaching transnational history in an environment still formed by a national history agenda poses many challenges, as Thomas Adam contemplates in his chapter. He develops an alternative approach to defining Atlantic History. He explains how we ought to think of the Atlantic no longer merely as a geographical space but conceive of it through the methodological approach of intercultural transfer. According to this premise the Atlantic World becomes 'a space created through human activity', namely the transfer and exchange of people and goods. It also means the modification, re-interpretation and sometimes rejections of cultural practices, ideas, and concepts in the process. Transatlantic relations in this context are treated as one example of transnational interaction. This framework not only allows for an interdisciplinary but also an inter-epochal exploration of the field.

Using a combination of methodological building blocks from cultural and intellectual history the contributors historicize the Atlantic and transatlantic discourse itself: in the realm of policy-making (Leendertz); mentality and identity (Scott-Smith and Chamedes); or the writing and teaching of history (Jarausch, Canny, and Adam). A number of the authors in this book reflect critically on the reasons for framing their questions in a transatlantic context (Scott-Smith, Leendertz, Chamedes, Jarausch). Others offer alternative ways to relate the transatlantic to a wider setting (Bailyn, Canny, Morgan, Maier), either by using the methodology developed along transatlantic examples for other contexts or by positing transatlantic relations as a stepping-stone to broaden the view.

The contributions of this volume also invite us to rethink spatial concepts and their geopolitical and ideological underpinnings which result in the framing of specific areas. (Trans-)Area studies are always a product of geopolitical and economic interest.[22] They come with powerful historical narratives. How those intertwine and shape the world is a subject for and of scholarly analysis. It is vital for Transatlantic Studies and Atlantic History alike to further reflect upon their historical and ideological baggage. A 'global' perspective can still be a 'colonial perspective' or a perspective marked by 'coloniality', as Walter Mignolo might put it.[23] Furthermore, future research can benefit from incorporating such concepts as South–South relations, the Global South, or the Western Hemisphere. As the dialogue between political realities and scholarly interpretations continues, we should reflect upon the 'transnational', the 'global', and 'globalization' as historical developments. Structurally they have grown out of the process of European expansion, colonialism, and imperialism between the fifteenth and the nineteenth centuries. Their narratives and historiographies, however, were shaped by the geopolitical context of the twentieth century, an amalgam of ideology and idealism which Walter Lippmann identified as the Atlantic World. In claiming a transnational and global perspective, in developing new approaches coupled with critical re-evaluations *The TransAtlantic reconsidered* engages with the Cold War shadow in the history of the Atlantic World and provides critical thinking for assessing the transatlantic crisis or – in a less pessimistic perspective – for reconfiguring transatlantic relations.

Acknowledgements

We wish to thank Volker Depkat and Michael Hochgeschwender for a critical reading of this Introduction.

Notes

1 S. Duke, 'Foreword: Time for a New Transatlantic Bargain?', in C. Wallin and D. Silander (eds), *Democracy and Culture in the Transatlantic World: Third Interdisciplinary Conference* (Växjö: Växjö University Press, 2004), pp. 1–13, here p. 1.

2 *Ibid*. See also T. Jäger, A. Höse, and K. Oppermann (eds), *Transatlantische Beziehungen: Sicherheit – Wirtschaft – Öffentlichkeit* (Wiesbaden: VS Verlag für Sozialwissenschaften, 2005).

3 C. S. Maier, 'Consigning the Twentieth Century to History: Alternative Narratives for the Modern Era', *American Historical Review*, 105.3 (2000), pp. 807–31.

4 J. Trautsch, 'The Invention of "the West"', *Bulletin of the German Historical Institute Washington*, 53 (2013), pp. 89–102.

5 *Ibid*., pp. 94–7.

6 *Ibid*., pp. 97, 99–101.

7 L. Hartz, *The Liberal Tradition in America: An Interpretation of American Political Thought since the Revolution* (New York: Harcourt Brace and Co., 1955).

8 E.g. V. Depkat and J. Martschukat, 'Introduction: Religion and Politics in Europe and the United States', in V. Depkat and J. Martschukat (eds), *Religion and Politics in Europe and the United States: Transnational Historical Approaches* (Baltimore: Johns Hopkins University Press, 2013), pp. 2–3.

9 E.g. G.-F. Budde, *Transnationale Geschichte Themen, Tendenzen und Theorien* (Göttingen: Vandenhoeck and Ruprecht, 2006); L. van Dongen, S. Roulin, and G. Scott-Smith (eds), *Transnational Anti-Communism and the Cold War: Agents, Activities and Networks* (Basingstoke: Palgrave Macmillan, 2014).

10 K. B. Bell, 'Developing a Sense of Community: U.S. Cultural Diplomacy and the Place of Africa during the Early Cold War Period 1953–64', in A. Jalloh and T. Falola (eds), *The United States and West Africa: Interactions and Relations* (Rochester: University of Rochester Press, 2008), pp. 125–46; J. Franco, *The Decline and Fall of the Lettered City: Latin America in the Cold War* (Cambridge, MA: Harvard University Press, 2009); A. Rubin, *Archives of Authority: Empire, Culture, and the Cold War* (Princeton: Princeton University Press, 2012); G. Scott-Smith and C. Lerg, *Campaigning Culture and the Global Cold War* (London: Palgrave Macmillan, 2017); O. A. Westad, *The Global Cold War: Third World Interventions and the Making of Our Times* (Cambridge: Cambridge University Press, 2005); H. L. Y. Zheng and M. Szonyi, *The Cold War in Asia: The Battle for Hearts and Minds* (Leiden: Brill, 2010).

11 See the TSA website: www.transatlanticstudies.com/. For different views on the concept of Transatlantic Studies see e.g. W. Kaufman and H. Slettedahl Macpherson (eds), *Transatlantic Studies* (Lanham, New York, and Oxford: University Press of America, 2000); M. Klepper and J. C. Schöpp (eds), *Transatlantic Modernism* (Heidelberg: Winter, 2001); F. Jaeger (ed.), *Kulturwissenschaftliche Perspektiven in der Nordamerika-Forschung* (Tübingen: Stauffenburg, 2001); S. Manning and A. Taylor (eds), *Transatlantic Literary Studies: A Reader* (Edinburgh: Edinburgh University Press, 2012); E. T. Bannet and S. Manning (eds), *Transatlantic Literary Studies, 1660–1830* (Cambridge: Cambridge University Press, 2012).

12 See also B. Bailyn, *Atlantic History: Concept and Contours* (Cambridge, MA: Harvard University Press, 2005); J. P. Greene and P. D. Morgan, 'Introduction: The Present State of Atlantic History', in J. P. Greene and P. D. Morgan (eds), *Atlantic History:*

A Critical Appraisal (New York: Oxford University Press, 2009), pp. 3–33; P. D. Morgan, 'A Comment', in S. Lachenicht (ed.), *Europeans Engaging the Atlantic: Knowledge and Trade* (Frankfurt/Main, New York, and Chicago: Campus and the University of Chicago Press, 2014), pp. 151–60.

13 E.g. K. Flint, *The Transatlantic Indian, 1776–1930* (Princeton and Oxford: Princeton University Press, 2009); W. Raussert and R. Isensee (eds), *Transcultural Visions of Identities in Images and Texts* (Heidelberg: Winter, 2008).

14 E.g. H. Slettedahl Macpherson, W. Kaufman (eds), *New Perspectives in Transatlantic Studies* (Lanham, New York, and Oxford: University Press of America, 2002); J. L. Venegas, *Transatlantic Correspondence: Modernity, Epistolarity, and Literature in Spain and Spanish America, 1898–1992* (Columbus: The Ohio State University Press, 2014); C. R. Rodriguez, D. Tsikata, A. A. Ampofo (eds), *Transatlantic Feminisms: Women and Gender Studies and the Diaspora* (Lanham, Boulder, New York, and London: Lexington, 2015); M. Heide and G. Pisarz-Ramirez (eds), *Hemispheric Encounters: The Early United States in a Transnational Perspective* (Frankfurt/Main and New York: Lang, 2016).

15 E.g. U. J. Hebel, K. Ortseifen (eds), *Transatlantic Encounters: Studies in European-American Relations. Presented to Winfried Herget* (Trier: Wissenschaftlicher Verlag, 1995); K. Hutchings and J. M. Wright (eds), *Transatlantic Literary Exchanges 1790–1870: Gender, Race and Nation* (Farnham: Ashgate, 2011).

16 E.g. E. Hochleitner (ed.), *Europa und Amerika: eine Beziehung im Wandel* (Maria Enzersdorf: Österreichisches Institut für Europäische Sicherheitspolitik, 2003).

17 B. Bailyn, 'Introduction', in B. Bailyn and P. L. Denault (eds), *Soundings in Atlantic History: Latent Structures and Intellectual Currents, 1500–1830* (Cambridge, MA: Harvard University Press, 2009), pp. 3–4. See also S. G. Reinhardt and D. Reinhartz (eds), *Transatlantic History* (Arlington: Texas A & M University Press, 2006).

18 E.g. V. Depkat, 'Remembering War the Transnational Way: The U.S.-American Memory of World War I', in U. J. Hebel (ed.), *Transnational American Memory* (Berlin: de Gruyter, 2009), pp. 185–213; T. Adam, *Intercultural Transfers and the Making of the Modern World, 1800–2000* (New York: Palgrave Macmillan, 2012); van Dongen *et al.*, *Transnational Anti-Communism and the Cold War*, pp. 7–11.

19 H. Bungert, 'Migration und Internationale Beziehungen im Kaiserreich: Wilhelm II, das Auswärtige Amt und ihr Interesse an den Deutschamerikanern', *Zeitschrift für Geschichtswissenschaft*, 63:5 (2015), pp. 413–34; L. Butler, *Critical Americans: Victorian Intellectuals and Transatlantic Liberal Reform* (Chapel Hill: University of North Carolina Press, 2009); E. Fuchs, 'Transnational Perspectives in Higher Education', *Comparativ* 22:1 (2012), pp. 7–14; David G. Haglund, 'That Other Transatlantic "Great Rapprochement": France, the United States, and Theodore Roosevelt', in H. Krabbendam and J. M. Thompson (eds), *America's Transatlantic Turn: Theodore Roosevelt and the 'Discovery' of Europe* (London: Palgrave Macmillan, 2012), pp. 103–19; M. Honeck, M. Klimke, and A. Kuhlmann, *Germany and the Black Diaspora: Points of Contact, 1250–1914* (New York: Berghahn Books, 2013); A. Iriye, 'Culture and Power: International Relations and Intercultural Relations', *Diplomatic History*, 10 (1979), pp. 115–28; C. Mauch, 'Oceans Apart: Paradigms in German-American History and Historiography', in T. Adam (ed.), *Traveling between Worlds: German-American Encounters* (Arlington: Texas A & M University Press,

2006), pp. 3–13; N. Renvert, 'Von Soft-Power zu Smart-Power: Zur Rolle der Mittler in den Transatlantischen Beziehungen', *Aus Politik und Zeitgeschichte (APUZ)* 61:51/ 52 (2011), pp. 30–5; D. T. Rodgers, *Atlantic Crossings* (Cambridge, MA: Harvard University Press, 2009); A. J. Williams, *France, Britain and the United States in the Twentieth Century 1900–1940: A Reappraisal* (London: Palgrave Macmillan, 2014).
20 See e.g. M. Heide and G. Pisarz-Ramirez (eds), *Hemispheric Encounters: The Early United States in a Transnational Perspective* (Frankfurt/Main, New York: Lang, 2016), pp. 1–31.
21 Bailyn, *Atlantic History*.
22 For a discussion of whether the Atlantic World is an area or a trans-area see S. Lachenicht, 'Transregions from Early Colonization to Post-Cold War: Multiple Atlantics', in *Handbook of Transregional Studies* (London: Routledge, forthcoming 2018).
23 E.g. W. D. Mignolo, *The Idea of Latin America* (Malden, MA and Oxford: Blackwell, 2005), pp. x–xi; S. Lachenicht, 'How the Americas became "the Americas"', in V. Depkat, H. Paul, and B. Waldschmidt-Nelson (eds), *Cultural Mobility and Knowledge Formation in the Americas* (Heidelberg: Winter, forthcoming 2018).

References

Adam, T. *Intercultural Transfers and the Making of the Modern World, 1800–2000* (New York: Palgrave Macmillan, 2012).

Bailyn, B. *Atlantic History: Concept and Contours* (Cambridge, MA: Harvard University Press, 2005).

Bailyn, B. 'Introduction', in B. Bailyn and P. L. Denault (eds), *Soundings in Atlantic History: Latent Structures and Intellectual Currents, 1500–1830* (Cambridge, MA: Harvard University Press, 2009), pp. 1–43.

Bannet, E. T. and S. Manning (eds), *Transatlantic Literary Studies, 1660–1830* (Cambridge: Cambridge University Press, 2012).

Bell, K. B. 'Developing a Sense of Community: U.S. Cultural Diplomacy and the Place of Africa during the Early Cold War Period 1953–64', in A. Jalloh and T. Falola (eds), *The United States and West Africa: Interactions and Relations* (Rochester: University of Rochester Press, 2008), pp. 125–46.

Budde, G.-F. *Transnationale Geschichte Themen, Tendenzen und Theorien* (Göttingen: Vandenhoeck and Ruprecht, 2006).

Bungert, H. 'Migration und Internationale Beziehungen Im Kaiserreich: Wilhelm II. Das Auswärtige Amt und ihr Interesse an den Deutschamerikanern', *Zeitschrift für Geschichtswissenschaft*, 63:5 (2015), pp. 413–34.

Butler, L. *Critical Americans: Victorian Intellectuals and Transatlantic Liberal Reform* (Chapel Hill: University of North Carolina Press, 2009).

Depkat, V. 'Remembering War the Transnational Way: The U.S.-American Memory of World War I', in U. J. Hebel (ed.), *Transnational American Memory* (Berlin: de Gruyter, 2009), pp. 185–213.

Depkat, V. and J. Martschukat. 'Introduction: Religion and Politics in Europe and the United States', in V. Depkat and J. Martschukat (eds), *Religion and Politics in Europe and the United States: Transnational Historical Approaches* (Baltimore: Johns Hopkins University Press, 2013), pp. 1–11.

van Dongen, L., S. Roulin, and G. Scott-Smith (eds), *Transnational Anti-Communism and the Cold War: Agents, Activities and Networks* (Basingstoke: Palgrave Macmillan, 2014).

Duke, S. 'Foreword: Time for a New Transatlantic Bargain?', in C. Wallin and D. Silander (eds), *Democracy and Culture in the Transatlantic World: Third Interdisciplinary Conference* (Växjö: Växjö University Press, 2004), pp. 1–13.

Flint, K. *The Transatlantic Indian: 1776–1930* (Princeton and Oxford: Princeton University Press, 2009).

Franco, J. *The Decline and Fall of the Lettered City: Latin America in the Cold War* (Cambridge, MA: Harvard University Press, 2009).

Fuchs, E. 'Transnational Perspectives in Higher Education', *Comparativ*, 22:1 (2012), pp. 7–14.

Greene, J. P. and P. D. Morgan. 'Introduction: The Present State of Atlantic History', in J. P. Greene and P. D. Morgan (eds), *Atlantic History: A Critical Appraisal* (New York: Oxford University Press, 2009), pp. 3–33.

Haglund, D. G. 'That Other Transatlantic "Great Rapprochement": France, the United States, and Theodore Roosevelt', in H. Krabbendam and J. M. Thompson (eds), *America's Transatlantic Turn: Theodore Roosevelt and the 'Discovery' of Europe* (London: Palgrave Macmillan, 2012), pp. 103–19.

Hartz, L. *The Liberal Tradition in America: An Interpretation of American Political Thought since the Revolution* (New York: Harcourt Brace and Co., 1955).

Hebel, U. J. and K. Ortseifen (eds), *Transatlantic Encounters: Studies in European-American Relations. Presented to Winfried Herget* (Trier: Wissenschaftlicher Verlag, 1995).

Heide, M. and G. Pisarz-Ramirez (eds), *Hemispheric Encounters: The Early United States in a Transnational Perspective* (Frankfurt/Main and New York: Lang, 2016).

Hochleitner, E. (ed.), *Europa und Amerika: eine Beziehung im Wandel* (Maria Enzersdorf: Österreichisches Institut für Europäische Sicherheitspolitik, 2003).

Honeck, M., M. Klimke, and A. Kuhlmann. *Germany and the Black Diaspora: Points of Contact, 1250–1914* (New York: Berghahn Books, 2013).

Hutchings, K. and J. M. Wright (eds), *Transatlantic Literary Exchanges 1790–1870: Gender, Race and Nation* (Farnham: Ashgate, 2011).

Iriye, A. 'Culture and Power: International Relations and Intercultural Relations', *Diplomatic History*, 10 (1979), pp. 115–28.

Jaeger, F. (ed.), *Kulturwissenschaftliche Perspektiven in der Nordamerika-Forschung* (Tübingen: Stauffenburg, 2001).

Jäger, T., A. Höse, and K. Oppermann (eds), *Transatlantische Beziehungen: Sicherheit – Wirtschaft – Öffentlichkeit* (Wiesbaden: VS Verlag für Sozialwissenschaften, 2005).

Kaufman, W. and H. Slettedahl Macpherson (eds), *Transatlantic Studies* (Lanham, New York, and Oxford: University Press of America, 2000).

Klepper, M. and J. C. Schöpp (eds), *Transatlantic Modernism* (Heidelberg: Winter, 2001).

Lachenicht, S. 'How the Americas became "the Americas"', in V. Depkat, H. Paul, and B. Waldschmidt-Nelson (eds), *Cultural Mobility and Knowledge Formation in the Americas* (Heidelberg: Winter, forthcoming 2018).

Lachenicht, S. 'Transregions from Early Colonization to Post-Cold War: Multiple Atlantics', in *Handbook of Transregional Studies* (London: Routledge, forthcoming 2018).

Maier, C. S. 'Consigning the Twentieth Century to History: Alternative Narratives for the Modern Era', *American Historical Review*, 105:3 (2000), pp. 807–31.

Manning, S. and A. Taylor (eds), *Transatlantic Literary Studies: A Reader* (Edinburgh: Edinburgh University Press, 2012).

Mauch, C. 'Oceans Apart: Paradigms in German-American History and Historiography', in T. Adam (ed.), *Traveling between Worlds: German-American Encounters* (Arlington: Texas A & M University Press, 2006), pp. 3–19.

Mignolo, W. D. *The Idea of Latin America* (Malden, MA and Oxford: Blackwell, 2005).

Morgan, P. D. 'A Comment', in S. Lachenicht (ed.), *Europeans Engaging the Atlantic: Knowledge and Trade* (Frankfurt/Main, New York, and Chicago: Campus and University of Chicago Press, 2014), pp. 151–60.

Raussert, W. and R. Isensee (eds), *Transcultural Visions of Identities in Images and Texts* (Heidelberg: Winter, 2008).

Reinhardt, S. G. and D. Reinhartz (eds), *Transatlantic History* (Arlington: Texas A & M University Press, 2006).

Renvert, N. 'Von Soft-Power zu Smart-Power: Zur Rolle der Mittler in den Transatlantischen Beziehungen', *Aus Politik und Zeitgeschichte (APUZ)*, 61:51/52 (2011), pp. 30–5.

Rodgers, D. T. *Atlantic Crossings* (Cambridge, MA: Harvard University Press, 2009).

Rodriguez, C. R., D. Tsikata, and A. Adomako Ampofo (eds), *Transatlantic Feminisms: Women and Gender Studies and the Diaspora* (Lanham, Boulder, New York, and London: Lexington, 2015).

Rubin, A. *Archives of Authority: Empire, Culture, and the Cold War* (Princeton: Princeton University Press, 2012).

Scott-Smith, G. and C. Lerg. *Campaigning Culture and the Global Cold War* (London: Palgrave Macmillan, 2017).

Slettedahl Macpherson, H. and W. Kaufman (eds), *New Perspectives in Transatlantic Studies* (Lanham, New York, and Oxford: University Press of America, 2002).

Trautsch, J. 'The Invention of "the West"', *Bulletin of the German Historical Institute Washington*, 53 (2013), pp. 89–102.

Venegas, J. L. *Transatlantic Correspondence: Modernity, Epistolarity, and Literature in Spain and Spanish America, 1898–1992* (Columbus: The Ohio State University Press, 2014).

Westad, O. A. *The Global Cold War: Third World Interventions and the Making of Our Times* (Cambridge: Cambridge University Press, 2005).

Williams, A. J. *France, Britain and the United States in the Twentieth Century 1900–1940: A Reappraisal* (London: Palgrave Macmillan, 2014).

Zheng, H. L. Y. and M. Szonyi. *The Cold War in Asia: The Battle for Hearts and Minds* (Leiden: Brill, 2010).

1

An interview with Bernard Bailyn

Susanne Lachenicht: What was Atlantic History about when you started the Harvard Atlantic History Seminar in 1995?

Bernard Bailyn: A general and at first vague awareness of Atlantic History as a distinct subject in itself had emerged after the Second World War from the convergence of developments at two levels, which I have sketched separately in my book *Atlantic History: Concept and Contours*: on the one hand, major developments in geopolitics centred on the Atlantic area, from the wartime Atlantic alliance to the Cold War and NATO; and on the other hand the dynamics within historical scholarship, that is, the great post-war proliferation of research and publication related to the region of the Atlantic generally. This intersection of academic proliferation and developments in world affairs created a general sense of a regional world, but the explosion of historical scholarship in this area had no governing concept. The books and articles that appeared were 'Atlantic' studies only in the sense that the contents related to things that happened within or around the geographical area of the Atlantic. There was no sense of the Atlantic region as a historical whole that could be defined and its history traced as a phenomenon in itself.

But the possibility of viewing the history of the Atlantic World in that way was latent from the start. I wrote about it first over sixty years ago, in my paper 'Communities and Trade: The Atlantic in the 17th Century', in the *Journal of Economic History* 13 (1953). Two years later I responded strongly to the first substantial effort to develop a truly regional concept sketched by Robert Palmer and Jacques Godechot in their essay 'Le Problème de L'Atlantique' presented to the *International History Congress* in 1955. I was shocked to find that their effort at conceptualization was ridiculed by the historians present at the Congress as pretentious, too 'philosophical', a mere response to Soviet policy, too vague and 'arbitrary'. But in fact the notion behind it was sound and important. Their essay suggested the concept of the Atlantic World as a coherent whole, with its own history involving intersecting aspects of Spanish, British, African, Dutch,

French, Portuguese, and Native American history. It offered a basic reference point for specific local studies, a way of thinking about events hitherto
explained in terms of local dynamics, as one historian has written, now 'revealed
to be above-water fragments of ... submarine unities'. I had 'Le Problème de
L'Atlantique' and other, lesser indications in mind when the Atlantic History
Seminar was established in 1995.

How revealing and useful the present concept of 'Atlantic History' as a
coherent historical region has been is testified to by the response to the Seminar
and by the publications that emerged as it developed. In all, 366 young historians
from Europe, Latin America, Africa, the UK and the United States participated
in the annual ten-day summer meetings, and many others contributed to the
Seminar's eighteen one-day conferences. The participants in the annual Seminar
meetings brought with them their own research-in-progress for the consideration of others from different academic backgrounds at work on similar themes
but drawing on different documentation and different approaches to history.
(Summaries of all of the 368 papers submitted, and of the eighty-two studies
presented at the Seminar's Tenth Anniversary Conference (2005), are available
on the Seminar's website, www.fas.harvard.edu/~atlantic/, *The Proceedings of the
Tenth Anniversary Conference of the Atlantic History Seminar*, as well as in a
comprehensive history of the Seminar, available in the Harvard College Library.)

The number of publications identified with Atlantic History after 1995 was
remarkable. Exploratory essays came first. No fewer than twenty-nine volumes
of collected essays on Atlantic History in three languages exploring aspects of
the subject were published between 2002 and 2010 (eight in 2007). And book-
length monographs followed: thirty such volumes were published in English
alone between 1998 and 2013 (six in the single year 2008). No doubt accidents
of timing in research, writing, and publishing account for much of the chronological clustering of such publications, but it is clear that the concept and formu-
lation of the Atlantic region as a coherent historical entity struck a responsive
chord, and that the Seminar, I believe, contributed something of a propulsive
effect on this historiographical development.

But to answer your question directly: much historical work concerning various
events and developments in the Atlantic region in the early modern period was
available in 1995, but it was scattered and without a governing concept of the
Atlantic region as a historical entity, with its distinctive origins, developments,
and evanescence.

S. Lachenicht: What were the major themes of the first ten years?

B. Bailyn: The topics chosen for the early years of the Seminar were as broad as
possible to allow for the widest participation and the exploration of the most
interesting themes, however unusual or strange. Thus the first Seminar, in 1996,
was devoted to the 'Movement of People, Mobility, and Migration, Recruitment
and Resettlement, 1500–1800', which involved developments in Europe and
Africa as well as the Americas. In 1997, we explored the imperial powers in
America: ideas and politics of empire in the Western world. Similarly broad

topics followed: 'Cultural Encounters', 'the Economy of the Atlantic World', and 'the Atlantic Revolutions' (the last emphasizing Latin America, which Robert Palmer had ignored in his famous *Age of the Democratic Revolutions*). In later years the topics became more narrowly defined but more challenging: 'The Atlantic as a Theater of War', 'The Americas in the Advancement of European Science and Medicine', 'Justice: Europe in America, 1500–1830'.

As to your questions about *what Atlantic History is today, what will it be in the near future, and where it should go*, the answers are closely related. We have just scratched the surface of the deep inter-involvements, the networks, in the vast Atlantic World, transnational and multinational in their essence. Thus, for example, we have David Hancock's fine book on the wine trade, that illustrates the close, intertwined connections among nations, ports, and domestic consumerism throughout the Atlantic; April Lee Hatfield's excellent *Atlantic Virginia*, on the 'vibrant interchange' among all the Western colonies of the seventeenth century and the networks that linked them to the European peoples; Stephen Behrendt's ingenious study of the calendar and phasing of the slave trade that involved intricate, coordinated timing of shipping in Europe, politics and markets in Africa, and the seasonal needs of planters in the Americas; Nuala Zahedieh's deeply researched study of London's role in the Atlantic economy 1660–1700, showing that commercial city's coordinating function in an increasingly coherent Atlantic system; Franco Venturi's brilliant tracing through the entire Atlantic World of Cesare Beccaria's *On Crimes and Punishments*; Horst Pietschmann's many works on the ramifications of Latin American trade, winding through the economies of two continents; John Thornton's *Cultural History of the Atlantic World, 1250–1820*, emphasizing the basic role of Africa in the general history of the Atlantic; and other networks in every sphere of life in the four continents of the Atlantic. The near future in my view is the recovery of these 'submarine' networks of multinational connections within the greater Atlantic region of the globe.

S. Lachenicht: Are there specific ways of enquiry in Atlantic History?

B. Bailyn: In my view, no. That is, traditional modes of research, documentation, and synthesis are as valid here as in any other field of history. Certain problems – statistical, demographic, linguistic (especially of indigenous cultures) – will require special skills, but they are within the range of traditional advanced historical research. The sociologists' more recent devising of techniques in 'network analysis' may prove to be especially helpful.

S. Lachenicht: Can other fields of research gain from 'Atlantic ways of enquiry'?

B. Bailyn: Yes, in the sense that other sub-global regional studies – several of which in other parts of the globe, especially Asia, are already well advanced – might find in the Atlantic region a model for further enquiry, and more important, useful contrasts and parallels.

S. Lachenicht: To what extent do we need interdisciplinarity?

B. Bailyn: It is essential for studies of any depth and range. I think that is now generally assumed.

S. Lachenicht: How does Atlantic History compare to Global History?

B. Bailyn: They are very different. On the occasion of the founding of *The Journal of Global History* (2006) several eminent historians wrote extensive explanations of what that subject is about and what it might achieve. Global history, the lead writer explained, is the study of connections and comparisons 'across continents, oceans and countries over very long spans of time ... for moral purposes, connected to the needs of a globalizing world' and leading to the creation of 'meta-narratives that might ... deepen our understanding of diversity and scale up our consciousness of [the] human condition'. The studies that have appeared in the journal, scattered across many areas of the globe and time periods, do follow that description in one way or the other; but they are related to each other only abstractly by degrees of similarity in scope and scale. This is very different from the conception, structure, goals, and purposes of Atlantic History, which is the history of the multitudes of networks that bound the four Atlantic continents together into an historical entity the stages of whose growth and evanescence can be traced.

The Atlantic region was never isolated, never wholly autonomous, without contacts with the greater world. Spanish commerce reached, tentatively, west into the Philippines and China, and Spain's rule in the Western Hemisphere was part of an empire that was centred deep in Eastern Europe. But the dynamics of the Atlantic region were not driven by global forces. Like the earlier Mediterranean world, of which so much has been written, it had its own historical identity, its unique contours, and its own interior propulsions. In time – with the end of imperialism in the Americas, the demise of the slave trade, and the transformation of the European economy – the region's integrity would be transformed and would become part of a greater system, a system which it had helped define.

S. Lachenicht: How does Atlantic History 'cope with' American History and European History?

B. Bailyn: I don't know what 'cope' means in this context, but it is an essential component of both. And it is essential in understanding African and indigenous American History.

S. Lachenicht: How much have different national academic traditions, from Europe and from the Americas, been important for Atlantic History?

B. Bailyn: The different national academic traditions do influence the approach to historical studies like this, but in the end, it comes down to traditional methods of research and writing that are universally shared by modern scholars.

S. Lachenicht: Is Atlantic History a US-American field of research?

B. Bailyn: It is not a US-specific field of research, nor is it a peculiarly British field of research. Atlantic History embraces in varying degrees all Western national fields and brings them together according to the problem at hand. And it is a mistake, I believe, to think of the subject as a combination or collection of individual national enclaves – Dutch Atlantic, French Atlantic, Spanish Atlantic, British, etc. That misses the point. The reason why it might seem a 'US Atlantic field of research' is simply that there are more historical researchers at work in the US than in other nations. I would guess that at least fifty historians in the US work in areas relevant to this field. Atlantic History is in no way a peculiarly 'American field of research'. The subject has no national boundaries.

S. Lachenicht: What does Atlantic History need to be successful as a field of research?

B. Bailyn: In the end it succeeds in so far as it establishes the origins of historical development of this great regional entity linking four continents and stretching over three centuries, and making clear how this region's history helped lay the foundations of the modern world.

For other discussion of these themes see Bernard Bailyn's *Atlantic History: Concept and Contours* (2005); 'Atlantic Soundings', in *Atlantic Studies* 7 (2010); the Introduction to *Soundings in Atlantic History: Latent Structures and Intellectual Currents, 1500–1830* (Cambridge, MA, 2009); and the history of the Seminar referred to above.

2

'Once more the storm is howling': On the political passions in Europe and America and their implications for Transatlantic History

Charles S. Maier

Contemporary developments as of early 2017, at a moment when this chapter is revised, must challenge the perspective that seemed appropriate when it was originally drafted over five years ago. To anticipate our conclusion, they do not make Transatlantic History less fruitful a pursuit, but they do suggest that the insights it generates should serve to open up even wider geographical frameworks for research. Transatlantic History has usefully helped scholars to transcend North-American particularism, but in turn, I will suggest, it should help historians to take account of the issues set by global frameworks.

To understand why, it makes sense to understand the ideological context within which transatlantic history developed. The field matured within the Atlantic political order advanced by the United States since its return to intervention in world affairs in the Second World War. And not only did the field develop within that political context; its premises built upon that context. Precisely the tremors of that geopolitical framework today reveal how implicitly connected were world politics and the progress of historical research. Up to a decade ago, perhaps until even more recently with the advent of the global financial crisis, the United States and Europe seemed to still share the successes of a liberal-democratic Atlantic Community, even if major challenges – a grave financial crisis, terrorism, turmoil in the Islamic world – were buffeting their common achievements. Today, the achievements of the shared political order of the Euro-American world are challenged fundamentally from within as without. We use the term populism to describe the discontents mobilized against the liberal order that seemed briefly to be gaining ground after 1989 but seems fragile and threatened in the middle of our century's second decade.[1] This new instability, however, lets us see more clearly the premises, promise, and limits of Transatlantic History. It also compels us to ask whether the enterprise of Transatlantic History rested on an overly optimistic liberal democratic teleology and whether we must revise its premises and implicit shared narrative.

Atlantic or Transatlantic History originated as a discipline that developed out of the perception that European and American development has been intimately 'entangled', and that a fuller comprehension required study as a common story. The early-modern age of encounter and transplantation (religious, ethnic, institutional) and the later decades of revolution in Europe and the Americas, even later the growth of welfare states and economic systems, cried out for a narrative that encompassed events on both sides of the ocean. This impulse produced several streams of research. British and American historians developed a transatlantic historical programme out of pre-war inquiries into the structure of the first British empire as documented by Charles M. Andrews and Lawrence Gipson. A generation later Bernard Bailyn and his students of American history, including Gordon Wood and my late wife, Pauline Maier, focused on Anglo-American ideological developments even as studies shifted and broadened their concerns – encouraged by the Institute of Early American History in Williamsburg – to scrutinize slavery, migration, and the encounters with indigenous peoples. What has emerged has been a powerful history of encounters, interlocking colonial regimes and their crises (including Spanish–British comparisons by John Elliott and Jeremy Adelman) and labour systems embedded in transoceanic exchange whether across the North Atlantic or the Caribbean. But other approaches that examined the interaction of continental Europe with the Americas also thrived: the massive outpouring of studies on Ibero-American slave circuits from the Portuguese onward (Joseph Miller), the comparative studies of the French and American revolutions – pioneered by Tocqueville's brilliant essays in the nineteenth century, taken up by R. R. Palmer and Jacques Godechot, extended to German-American liberal thought, then to the late nineteenth-century interactions as studied by James Kloppenburg and Daniel Rogers.

Over the past decades, therefore, practitioners brought ever more themes under scrutiny: commodity transfer, environmental practices, the massive forced transportation of African slaves, the multiple migrations and diasporas, and the development of welfare states. Of course, historians had long studied comparative revolution, immigration, the 'triangle' trade, and diplomatic and military affairs. But the sensibility changed a generation ago; the story was no longer one of European institutions transformed by being brought to the Americas. And it certainly could no longer be just a story of British transplantation: French, Dutch, Iberian participation became important, as did the development of indigenous peoples and the massive reliance on slavery in the transatlantic and indeed the global economy.

This development brought a significant enrichment of American History. Nonetheless, it still rested on an implicit teleology for a 'Western' or Atlantic History – liberal and democratic institutions developed together as part of what might be thought of as an irreversible force. The overthrow of communist regimes in Eastern Europe in 1989 reinforced this success story. But historians today need to ask in the light of contemporary 'populist' challenges whether these optimistic premises were flawed as the basis of a historiographical programme. And a further question arises: even if we can rescue the transatlantic project, is it a sufficient basis for historical research? Without denying the contributions Atlantic History has brought to earlier self-enclosed and often smug narratives, is it an adequate basis for understanding American and indeed much of European history? To anticipate the response offered here: even as a volume such as this one implicitly celebrates the maturity of Transatlantic History, researchers should take account of the precariousness of the Atlantic institutional achievement. At the same time they will do well to expand the geographical frame once again – this time to create an awareness of 'entanglement' (the term now so prevalent for trans-national history; the French equivalent is *histoires croisées*) in a wider framework that will embed the Atlantic arena within global developments.

I hope to engage these propositions by following a political theme that should seem urgent in light of political violence and even the recent electoral results in Europe and the United States: the passions of politics. Consider as an introduction a different evocation of the Atlantic. Almost a century ago William Butler Yeats cited the ocean's daunting tempests to evoke the turmoil in Ireland and the wider world:

> Once more the storm is howling, and half hid
> Under the cradle-hood and coverlid
> My child sleeps on. There is no obstacle
> But Gregory's wood and one bare hill
> Whereby the haystack- and roof-levelling wind,
> Bred on the Atlantic, can be stayed;
> And for an hour I have walked and prayed
> Because of the great gloom that is in my mind.
> I have walked and prayed for this young child an hour
> And heard the sea-wind scream upon the tower,
> And under the arches of the bridge, and scream
> In the elms above the flooded stream,
> Imagining in excited reverie
> That the future years had come,
> Dancing to a frenzied drum,
> Out of the murderous innocence of the sea.

Yeats was preoccupied by violence and revolution on his Atlantic island. In 1919 he wrote his other prophetic poem 'The Second Coming': 'Things fall apart; the center cannot hold,/ Mere anarchy is loosed upon the world,/ The blood dimmed tide is loosed, and everywhere/ The ceremony of innocence is drowned;/ The best lack all conviction, while the worst/ Are full of passionate intensity...' Three years earlier Yeats had written his great lines about the Easter Rebellion of April 1916, which recorded how the Irish who seized the Post Office had been transformed into revolutionaries: 'All changed, changed utterly:/ A terrible beauty is born.'[2]

At the origin of that transformation, Yeats placed not any institutional situation, not, say, the prolonged British domination of Ireland, or the claims of national groups that had become so strident in the years before the First World War, whether in Ireland or the Balkans or Asia, but rather the transformation of individuals through politics and ideology. Single-minded political commitment had withered human sensibilities. 'Hearts with one purpose alone/ Through summer and winter seem/ Enchanted to a stone/ To trouble the living stream ... Minute by minute they live:/ The stone's in the midst of all.// Too long a sacrifice/ Can make a stone of the heart.'[3]

Atlantic History, then, is not just the narrative of Western values. It is a history of stormy weather: revolutions, wars, mass migrations under the duress of poverty, and passionate political convictions as well as a gentle liberalism. Anyone living through the classical revolutionary epoch of 1789 to 1815 or later agrarian unrest, the US Civil War, the protests of industrial labour would have understood this intuitively, as did most adults experiencing the 1930s and the successive decades of the Second World War and the Cold War. The optimism created by the collapse of communist regimes in Europe, however, allowed ideas of a halcyon outcome to take root. By the mid-1990s with democratic transformations in Eastern Europe, apparently in Russia, South Africa, and Latin America, observers could well envision transnational democratization and international harmony close at hand, indeed a possible 'end of history'. Not long into our current millennium, however, we have had to learn anew that 'dancing to frenzied drums' was likely to resume.

For Yeats the dangers and the menacing threats of 'things falling apart' and 'the blood-dimmed tide' were rooted in personal fanaticism, the 'passionate intensity', and 'the stone in the heart'. Lovers of English-language poetry cite these evocative verses often, but historians cannot be content with Yeats's genealogy of anarchy and violence. Nevertheless, he opens or re-opens the issue of what role the passions play in politics. Yeats compels us to turn, if only provisionally, from social institutions to basic individual impulses, likewise from social structures to intellectual structures or ideologies, that is, to ideas that are so coherent and totalizing they evoke the passions, by which I mean feelings that seize control of our rational faculties, that obsess us. What I call the public passions have the same power as the private passions – love, sexual longing, jealousy, hatred – but they require a wider stage for their satisfaction. What Yeats understood, moreover, was that the public passions crowded out the private passions and normal affections – they erased love and personal connections and made, as he was so concerned to document, 'a stone of the heart'. The poet Rilke wrote similarly that the outbreak of the First World War 'planted within our no longer individual breasts, as if with by some meteor from space, a hot iron heart'.[4]

My theme then concerns the ideological storms arising over the Atlantic, or more precisely in the societies that recognize themselves as part of a transatlantic community, but in this case as a community of political passions. We are familiar with the political passions from the great philosophers and also from the poets and novelists and playwrights, as well as from historical documentation. Shakespeare and Schiller both built many of their dramas around political passions, as did Verdi his operas. Recall Philip II and Rodrigo in *Don Carlo*, the conspirators in *Julius Caesar* or *Un Ballo in Maschera* – all excited by political and personal passion to carry out a spectacular assassination. Their passions include jealousy and ambition in the first instance, the lust for power or for glory and preeminence, or alternatively the hatred of inequality; sometimes the thirst for liberty and hatred of authority, the commitment to national fatherland, and occasionally the belief in some vague total transformation of the present order.

Characteristic of the political passions is that they are often held collectively. Jealousy and hopeless love are personal passions; so too usually is ambition. But hatred of an enemy, or the desire to overturn a social order are impulses that are cultivated by a party or a group whose members often raise the level of commitment. Political passions not only have collective ends, but often depend on collective commitment or on group interaction: as does terrorism, whether the Red Brigades of the 1970s or the Jihadists of today.

Most of us academics hardly know how to deal with these impulses. These are forces that seem far too primitive for us as scientific historians to devote much time to. We deal with structures, not passions, that is with the organizations that are left once passion has congealed into nations, religions, or social classes. And yet just as Yeats sensed these basic political passions were arising again, 'dancing to a frenzied drum', and emerging out of the Atlantic storms, so we have had to reckon with them once again. Of course, first-rate social scientists always sensed their power and never neglected them: Alexis de Tocqueville, Hannah Arendt, and Judith Shklar, Albert Hirschman in his gem-like book on *The Passions and the Interests*, Pierre Hassner in an essay on the return of the political passions.[5] Our great moral philosophers –excepting perhaps Nietzsche – have believed that mastery of the passions was the crucial moral task for mankind – whether Plato or Spinoza or Kant. After all, the word passion did not imply self-mastery, but rather the opposite – passivity, being a slave, losing control.

But it is not clear when passion takes over in that sense. It might be appropriate to define a political passion as an impulse that justifies political imprisonment or even killing, but obviously in many cases we recognize these extreme measures as rational ones, whether by states or resistors. Most of us are not ready to rule out political violence as a recourse. Not all situations allow the non-violent tactics of Gandhi or Martin Luther King to promise political change. And not all recourses to violence are products of passion in the ordinary sense. They may arise from what ultimately is a passionate conviction, but still represent reasoned responses, not what we think of as mere fury and rage. Were the Resistance forces of the Second World War caught up in the throes of political passion? When President Obama decided to deploy air power against IS, was he possessed by a political passion? Ultimately we rely on our own judgement, and the line between reason and passion is hardly a firm one. Alternatively, there are societies that engage in cycles of revenge, murder, and cruelty that exceed ideological passion. The Balkans were gripped by murderous civil wars before the First World War and then after the Second World War, but it is not clear that actors there were motivated by what might be thought of as political goals. From 1946 to 1958 *La Violencia* in Colombia cost perhaps 200,000 lives, many in sadistic rituals of reprisal, whereas the successive uprising by the FARC that lasted from 1964 to 2016, brutal though it was, seems to have remained more subject to an instrumental calculus of violence.

It is important not to equate the political passions solely with the recourse to violence. Even when non-violent, the persistence and resurgence of political passions engages us with an aspect of political behaviour that historians usually think of as standing in the way of the dominant Atlantic narrative, which until the new century focused on the progress of liberty and democracy. Social scientists have tended to treat the outbreak of passionate collective mobilization as a distraction from a master narrative of democratization, or else have tended to focus on the passions when they advanced the progressive agenda as in the movements for African-American political rights and later minority rights more generally. In fact, I am thinking not only of cases where passions seem to rule continuously, but others where political impulses seem rather just to explode the framework of day-to-day compromise and motivate transformative collective actions, which may be non-violent as well as violent. The political passions refer to the mobilization of the public mind by the great themes of politics even when they do not result in profound change, but merely fill its media, provoke intense debate, and lead us to believe that the decisions of the community are as important as the choices of our individual lives.

The question appropriate for an investigation into Transatlantic History is whether politics evokes equal passions on both sides of the Atlantic, or whether our respective continents regulate public affairs with differing levels of what Yeats called 'passionate intensity'. In the century that has almost passed since Yeats envisaged the personal catastrophes – the 'stones out of hearts' – that the political passions had unleashed in Ireland and over the Atlantic, have the United States and Europe been subject, if not to the same ideological commitments, the same intensity of commitment? What have we shared, what has separated us?

Think first about the great divisive political issues that have emerged on one or both sides of the Atlantic since the development of settler societies. Within the framework of a shared narrative, an Atlantic political history, what overarching themes emerge? Following Seymour Martin Lipset and Stein Rokkan a generation ago, I would propose that the basic issues that were up for debate in the past four centuries or more of transatlantic community-building fall into four major clusters: originally the role of religious authority and uniformity; second the rights of populations to self-government and free expression; then, in the nineteenth century and with revived force today, the question of who was inside and who outside of a national community; and later the issue of how to adjudicate the contending claims to national wealth and production.[6] These debates have sometimes been tackled in sequence and sometimes simultaneously. They have seemed resolved at times and lying far in the past only to be resurgent within a new context. Thus the question of who belongs to a national community was central in the era of nation-building in the nineteenth century and has repeatedly emerged in eras of migration, including our own. These are the issues that generate strong political passions on both sides of the ocean, not always murderous, but certainly engaging fundamental commitments.

The first and earliest agenda, as noted, formed around the claims of state-enforced religious authority. For two and a half centuries religious conflicts wracked the European world and were echoed in the Americas. But rival faiths that contested proximate territories in the Old World usually lived in widely separate regions of the New. Religious warfare in Europe was transformed into colonial contests in the Americas. Within the North American colonies, the preoccupation with communal uniformity gave way sooner or later to acceptance of the faiths brought by different groups of migrants. But toleration has to be followed at different levels, whether as a political and legal regulation of minority rights or the willingness of communities to accept alien congregations in their own home regions.

Outside the vast Iberian and Iberian-American world Protestant–Catholic divisions had come to be regulated by principles of geographical partition between 1555 and 1648 although only after long and often cruel conflicts. Efforts by rulers, such as Louis XIV or later the Prince-Archbishop of Salzburg to deny the rights of minority sects in their long-established enclaves went against the spirit of eighteenth-century intellectuals. But at the same time, efforts by rulers to extend further rights to religious dissenters often aroused the hostility of the popular urban classes and provoked demonstrations. Religious uniformity had been an issue in seventeenth-century New England – British dissenters were hardly tolerant in their own colonies. By the time, however, that Jefferson wrote the Virginia charter of religious freedom and Enlightenment intellectuals were celebrating toleration, it was becoming a back-burner question that was largely quiescent. Geographical sorting tended to prevail in the North American colonies as well, largely by virtue of settlement patterns. The Quebec Act of 1774, in which the British hoped to reassure their recently acquired French Catholic subjects in Canada, seemed to threaten the prevailing Protestant culture of New England and aroused sharp protest. Popular protest and violence, however, often accompanied the appearance of minority communities and revived in the early nineteenth century all the way from the Jewish communities of Central Europe to the convents of the American cities to the Mormon settlements in the western regions of the United States. Religion remained a potential fuel for the political passions across the Atlantic World even as ideas of diversity seemed to gain traction.

The second agenda, centring on the nature and extent of state control over freedom of expression and the role of popular government led to the great conflicts that marked the age of revolution on both sides of the Atlantic from the late eighteenth century until the mid-nineteenth century in Central Europe. America and France clearly led in mobilizing democratic political passions and defining the role of a constituent people, while the other societies were left to catch up over a period of almost a century. Ideologically, the ideas mobilized on both sides of the Atlantic were roughly equivalent; it was the tempo of their mobilization that varied. And the fact that the liberal left in this great struggle met more resistance inside Europe than within the American republic meant that the struggle was harder and mobilized revolutionary passions throughout the first half the nineteenth century.

The third great agenda involved the issue of inclusivity – who would be inside and who outside a legitimate constitutional community, that is, the question of nation-building and nationalism. But it was also an issue of citizenship. What peoples were to be inside a given national community whether in terms of language and tradition in Central Europe, or in terms of race in the United States? These issues seemed resolved in America by 1865 with the conclusion of the Civil War, and in Central Europe by 1870 – only to be contested anew in different frameworks over the next century. This issue has returned today as societies face levels of migration – and from non-Christian societies – that bring challenges to jobs and community values.

The fourth issue – that of how to allocate claims to wealth and income – has usually run parallel with the others, but became the focus of conflict and ideological contestation in the twentieth century. Its particular bitterness helped create the level of conflictuality and passion that Eric Hobsbawm characterized as the age of extremes from 1914 to 1989. It helped generate the two totalizing ideologies of the twentieth century: communism, and indirectly, fascism. And it was with respect to these commitments that the history of the United States and of Europe seemed most divergent. It was in fact the impact of this agenda that created the misleading impression that Americans were far less prone to ideological politics than Europeans.

Economic conflicts naturally arose first between the classes contending for the surplus created in the countryside – in Europe between the feudal and early-modern state and its privileged often aristocratic landowners, then between landowners and direct cultivators. In so far as the economic agenda concerned the claims of smallholders in the countryside, the United States did become an arena for hot-blooded politics and passionate commitments, a contest that reached its high point in 1896, when visions of an agrarian voice over national development were fundamentally defeated.

As for class conflicts within the industrial sector, it became commonplace to note that America had no successful working-class parties. Sombart had noticed from the beginning of the century that socialism had little chance in America: it foundered on the reefs of prosperity. In the 1960s, American historians on the Left excavated the history of socialism and found that in areas such as Milwaukee or among the New York working classes (especially the Jewish immigrants from Eastern Europe) there were strong socialist subcultures, and that only the First World War and the subsequent Red Scare had suppressed them. But even the 1912 vote for Eugene Debs in the presidential race and for the American Socialist Party in general amounted to only a small fraction of what the SPD was achieving in imperial Germany. Of course, there was an American Socialist Party, and during the period of the Third International, an American Communist Party, but with none of the mass constituency that Europe's parties had. America, to put it crudely, had no socialism. Neither did America have a mass fascist party, nor even a highly nationalistic right-wing grouping. Americans, we were taught as students, had no feudal tradition, thus enjoyed a liberal consensus from the beginning and hence offered stony ground for socialism and for its fascist adversary.[7] Political passions, I was taught in the late 1950s, supposedly had little traction in the United States.

Such an innocent – or wilfully myopic – historical belief was destined to be buffeted by the controversies over the rights of African-Americans and then US intervention in Vietnam – only the most salient conflicts that opened up in the American society of the 1960s. The political passions these fractures revealed led to urban civil strife and polarized universities in the 1960s and 1970s – America's version of a worldwide upheaval against the post-war structures of Cold War authority. By the late 1970s the American insurrections seemed finally to have exhausted themselves, or perhaps more accurately to have been adequately channelled into reforms that could be accommodated by traditional institutions. What political observers overlooked, however, were the countervailing resentments and resistance entrenched in churches and local communities, many of which were profoundly transformed by the economics of globalization and technological change – seismic forces for change less overt than street demonstrations but just as subversive.

Half a century after the 1960s, the so-called populist trends, which made an initial splash with Newt Gingrich's 1994 congressional campaign, then manifested themselves in the so-called Tea Party, and have most recently produced the spectacular presidential victory of Donald Trump, require us to reconsider the alleged American immunity to anti-democratic movements. Fascism and communism were the great rival political passions of the twentieth century, and it is true that the United States did not experience their impact as did the continental European political systems. Both communism and fascism were doctrines that reversed Clausewitz's famous dictum to insist that war should be thought of as politics, i.e. the pursuit of rational policy, by other means. They both envisaged politics as war by other means; they both tended to fulfil Carl Schmitt's notion that the political was about annihilation of the enemy. Fascism arose in Europe not merely as a party to oppose Marxism; it also emerged as a response to unresolved issues of national belonging and popular participation. Fascism and communism alike did make – to echo Yeats – a stone of the heart, at least in their initial decades of militant struggle. Both emerged as plausible recourses with the First World War and the stark opposition that the war apparently revealed between dangerous and manly military action on the one hand and feckless parliamentary governance on the other. Both communism and fascism defined their mission in terms of continual adversaries, whether other classes or other nations or other parties, and envisaged their mission as politically and sometimes physically liquidating their adversaries.

Did the communist intellectuals and the non-party sympathizers ('fellow travellers' to use the later term) somehow crave self-abasement, as critics such as the Polish exile Czeslaw Milosz later suggested with his wonderful fable of the magic pills that made intellectuals happily yield to the charms of totalitarian power?[8] Was it the merciless logic imposed, as they believed, by the unyielding laws of history? Good communists took pride in their commitment to a disciplined body that demanded obedience even as it reassured members they alone understood and were advancing the inexorable processes of history. In his 1922 book, *History and Class Consciousness*, the communist philosopher Georgy Lukács – who after a subsequent generation of Stalinist repression would actually strive to moderate dictatorship in 1956 in Hungary – set out the dialectical logic of a party dictatorship already emerging in Russia as the Bolsheviks shut down alternative parties, established their Cheka or secret police and used military force to suppress the Kronstadt fortress mutiny: 'The forms of freedom in bourgeois organizations are nothing but a 'false consciousness' of an actual unfreedom ... Only when this is understood can our earlier paradox be resolved ... the unconditional absorption of the total personality in the praxis of the movement, was the only possible way of bringing about an authentic freedom'. Praxis meant discipline and subservience, but to policies that in the long run had to be objectively correct.[9]

Fascists, on their side, affirmed that not only was war an experience important for manhood (that belief had long had advocates), but that politics at its most basic must be akin to war, was in fact a form of war itself. War called forth the essentials demanded by manhood: loyalty and comradeship, command and obedience, and courage. Soldiers sacrificed themselves for their nation and for their fellow comrades. Liberal politicians in the First World War had stayed at home, immune from danger, chatting away in their feckless parliaments while the youth of their societies were consumed in distant battlefields. In so far as there was a common content to the doctrines we think of as fascist (and here I am including National Socialism as well), it lay in this belief. Political life must be waged as a struggle, a search to dominate, not just legislate. It was adversarial and hard, it demanded obedience to a party and leader just as military organization did, and indeed one donned quasi-military uniforms for party gatherings. Both movements rejected the premises of political liberalism as developed since the late eighteenth century. Both claimed to leave bourgeois sentiment behind – the communists in favour of a new proletarian collectivism, the fascists on behalf of a contradictory mix of values rooted in the ancestral soil but also in the modern claims of technological innovation.

Many brilliant social theorists strove to explain why the United States had remained relatively immune to these movements. What they accounted for, however, was not the absence of a fascist or socialist mentality, but the failure to develop a collective movement. Americans often responded to the authoritarian passions that informed both movements. But building a successful party on the basis of those passions proved impossible. Americans enjoyed a political system and institutions, such as a popularly elected presidency and single-member congressional districts that rewarded capturing the 'vital center', to use Arthur Schlesinger Jr.'s term, and that made it hard to raise left–right politics to the same sort of ideological pitch that European conditions had permitted. There were many efforts to explain so-called 'consensus' politics in the 1950s and 1960s. Louis Hartz argued that the absence of a feudal society, an *ancien régime*, in America had fundamentally determined a much narrower political spectrum. Seymour Martin Lipset returned to the old diagnosis that Sombart had offered: general prosperity and the possibility of social mobility inhibited the development of collectivism among the working class, and the absence of a plausible revolutionary threat inhibited the extremism of the middle strata. Richard Hofstadter suggested that the European political passions that culminated in fascism and revolutionary politics were channelled into what he termed the paranoid style in American politics. Earlier he would cite Adlai Stevenson to agree that US liberalism represented a sort of conservative instinct in a society that had never been feudal. Most astutely he analysed populism not only as the People's Party of the 1890s, but the source of 'an undercurrent of provincial resentments, popular and 'democratic' rebelliousness and suspiciousness, and nativism'. 'Such tendencies in American life as isolationism and the extreme nationalism that usually goes with it, hatred of Europe and Europeans, racial, religious, and nativist phobias, resentment of big business, trade-unionism, intellectuals, the Eastern seaboard and its culture – all these have been found not only in opposition to reform but also at times oddly combined with it.'[10] Anti-communism did become an American political passion in those years, but less as a left–right issue than as one subsumed under the distrust of elites that has mobilized Americans since the Jacksonian era. McCarthyism took shape not as a proto-fascism but as a latter-day anti-Masonry, or battle against the Philadelphia Bank of the United States. The destructive passions of Left and Right were transformed into a sort of psychopathological fringe, which found its recurring phenomenology in beliefs in conspiracy theories. The ideological passions that roiled Europe could only surface as pathologies in the United States.

Earlier theories focused less on the specific resistance to political extremism than the conditions that were conducive to democracy. As Frederick Jackson Turner had argued (borrowing from Achille Loria, the Italian advocate of cooperatives), access to free land also made a difference. By making it possible for rural settlers to become yeomen, the plentiful lands of North America (once wrested from the indigenous polities) enabled America to bypass the centuries-long conflicts of agrarian systems in Europe. The need to confiscate Church lands did not exist in the United States.

Less noted in the historiography until recently, the land issue also changed the concept of empire in the United States. Historians tended to overlook the fact that the great American imperial venture was not really the acquisition of colonies abroad, despite the territories that were annexed permanently or temporarily in the years between 1898 and 1916, but was the acquisition of the inner domain, which could be conceived of as fulfilment of the country's 'Manifest Destiny' and which took place at the expense of sparse populations of indigenous North Americans. Continental expansion benefited from the British, French, and Spanish imperial rivalries that led the European powers to shed their North American claims. France and Spain sold or negotiated their rights; the Mexican state that originally inherited large tracts could not withstand US pressure. The virtual completion of this process before the so-called age of imperialism meant that the nation did not face the same great-power military rivalry as the Europeans did. The British welcomed the Americans to the club of empire; the French and Germans saw no real conflict as of 1900; the Spanish by then were a push-over. The acquisition of overseas territory was so painless that the internal opposition remained a feeble intellectual movement. In foreign as domestic affairs, institutional or territorial good fortune impeded building durable political structures based on the political passions that in Europe became the basis for successful movements. Americans did not lack the mentalities that might conduce to extremism. After all, they could suppress blacks, battle Indians, try to isolate themselves from East European immigrant hordes, employ violence against labour movements, or conversely castigate the wealthy and envisage dark conspiracies by monopolists. But they found it hard to construct durable political movements on these passions. Whether they are doing so today remains in question.

A comparative analysis requires addressing two further questions. Have there been political passions that Americans had, which Europe was spared? And have the United States and Europe shared political passions in the last decades? Does our recent transatlantic history reveal a convergence of the societies on both sides of the water? Certainly there are political responses that have characterized American political passions. Most obviously race has played a political role throughout American history that had no counterpart in Europe, but I will cite only the latest phases of this 'American dilemma', to cite Gunnar Myrdal's famous study that now lies halfway back to the Civil War, and I will not bother to sketch the history. Prohibition in America took on dimensions that the European temperance movement never did.[11] It built on the Protestant (but non-episcopal) culture that feared eclipse in the early years of the twentieth century.

Even in Protestant northern Europe the cultural forces behind temperance could not succeed in national bans on alcohol. The American political system – in particular the resilient structures of state and local power – have long been conducive to evangelical politics often on highly charged issues of belief and lifestyle. Whether the effort to combat the teaching of evolution (e.g. the 1925 Scopes Trial) or today's Tea Party successes, American politics has allowed a mobilization around moral issues that is far less promising in Europe. The historian of divergence can also turn to McCarthyism as a peculiarly American episode. Certainly there was no lack of anti-communism in Europe, where the strength of the communist parties polarized Italy and at times France. But European anti-communism involved a battle against party structures and affiliated labour unions; in the United States it became a panic over subversion. It did not engender the same need to interrogate political dissenters, to rake over the past, to maul government agencies and impose loyalty oaths on universities that the hunt for communists did in the United States.

As for the second question – have our societies shared political passions in recent decades – the answer, I believe, must be clearly yes. Turn back to the late 1960s and 1970s. Both sides of the Atlantic lived through a degree of political mobilization that was profoundly disturbing to those citizens who prized political order. At first glance the reasons seem quite diverse. The American civil rights struggle emerged from America's particularly racial institutions: the never quite resolved legacy of black slavery. Had it not been for the fact that American Civil Rights leaders were discovering the effectiveness of non-violent protest, as represented by Martin Luther King's movement, far greater violence might have been mobilized. Non-violent strategies notwithstanding, the insurgency in America's northern cities in the late 1967, the so-called ghetto riots in Detroit or Los Angeles, revealed that the institutions designed in the founding era, then amended in the 1860s and the 1960s to assure legal equality, might not guarantee civil tranquility. So, too, the tensions over the Vietnam War raised political passions to a degree not seen since the 1850s. But how, then, can we explain the European mobilization of the late 1960s and early 1970s? The passions that racked the American universities and racial ghettos should have found no echo in Europe, any more than fascism and mass communist parties had found a United States counterpart between the wars. In fact the American clashes were part of a global movement, that included the uprisings in Prague, in Western Europe, and Mexico and South America, Egypt, the Near East, and sites in Asia. What was at stake?

At this point, we must seek some answers that go beyond the comparative frameworks that historians and political scientists developed in the 1950s and early 1960s. My own conviction is that the inquiries suggested by Transatlantic History must be set within a wider global context. First, perhaps, was the all-encompassing nature of the Cold War, which lasted far longer than the hot war against fascism. The intensity of this struggle – the level of resources devoted to sustaining it for forty-five years; the ideological mobilization involved as it generated one crisis after another; the dangerous accumulation of nuclear armaments, and the global dimensions of rivalry whether over Eastern Europe and Germany after the collapse of the Nazi empire, then over Asia and the Middle East from 1950s on, finally as a contest for influence in Africa and Latin America from the 1960s – obscured a major fact.[12] At the same time that it was a struggle between contending ideological systems and contending geopolitical hegemons, it was also a struggle over the legacy of colonialism, which had formally disintegrated but in many ways continued as a conflict over the global distribution of wealth. It built on and helped to deepen a North–South division, not just an East–West one. Thus the question emerges whether Transatlantic History can adequately take account of this North–South confrontation. Or perhaps, whether and how those who pursue Transatlantic History can enlarge their framework to encompass the range of North–South issues.

One possibility perhaps is to recognize that post-Cold War developments – that is, world history since 1989 – have recapitulated each of the great agendas that set the terms for transatlantic politics, as shared by Europe and America, but now on a wider scale: first, the great contest over the claims of religious authority, which the Western world thought to have settled between the eighteenth and early twentieth centuries, has re-emerged with the claims of militant Islam and must be negotiated in the decades to come. The question of who belongs to a particular national community and who does not – indeed what is a national community – becomes urgent, not because we believe every people needs a state (this remains troubling enough) but because so many peoples maintain a diasporic identity – whether Latinos in the United States, Turks in Germany, Chinese in Southeast Asia – and the claims of this national pluralism are hard to accommodate in those countries that formed their nations around single ethnicities. Acceptance of pluralism, of the legitimacy of multiple loyalties, of cosmopolitanism, seems confined to beleaguered elites. Indeed, for the last thirty years, our political conflicts have become waged more over identity than distribution: not about what we get, but who we are. We are passionate less about payrolls and more about passports. Borders are fluid, more migrants believe they should have diaspora status, and obviously these issues have ignited new passions that have supplemented and perhaps superseded the ones largely burned out after Hobsbawm's short twentieth century.[13]

Nonetheless, the issues of distributive politics, that is of what groups are entitled to what rewards, have also re-emerged. Such conflicts may for now no longer produce left-wing ideologies of collectivism to shatter the West's neo-capitalist consensus (although these movements have recently taken on signs of life). But economic struggles have also been enlarged by questions of access to resources that raise environmental issues. Since the 1960s or 1970s, distributive politics has become less of an issue between classes than between blocs of states. In so far as the contests involve the claims of advanced and emerging economies on a common environmental legacy now in danger, they will, however, be very thorny indeed. So far many of these issues have mapped uneasily over the familiar contending political coalitions of haves and have-nots that marked Transatlantic History. But how we organize politics to contest the alternatives in the contemporary world is far from clear.

All these challenges, I believe, mean that we should no longer be content to investigate comparative history, or entangled history, as just a transatlantic game. Any American-European set of investigations really must be open to a broad framework of global influences. At the very moment that Transatlantic History has opened up traditionally parochial perspectives and inquiries, it reveals new questions that cannot be addressed within this new capacious framework. The history of slavery involves Africa and the Americas, but also Africa and the Middle East; the history of overseas migration links both shores of the Atlantic, but rightly understood both sides of the Indian Ocean and the Bay of Bengal; the history of commodities, whether precious metals or grains or cotton, takes in South and East Asia and Africa; the history of corporations or international law emerges from explorations and conflicts on all continents. We can take stock of the achievements of Transatlantic History, but we cannot finally rest there, no more than we can take our wealthy societies of the West as a teleological endpoint, in the way that certainly our Cold War historiography did, as did our theories of modernization, as did perhaps even the brief sense of euphoria we enjoyed in 1989–90.

Yeats wrote his poem about 'the storm bred on the Atlantic', but now the winds blow from many different oceans. The storms over the Atlantic have perhaps abated, nonetheless, but there are still leaders 'who peddle arrogance and hatred in the thoroughfares'. To understand them we shall have to listen to the storms that arise over all the world's oceans and seas – Pacific, Indian, and Mediterranean as well. Storms arise whenever and wherever the world's oceans touch upon land masses. And as historians we must be willing to study each of those great zones that generate tempests and typhoons and tsunamis. So even as we recognize the insights generated by Transatlantic History, I believe that as a research programme it must look across many oceans to understand and contextualize our own.

Acknowledgements

This address was presented at the invitation of Christof Mauch for the opening of his LMU Schwerpunkt in Transatlantic History – 'Ideas and Cultures in Motion'. With slight revisions it is published in the form it was given – as a keynote reflection – and I have notation only for direct quotations. I acknowledged in my presentation the great service that Christof had rendered by guiding a major transatlantic historical enterprise through a long transition, namely the German Historical Institute of Washington, which has functioned as a centre of cooperative scholarship under a succession of remarkable directors: Hartmut Lehmann (Heidelberg), Christof Mauch, Hartmut Berghof, and currently Simone Lässig. It represents the best of a generation's exploration of our connected history.

Notes

1   Useful for defining the phenomenon internationally: J. W. Müller, *What is Populism?* (Philadelphia: University of Pennsylvania Press, 2016).
2   'A Prayer for my Daughter'; 'The Second Coming'; 'Easter 1916' all in *The Collected Poems of William Butler Yeats*, R. Finneran (ed.) (New York: Simon & Schuster, Inc., 1996), pp. 188, 187, 180–1 (in order of citation).

3 'Easter 1916–81', in *ibid.*
4 Perhaps the best German-language counterpart to Yeats's evocation of hearts made stone (best in quality and closest in concept) were Rilke's *Fünf Gesänge*. Writing five years earlier at the beginning of the First World War, the poet envisioned the war god transforming individuals into common purpose: 'Andere sind wir, ins Gleiche Geänderte: jedem/ Sprang in die plötzlich/ Nicht mehr seinige Brust meteorisch ein Herz./ Heiß, ein eisernes Herz aus eisernem Weltall.' 'We have become different, changed into equals; into each one's suddenly no longer individual breast a heart has sprung. Hot, an iron heart from an iron universe.'
5 P. Hassner, *La terreur et l'empire: La violence et la paix* II (Paris: Seuil, 2003); and P. Hassner, 'La revanche des passions', *Commentaire*, 110 (2005), pp. 299–312.
6 S. M. Lipset and Stein Rokkan (eds), *Party Systems and Voter Alignments: Cross-National Perspectives* (New York: The Free Press, 1968); and Stein Rokkan, 'The Structuring of Mass Politics in the Smaller European Democracies: A Developmental Typology', *Comparative Studies in Society and History*, 10:2 (1968), pp. 173–210.
7 L. Hartz, *The Liberal Tradition in America: An Interpretation of American Political Thought since the Revolution* (New York: Harcourt, Brace, 1955).
8 C. Milosz, *The Captive Mind*, Jane Zielonka, trans. (New York: Vintage, 1955). Many similar critiques emerged by the 1940s and 1950s, among them Arthur Koestler's fictional account, *Darkness at Noon*, and George Orwell's *1984*.
9 G. Lukács, *History and Class Consciousness*, Rodney Livingstone, trans. (Cambridge, MA: MIT Press, 1971), pp. 319–20, 326–7.
10 Again Hartz and also R. Hofstadter, *The Age of Reform from Bryan to F.D.R.* (New York: Knopf, 1959), pp. 5, 9–13, 20.
11 Most recently see L. McGirr, *The War on Alcohol: Prohibition and the Rise of the American State* (New York: W. W. Norton & Company, 2015), who stresses the legacy of the enforcement effort on American state-building.
12 For a masterly survey of the non-European dimensions see O. A. Westad, *The Global Cold War: Third World Interventions and the Making of Our Times* (Cambridge: Cambridge University Press, 2005).
13 For more extensive discussion of the political ramifications, C. S. Maier, 'Territorialisten und Globalisten: Die beiden neuen "Parteien" in den heutigen Demokratien', Bodo Schulze, trans. *Transit*, 14 (1997), pp. 5–14; Maier, '"Being There": Place, Territory, and Identity', in S. Benhabib, I. Shapiro, and D. Petranovic (eds), *Identities, Affiliations, and Allegiances* (Cambridge and New York: Cambridge University Press, 2007), pp. 67–84; also Maier, *Once within Borders: Territories of Power, Wealth and Belonging since 1500* (Cambridge, MA: Harvard University Press, 2016), pp. 277–96.

References

Finneran, R. (ed.), *The Collected Poems of William Butler Yeats* (New York: Simon & Schuster, 1996).
Hartz, L. *The Liberal Tradition in America: An Interpretation of American Political Thought since the Revolution* (New York: Harcourt, Brace, 1955).
Hassner, P. 'La revanche des passions', *Commentaire*, 110 (2005), pp. 299–312.

Hassner, P. *La terreur et l'empire: La violence et la paix* II (Paris: Seuil, 2003).

Hofstadter, R. *The Age of Reform from Bryan to F.D.R.* (New York: Knopf, 1959).

Lipset, S. M. and Stein Rokkan (eds), *Party Systems and Voter Alignments: Cross-National Perspectives* (New York: The Free Press, 1968).

Lukács, G. *History and Class Consciousness*, Rodney Livingstone, trans. (Cambridge, MA: MIT Press, 1971).

Maier, C. S. '"Being There": Place, Territory, and Identity', in S. Benhabib, I. Shapiro, and D. Petranovic (eds), *Identities, Affiliations, and Allegiances* (Cambridge and New York: Cambridge University Press, 2007), pp. 67–84.

Maier, C. S. *Once within Borders: Territories of Power, Wealth and Belonging since 1500* (Cambridge, MA: Harvard University Press, 2016).

Maier, C. S. 'Territorialisten und Globalisten: Die beiden neuen "Parteien" in den heutigen Demokratien', Bodo Schulze, trans. *Transit*, 14 (1997), pp. 5–14.

McGirr, L. *The War on Alcohol: Prohibition and the Rise of the American State* (New York: W. W. Norton & Company, 2015).

Milosz, C. *The Captive Mind*, Jane Zielonka, trans. (New York: Vintage, 1955).

Müller, J. W. *What is Populism?* (Philadelphia: University of Pennsylvania Press, 2016).

Rokkan, S. 'The Structuring of Mass Politics in the Smaller European Democracies: A Developmental Typology', *Comparative Studies in Society and History*, 10:2 (1968), pp. 173–210.

Westad, O. A. *The Global Cold War: Third World Interventions and the Making of Our Times* (Cambridge: Cambridge University Press, 2005).

3

Atlantic History: The evolution of a subject

Nicholas Canny

Several of those who have set out to explain the emergence of Atlantic History as a distinct subject of enquiry have begun by seeking to establish when the concept of an Atlantic World first came into vogue. Those who have done so have found that the concept of an Atlantic Community, if not of an Atlantic World, was first popularized in the aftermath of the Second World War by scholars who considered that the liberal-democratic values that had been gradually enshrined into law by governments on both sides of the Atlantic Ocean from the late eighteenth century forward had given a unique character to political life in this part of the world and had provided its inhabitants with the will to confront totalitarian forces such as those that had just then been defeated in Germany and Japan.[1] More to the point it was being argued that attachment to those values was all the more critical at that moment when totalitarian regimes were engulfing much of Eastern Europe and other parts of the globe under the guise of communism. This outlook permeated the influential two-volume study by R. R. Palmer, *The Age of the Democratic Revolutions*.[2] This major comparative study proceeded from the assumption that those individuals in Western Europe and in the Americas who set out to establish new polities during the closing decades of the eighteenth and the early decades of the nineteenth centuries were concerned to promote modern democratic states which would uphold the rights and liberties of the individual citizen against the threat of tyranny. Such states, as Palmer's contemporaries well knew, had just then endured the greatest challenge that had yet presented itself, and many of them believed that democratic states would endure into the future only if they offered each other mutual assistance as they had done during the course of the Second World War; this time under the umbrella of the North American Treaty Organization (NATO) that had been designed to counter the communist menace.

Robert Palmer, unlike other promoters of the concept of an Atlantic Community, made no specific mention of NATO in his publications and advanced his moralizing project not by exhortation but by studying, and illuminating, examples from the past. However he identified himself as a liberal in the Anglo-Saxon tradition, particularly in the eyes of many French historians of his generation, first by interpreting the French Revolution, which lay at the core of his study, as having been concerned essentially with promoting the liberty of the individual rather than achieving a more equitable distribution of wealth, and second by continuously implying, and occasionally asserting, that it, and all other revolutionary movements that occurred in the Atlantic basin at that time, had been inspired by the American Revolution. This, he argued, had led not only to the creation of the United States as an independent political entity but also to the framing of the US Constitution, which Palmer considered an exemplary foundational document that had been, and might in the future be, imitated by any political communities wishing to constitute themselves as independent democratic republics. Indeed he brought his massive study to an end by concluding that after the early 1800s, by which time counter-revolution had put a temporary halt to democracy in most of the Western world, the United States, which then stood alone as a truly republican democracy, 'had a kind of duty meanwhile to develop it and to promote it, so that peoples of other nations, old and new, might someday move in the same direction'.[3]

It is probably doing less than justice to the formidable research and reflection of Robert Palmer to depict *The Age of the Democratic Revolutions* as the product of the time and place in which it was conceived and written. Account must also be taken of the fact that it derived from a long scholarly tradition fostered both within and outside the walls of universities in North America that had treated every protest registered by English settlers in North America from the moment that the passengers on the *Mayflower* had disembarked on American soil in 1620 to the end of what was then described as the Colonial Period of American History, as but one further move towards the achievement of individual liberty and the ultimate attainment of American political independence from Britain. Those who espoused this teleological narrative placed a premium on political, constitutional, and religious developments, especially within the New England colonies, which were taken to be a microcosm of what would ultimately become the United States of America. Succeeding generations of scholars who, until the 1960s or beyond, traced the unfolding of America's manifest destiny, remained chauvinistic in their outlook and preoccupations. However some of them developed an Atlantic dimension, or at least an English/British Atlantic dimension, to their work by linking whatever bids for greater political autonomy and individual freedom were voiced by colonists in America to the challenges to established authority enacted in England during the course of the English Civil War of the mid-seventeenth century and of the Glorious Revolution at the close of that same century. In this way, the authors dovetailed America's march towards political independence with the efforts of successive generations of English people, both at home and abroad, to curb the absolutist tendencies of monarchs. Thus the colonial dimension to a Progressive history of the United States[4] was blended with English Whig history[5] and it became possible for the historical exponents of American exceptionalism to trace the constitutional history of their young country backwards to Magna Carta of 1215[6] and even to the dark forests of Germany where the Anglo-Saxon peoples had originated.

This brief depiction of what was being written from the seventeenth to the mid-twentieth centuries on the history of England's (or more accurately Britain's) colonies in North America will serve to explain how Robert Palmer, a historian of Europe based in the United States, could conceive of the existence of an Atlantic Community in past centuries when such a concept had little meaning for most of his European counterparts, particularly those of them who, like Palmer, were historians of countries on the European continent.[7] However at the very moment that Palmer was formulating his thesis, the premise on which it rested was being challenged by other scholars and from two different angles.

The challenges closest to him at Princeton University, where Palmer made his academic career after his big book appeared, came from colleagues who specialized in the history of colonial North America. These had slowly, and then more rapidly, begun to counter the version of events that had been handed down to them by previous generations first by developing a social dimension to that history, and second by decrying the teleology that had inspired it. Instead of presuming that Britain's colonies in America had been destined from the outset to become independent of the mother country, these pointed to the fact that whatever disturbances characterized the history of the colonies were as likely to have been provoked by socio/economic dislocations within the colonies as by resentment over being governed from London.[8] Some historians, with Jack Greene a leader among the challengers, also pointed to the strong attachment of American colonists to English political and constitutional procedures even it they had to modify them to suit their particular requirements.[9] Then, those who studied the American Revolution itself pointed to the normally harmonious relations that had existed between Britain and its colonies and found that when the relations became seriously disrupted after 1763 it was more due to the bungling by inept and insensitive British officials then because of any anxiety on the part of some colonists to establish an independent polity.[10] This new generation of historians also pointed to the reality that only thirteen of Britain's Atlantic colonies sought to become independent of the mother country and that those in the West Indies and in Canada remained loyal.

Another challenge to the received version also came from those historians of colonial North America who questioned the assumption that the descendants of the New England Puritan migrants of the seventeenth century alone could be considered the progenitors of the American nation. Those most effective in countering this assertion were those who had dedicated themselves to studying the history of English settlement in the Chesapeake Bay area that encompassed the coastal regions of Virginia and Maryland. These could show that the English settlement at Jamestown had pre-dated the arrival of the first Puritans in New England; that early colonists in the Chesapeake proved every bit as ready as their New England counterparts to resist any unwarranted interference by the British authorities; and that when the revolutionary moment came they supplied a disproportionate number of the leaders that led to the thirteen colonies achieving their independence from Britain.[11] These however clung to the concept of a British Atlantic based on liberal principles but with Virginian gentlemen rather than New England Puritans sustaining the intellectual contact with developments in Britain and then in France.

This latter challenge which was based to an extent on sectional jealousy became more fundamental when some historians pointed to the presence in the Chesapeake of a considerable body of slaves of African descent, especially from the late seventeenth century forward, and, previous to that, large workforces of white indentured servants[12] whose labour was, in each case, the principal contributor to the wealth of the Virginian elite who simultaneously remained familiar with, and even participated in, social and political discourse in Europe.[13] This growing realization that the prosperity of Britain's colonies in America was based on the harsh exploitation of subservient workforces became indisputable when account was also taken of developments in the British colonies on the islands of the West Indies where the exploitation of slave labour (native American as well as African) was even more extreme and more vital to the very considerable wealth of the colonial elite than had been the case in the Chesapeake. Moreover as research attention was focused on Britain's colonies in the West Indies it became increasingly clear that the New England colonies were also caught in that nexus as it was revealed how the New England colonies had survived, and even prospered, by becoming suppliers of provisions to the slave colonies in the West Indies.[14] By this stage, in the 1960s and 1970s, scholarship within the United States was leading to the conclusion that if historians wished to foster the concept of an Atlantic World in past time they should think of a world based on slavery rather than on liberty and one that encompassed Africa as well as Europe and America.

This conclusion was not very different from that being advanced at much the same time by scholars in Europe (especially in Britain) who had been contemplating the involvement of Britain and of other European powers with the Americas during the early-modern centuries. Most of these had come to the subject from backgrounds in Imperial History where the triumphalist attitude that had once dominated the study of British involvement beyond the confines of Europe had fallen into disrepute during the post-war decades when decolonization rather than colonization impacted upon the everyday lives of people in Britain, as it did also upon the populations of the other European countries with an imperial past. In so far as England's, and Europe's, overseas expansion during the early-modern centuries continued to be studied it was to ask questions concerning how this involvement had influenced the economic developments in particular countries in Western Europe and in the world at large, and also how such developments had impacted upon the lives and cultures of non-European peoples who, willy nilly, became involved with European overseas expansion.

Some of this interest was stimulated by the protracted, and ultimately inconclusive, debate among economic historians concerning the extent to which the prolonged Spanish importation of silver from the New World triggered the inflationary spiral, and the resulting societal change, that had unquestionably been experienced by almost every country of Western Europe from the late fifteenth to the mid-seventeenth centuries. It was this debate, which persuaded the Chaunus, a French husband-and-wife team, to attempt, in so far as the surviving evidence permitted it, to reconstitute the totality of Spanish transatlantic traffic on the Atlantic during this crucial era.[15] At the same time English economic historians, notably Ralph Davis, sought more modestly to identify the scale and nature of the imports to, and exports and re-exports from, England that were related to its transatlantic engagement during this same period.[16] Davis, like several of his British contemporaries, was interested in identifying the factors (other than the sudden availability of Spanish silver) that contributed to the inflationary spiral that could be identified when he tracked the price of essential goods over time. However economic historians were also provoked into paying greater attention to trade on the Atlantic by the publication in 1944 by Eric Williams, a West Indian historian of African descent, of the so-called Williams thesis which contended that the First Industrial Revolution, which was then thought to explain the global hegemonic position that Britain came to enjoy during the nineteenth century, would never have been achieved had not British traders had money available for re-investment due to the profits they had garnered from the slave trade.[17]

While many historians in Britain (particularly economic historians) wished to qualify or discredit the Williams thesis, that author had succeeded in bringing some scholars to pay greater attention than they had done previously to the increasing economic importance of Atlantic trade as the seventeenth century proceeded; to the central position of the Caribbean as the source of the commodities that lubricated that trade; and to the importance of the link with Africa that was forged by European traders in search of the slaves who provided the workforce required to cultivate and process the crops from which the trade goods were derived. Historians who wrote in this tradition, the most accomplished of them being Richard Pares, may not have used the term the Atlantic World and made no claims to be writing Atlantic History. However it is certainly true that scholars of later generations who began to consider themselves to be Atlantic historians were greatly indebted to the insights and research of Pares and his contemporaries.[18]

While economic historians saw the need to challenge the Williams thesis those who identified with political causes of the Left, or had been inspired by Marxism, tended to look more favourably at Williams's critical attitude towards colonization even when they fell short of endorsing his conclusions. Of those historians who appear to have drawn some inspiration from Williams we will look at the contributions of David Beers Quinn and Kenneth Andrews who were concerned particularly with the origins of British overseas expansion. Each of these set out to re-interpret England's encounter with the wider world (and particularly the world on the far side of the Atlantic) at the point when they, as historians, had been liberated from the jingoism that had characterized what authors of previous generations had written on Britain's imperial past. They sought to take account of the impact of the initial encounter upon the lives and habitats of those who were forced to become subservient to the English, and to appraise the motivation and achievements of those English who entered upon such ventures. Quinn promoted his re-interpretation most effectively by displaying an interest in, and concern for, the native populations and cultures (Native American or Irish) that fell foul of the acquisitiveness of English adventurers during the sixteenth and seventeenth centuries. Andrews, on the other hand, alluded repeatedly to the plunder and piracy that was pursued by the well-known Elizabethan sea adventurers such as Drake, Raleigh, and Hawkins, and he demonstrated how some of London's leading merchants and several senior figures at court invested in, and profited from, extra-legal activities.[19]

When they are considered together, the publications of these two authors combined to sustain the general proposition that England's capitalist system was based on theft either from native populations or from European competitors. As they made their case, each exposed the darker side to the 'sea dogs' of the later years of Queen Elizabeth's reign who previously had been portrayed as unblemished heroes. Quinn and Andrews depicted them rather as products of their generation who repeatedly, and in different contexts, proved themselves to be enterprising, skilled, brave, curious, and unscrupulous in their single-minded pursuit of glory, gain, and social uplift. While Quinn reduced Humphrey Gilbert and Walter Raleigh to human dimensions Andrews did the same to Francis Drake. Not all was debunking, however, and while Quinn appraised the way in which Raleigh, and his principal agents, set about establishing English colonies both in Munster in Ireland and on Roanoke Island, off the coast of present-day North Carolina, Andrews admired Drake's seamanship as this had been demonstrated both by his global circumnavigation of 1580, which Andrews ranked 'among the greatest feats of early European oceanic enterprise', and by his ability to outwit and outmanoeuvre his Spanish opponents at close quarter and in confined space.[20]

Neither Quinn nor Andrews ever described himself as a student of an Atlantic World but each was keenly conscious that the actions they described involved, and had consequences, for people of many nationalities and social origins, including indigenous, European, and African. They were also aware that the English actors whose deeds they described believed themselves to be in competition with other Europeans whether with Basques and Normans seeking for advantage in the fishing grounds off Newfoundland or with Spaniards seeking to control passage through the Caribbean to the coastline of Central and South America. And each was also aware that if they were to prove themselves more sympathetic than previous scholars to all participants in the encounters they were describing, they would have to seek to enter into the mindset of more than the English adventurers. Quinn did so in exemplary fashion by linking his close study of the John White drawings of the Native Americans on Roanoke Island with recent archaeological investigations into indigenous cultures. The special contribution of Andrews was that he sought to come to grips with Spanish as well as English motivations and fears by delving into Spanish as well as English archives when describing the struggle between actors from those two countries for dominance in the Caribbean which, in one of his books, he described as an 'American Mediterranean'.[21]

This telling phrase suggests that as Andrews presented England's involvement in the Caribbean in an Atlantic setting he was looking enviously at the ease with which Fernand Braudel had won professional acceptance for his locution 'the Mediterranean World'; a term that would have been incomprehensible to earlier generations of scholars whose study of the Mediterranean had treated principally of the conflicts between Christianity and Islam for domination in that sea.[22] Some historians of the Atlantic, and most emphatically Bernard Bailyn, question the geographic determinism employed by Braudel to legitimize his usage. Bailyn's hostility to determinism may have decided him against conceptualizing an Atlantic World as a closed space, analogous to Braudel's Mediterranean, when in the mid-1980s he launched a recurrent international summer school in Atlantic History at Harvard University supported by the Mellon Foundation.[23] His conservatism was ultimately justified by the findings of several members of the Harvard summer school which showed that trade conducted within the Atlantic basin during the early modern centuries traversed a vast array of climates and habitats and that, unlike in the Mediterranean Sea as described by Braudel, people who used the Atlantic strove always to overcome the hindrances to human movement imposed by nature.[24]

It may be precipitate to describe the scholarly approach to Atlantic History encouraged by the Harvard summer school because well before then, and continuing to the present day, some historians had been developing a wider frame for their investigations of the colonial endeavours in the Atlantic of entrepreneurs from particular European nationalities. This approach has resulted in a plethora of journal articles, book chapters, and books devoted to the 'worlds' of the English/British Atlantic, the Spanish Atlantic, the Portuguese Atlantic, and the Dutch Atlantic. These various studies have proven useful in bringing scholars to appreciate that adventurers from any one European country who engaged with the Atlantic during the early-modern centuries were necessarily involved with a range of geographic areas and climates, with an array of settlement types, and a diversity of processing and trading possibilities. These latter ranged from slaves, animal pelts and sugar to tobacco, salted fish, and flour; both that made from manioc or maize and that milled from European wheat grown in an American environment.[25] However the fact that they chose national titles for their books, chapters, and articles might lead readers to believe that they were taking up where the imperial historians of a previous generation had left off. If they are so doing they differed from them, however, by concentrating on those parts of the various European sea-borne empires that were located on either side of the Atlantic Ocean and they usually considered the European presence and activities in Asia of the same time as separate, if interrelated, in that they were usually pursued by different traders, in different kinds of ships, and in distinct circumstances.

Moreover, many scholars of Atlantic activities who have located their work in such contexts have come to realize that segmenting the Atlantic along European national lines for the purposes of study may make archival sense but that it can prove misleading because it suggests that each such world was self-contained, which, obviously, was never the case. This is not to deny that much good research can be accomplished, for example by studying the Spanish Atlantic World in isolation as a zone that spread outwards from Seville towards the Caribbean and from thence to the isthmus of Panama and the vast territories that lay to the north and south of that point, and even westwards from Peru into the Pacific and as far as the Philippines. It has now come to be accepted that those wishing to track such 'national' endeavours can do so most profitably when they recognize that these ran parallel to, and were interrelated with, Atlantic endeavours of other European groups. It is now also accepted that such scholars must recognize that the various enterprises promoted by Spanish colonists in this vast expanse of land and sea were greatly assisted by indigenous populations, and also relied heavily upon a supplementary labour force from Africa that was supplied to the Spanish colonists initially by Portuguese traders, and then, after 1713, by British slave traders to whom the Spanish government had ceded the right of supply by formal treaty.

The older impression that each designated 'national' Atlantic World was self-contained was again conveyed by the attention traditionally given by authors to the various systems introduced by most European imperial powers to regulate trade with their respective colonies and to exclude foreign competition from them. Those scholars who have more recently examined the operation of such regulations have demonstrated that any such impression is false since they find that the machinery to achieve exclusivity was never sufficient to keep determined traders from interloping in prohibited markets. Thus it has been made clear that the Dutch were persistent intruders upon Spain's Atlantic dominions in the sixteenth century and that the Dutch also became the most successful and persistent trespassers upon British and French settlements in the Atlantic in the seventeenth century when their own Atlantic possessions were being wrested from them, principally by British naval action. Then, to further complicate matters, it has been shown, as has been emphasized by Thomas Adam in this volume, that traders from various German ports who had no Atlantic possessions become involved with Atlantic trade, sometimes under licence from European governments. These German traders were concerned both to find a market for the provisions and the manufactured commodities, notably linen and metal goods, that could be provided by their own hinterlands or back countries, and to gain direct access to those American commodities that were in increasing demand in areas of Europe remote from the ocean. The Atlantic commodities most in demand were tobacco, indigo, cotton, and sugar. And trade, as is well recognized, led to knowledge throughout the Germanic speaking areas of Europe of the career opportunities that America presented which led to significant 'German' emigration to the Americas, particularly from those areas close to navigable rivers that flowed in the direction of Atlantic sea ports.[26]

The other complicating factor that has come to the attention of those who continue to study these various nationally designated Atlantic worlds, is that the ambitions of European settlers in the various colonies established by several European governments were often at variance with those of the metropolitan authorities and that the settlers frequently conspired to promote their own interests by breaching regulations and restrictions laid down by metropolitan governments. Such ambivalence created an environment where illicit inter-colonial trade and even transatlantic smuggling could flourish. Marginalized groups such as French Huguenots and Irish Catholics who had been forced into exile for their beliefs and who had kinship connections in several Atlantic empires and in several European ports are seen to have become active in exploiting such opportunities, and many are known to have made handsome profits from their involvement with high risk/high gain activities that recognized no artificial boundaries before they refashioned themselves as legitimate traders.

Now that attention has been drawn to the porous nature of the borders between the various nationally designated 'European' trading empires in the Atlantic, it has encouraged historians to seek a more appropriate framework within which to study the entire spread of European influence into and across the Atlantic. At the same time historians are being made increasingly aware, especially by anthropologists and archaeologists, that much of what their predecessors have written on European involvement with other populations in the Atlantic basin is unpardonably Eurocentric and that they need urgently to take account of the contributions made by African slave populations and Native American populations to the creation of the various worlds that historians had been describing. As these calls for revision were being issued, other scholars, notably Ian Steele and Nicholas Rodger, who were experts on such matters as maritime navigation, climate, wind systems, and prevailing ocean currents, explained the extent to which the efforts of Europeans to shape an Atlantic World were influenced and constrained by natural forces.[27] In making such points these historians were not being as deterministic as Braudel had been when delineating the patterns of both settlement and navigation within his Mediterranean world, and they were conscious that scholars who had worked on trading patterns in the Indian Ocean (some of whom had studied with Braudel) had been able to show how, in the age of sail, the efforts of humans to traverse long distances on a large body of water had been both assisted and limited by seasonal climatic conditions. Thus informed and encouraged, those scholars who set out to retrace the paths of those involved with the various kinds of traffic that were promoted on the Atlantic Ocean during the early modern centuries, were able to show that in the age of sail, regardless of nationality or ship type, all European mariners who crossed the Atlantic in either direction between Europe and America, or who travelled southwards from Europe along the coast of Africa to secure slaves and provisions before they headed westwards across the ocean with their cargoes, traversed much the same routes, frequently within hailing distance of each other's vessels.[28]

All of these factors brought historians of European expansion and of Europe's Atlantic empires to appreciate that an Atlantic World existed throughout the early-modern period even if the concept and term had not been invoked at the time. As a consequence, several scholars devoted attention to considering how this new subject might best be approached and what its study encompassed. Bernard Bailyn was possibly the person who gave greatest thought to definition because as Director of the International Seminar on the History of the Atlantic World at Harvard University, he had a special responsibility to do so. As he and the members of the Harvard seminar came to grips with their subject they attached considerable importance to the voluntary and involuntary movement of peoples that became a constant feature of life within the Atlantic basin during the early modern centuries. It became so because promoters of colonial undertakings sought to satisfy the labour shortages that arose when they required people with particular skills to develop the various commercial projects they were undertaking, and when they had to re-people territories that had become depopulation because Native American populations had succumbed to European disease or had fled to escape European exploitation.[29] This attention to the movement of peoples led inevitably to a discussion of mortality rates experienced by Native American, African, and European populations respectively in different circumstances and in different environments and to the human hybridization that invariably occurred whenever mortality rates or sexual balances became skewed, as they frequently did. Trade within the Atlantic World, and from the Atlantic outwards to Asia, continued to be of core importance to Atlantic History as it had been to the older imperial history, but greater attention was now given to illicit as well as to licit trade, to the multicentric trading patterns that developed over time, and to the involvement of indigenous peoples and of Africans, as well as Europeans, in whatever trade occurred. Great attention was given to the undisciplined, sanguinary, and exploitative aspect of life within almost all parts of an Atlantic World where life became even more harsh and uncertain than within war-torn Europe. However, on the positive side those associated with Atlantic History have been taking an interest in explaining how, over time and in several different circumstances, people began to create a more certain and even a more caring Atlantic World despite its harsh and brutal beginnings. This has led to a consideration of the role within the Atlantic World of the Christian and Muslim religions, of administrative, including legal, institutions, and of Enlightenment thought (in the Americas as well as in Europe) in championing more humane values.

Jack P. Greene, together with colleagues at Johns Hopkins University, was another of the pioneers of Atlantic History and had promoted a seminar and a lecture series in Atlantic History long before the Harvard seminar on the History of the Atlantic World was established. The distinguishing mark of the Johns Hopkins seminar was its insistence upon the central role of Africa and Africans in the creation of an Atlantic World, but it, and certainly Jack Greene, also devoted attention to the political and administrative institutions that were established in and that developed in most Atlantic colonies. By virtue of the emphasis they placed upon what became 'normal', Greene and his colleagues do not appear to have dwelt as much as their opposite numbers at Harvard upon a caesura between a harsh beginning and more gentle maturing that characterized many colonial experiences in the Atlantic.[30]

All parties to the discussion of what Atlantic History entails are today agreed that the subject they would like to see developed would require a greater range of linguistic and methodological skills than most historians can master in a lifetime. They also agreed that their subject can be advanced most readily through comparative work of the kind exemplified by Sir John Elliott in his *Empires of the Atlantic World*. In that study Elliott combined a mastery of the extremely bulky secondary literature on each of the Spanish and British Atlantic empires with his own investigation into much primary literature relating to each of the two empires.[31] His, like all good comparative studies, sheds light on many differences between the two experiences. Of these, three leave a lasting impression. The first he identified was the good fortune of the Spanish in encountering and mastering sophisticated, populous, and highly urbanized preexisting empires whose populations had ready access to precious metals, as opposed to the British who, in those various parts of America in which they attempted to introduce settlements, met with relatively poor and unsophisticated populations who did not have access to precious metals. The second was the advantage the Spanish enjoyed over the British in having ready access to educated clerics and lawyers from Spain to oversee, administer, educate, and evangelize their new subjects, where the British always experienced difficulty in attracting skilled personnel to take up residence in the various colonies they promoted. And the third outstanding difference was the greater talent of Spaniards, and soon also of their new subjects in the New World, at creating visual representations of what they were engaged upon. While John Elliott alluded in his book to many differences in the two experiences at creating European-dominated empires in America, his most dramatic conclusion was that, regardless of the differences in time and context within which these two great undertakings were enacted, and notwithstanding the different religious and cultural backgrounds from which the original colonists had sprung, the Atlantic worlds that had been created respectively by the Spanish and the British at the close of the eighteenth century had more in common with each other than has traditionally been acknowledged. Moreover, he found that each of the two Atlantic empires had come to depend on each other to the point where a bid for political independence by one section of Britain's Atlantic empire after 1776 led to the rapid political unravelling also of most of Spain's Atlantic empire.[32] Such similarities, as Elliott would have it, had emerged because each had gone through similar processes, which, in the words of Bernard Bailyn, involved 'the fusion of exploitative economic force … and the shared idealism of the Enlightenment'.[33]

As I have described how the subject of Atlantic History has evolved over the past half-century or more, I have shown how, in recent years, it has been brought more sharply into focus principally by historians who in their earlier careers wrote concerning the histories of Atlantic empires dominated by particular European countries. To this extent Atlantic History is, as Thomas Adam has stated in this volume, an outgrowth of colonial history, but, as I have suggested, those involved in this enterprise who were trained as colonial historians have been transformed by the experience of coming to recognize a subject that involved African and Native American peoples as well as those from several European national, religious, and cultural backgrounds who had been the principal subject of interest to colonial historians. As the subject has developed it has, as Philip Morgan has shown in his contribution to this volume, promoted an extraordinary output of books and papers that are brimming with ideas by scholars who approach the subject from many different perspectives and with various methodologies. It has also, as Philip Morgan and Thomas Adam agree, encouraged the development of some academic programmes where early stage researchers are being trained to view developments from an Atlantic perspective. Equally important publications on Atlantic History have begun to exert some influence on how other historians approach their 'national' histories.

Thomas Adam seems confident that some practitioners of the history of the United States during the nineteenth and twentieth centuries recognize the need to introduce an Atlantic dimension to their work but he clearly would like to see more such impact and understanding. However more than the history of the United States is being influenced by the new knowledge of developments in the Atlantic that is being produced. The change that is underway can, I believe, also be illustrated to the case of France, where historians have been concerned overwhelmingly with the domestic history of the French state and its people, and, for the early modern period, the only overseas activity that has customarily received any serious attention has concerned France's involvement with Canada. This has been corrected more recently by a renewal of interest in France's engagement with the Caribbean, and by a growing recognition of the economic importance to France of its possessions in the Caribbean until the profit that French planters, traders, and entrepreneurs had been deriving from that source was jeopardized by the long drawn out revolution on the island of St Domingue that led ultimately to the creation of the independent state of Haiti. While historians have yet to assess the economic consequences for France of the loss or disruption of its most productive colonies, there is also a growing appreciation, which has been sustained by several studies, that those who promoted revolution in St Domingue carried the principles and practice of the French Revolution to further extremes than happened anywhere in the metropole.[34]

Historians from other European countries have also begun to look more closely at how the expansion of the various economies based on the Atlantic created both a demand throughout the Atlantic World for the commodities (ranging from provisions, to linen fabric and ironware) that the hinterlands to the great trading ports of Northern Europe could provide, and a domestic appetite for the consumer products (tobacco, sugar, dye stuffs, and cocoa, for example) that were becoming more readily available from various colonies in the Americas. As historians of particular European countries take such factors into account they are in effect demonstrating that the countries and regions whose history they study were being absorbed into an Atlantic World. This reality has became even more apparent to historians of Germany who now take account of the increasing number of people from the Germanic speaking areas of continental Europe who opted to make their homes in America – most noticeably in Pennsylvania – as readily as if their own governments had had colonies there. Then also historians from those countries, including the Netherlands and Denmark, that had less-consequential, but nonetheless formal, involvement with the Atlantic, have rekindled an interest in the study of the companies that had been chartered to promote Atlantic trade and colonization, including with the slave trade.

The chapter by Philip Morgan in this volume charts the sharp increase in publication on Atlantic subjects that has occurred in the recent past. His compilation shows, however, that relatively few authors have attempted to write on developments within the entire Atlantic World, even for a short period of time, possibly because of the formidable linguistic and methodological challenges that such a task would present. Given such challenges some historians persist with the study of Atlantic worlds supposedly constructed by particular European nations which, in a sense, contradicts what Atlantic History involves; others write broadly based studies of the production of, or trade in, single Atlantic commodities ranging from sugar, slaves, salt, rice, and rum to Madeira wine and pearls, while those who want a more comprehensive Atlantic perspective have, for the moment, to satisfy themselves with collections of essays by specialist authors who have combined their talents and interests to achieve the panoramic view that no one author seems capable of representing. But even with all such approaches and with the formidable output in publications on Atlantic History that Philip Morgan describes in this volume, some historians with Atlantic experience challenge the validity of the Atlantic framework and suggest that the evangelists for a new subject should instead be promoting global history.[35]

Such criticism is welcome, as is the suggestion made by Thomas Adam in this volume, that Atlantic historians, who usually terminate their enquiry about 1820, would be well advised to extend their investigations into the nineteenth and twentieth centuries when, as he puts it, 'transatlantic dialogue' was more active and audible than previously. I have no doubt that he is correct on this point since European migration to America was on a scale in the nineteenth century that was inconceivable in the age of sail. These very words make the point, however, that the dramatic developments the fifnteenth, sixteenth, seventeenth, and eighteenth centuries that command the interest of Atlantic historians were fundamentally different from the transatlantic contacts that developed in the nineteenth century.

The first difference was that those who ventured on long distance travel during these earlier centuries were frequently seeking to make their way into the unknown or the little known, and crossed the Atlantic under sail in wooden craft without the aid of reliable instruments to measure longitude. This was entirely different from the experience of those who undertook long journeys in the age of steam when mariners had better navigational instruments available to them and when would-be migrants from Europe to America could make their way by train to port cities from what previously had been considered inaccessible parts of Europe. From the ports they might then undertake transatlantic voyages that became ever more predictable as steam-powered ships with sophisticated navigational instruments took over from sailing vessels, as greater attention was given to hygiene, and as more use was made of ironclad vessels. Those who made the voyage in the nineteenth century were also travelling increasingly to locations where people of their acquaintance had preceded them and where a European style infrastructure had been put in place. The other essential difference was that migration for most of the nineteenth century involved the movement of free people whereas the majority of those involved in the re-peopling of the Americas in the seventeenth and eighteenth centuries arrived as unfree people at destinations that were usually not of their own choosing either because they had contracted away their labour to become indentured servants, or because they were being conveyed in chains from Africa as chattel slaves to serve as labourers on plantations in America. The close off of the transatlantic slave trade almost everywhere during the early decades of the nineteenth century meant that, thereafter, the transatlantic connection was principally one between Europeans and Americans of European extraction. This was very different from the lively cultural interaction on American soil between peoples who were indigenous to the three continents of Europe, Africa, and America. This interaction, which has become one of the principal matters that concern historians of the Atlantic World, would hardly have been comprehensible to European emigrants to the Americas of the nineteenth and the twentieth centuries. This, I would suggest, justifies the efforts of the practitioners of Atlantic History to designate some point in the 1820s as a terminal date for their subject because it is only by doing so that they can hope to maintain the integrity of their subject, and prevent their historical enquiry from being re-submerged in the teleological morass from which the scholars of the 1960s and 1970s rescued it.

Notes

1   The genealogy of the term has been traced in B. Bailyn, *Atlantic History: Concept and Contours* (Cambridge, MA: Harvard University Press, 2005), and in W. O'Reilly, 'Genealogies of Atlantic History', *Atlantic Studies*, 1 (2004), pp. 66–84.

2 R. Palmer, *The Age of the Democratic Revolution: A Political History of Europe and America*, 2 vols: Vol. 1, *The Challenge* (Princeton: Princeton University Press, 1959), Vol. 2, *The Struggle* (Princeton: Princeton University Press, 1964).

3 Palmer, *The Age of the Democratic Revolution*, Vol. 2, p. 546.

4 On the impact of Progressivism (the belief that each generation does better than its predecessor) on American historical writing see R. Hofstadter, *The Progressive Historians, Turner, Beard and Parrington* (New York: Cape, 1968).

5 The term 'Whig history' was popularized in H. Butterfield, *The Whig Interpretation of History* (Cambridge: Bell, 1931) where the author criticized the tendency of some nineteenth-century British authors, and some of his contemporaries, to attribute the power and influence that Britain enjoyed in the nineteenth century to constitutional choices made by English people in earlier centuries.

6 *Magna Carta Libertatum* or the Great Charter of Liberties was a document, probably composed by Stephen Langton, Archbishop of Canterbury, that was conceded by King John of England on 15 June 1215 to a rebellious group of English Barons at Runnymede, on the River Thames near Windsor, when they were at the point of deposing him. The document provided assurance that all people, including the king, were subject to law. It, and variations upon it, were subsequently disputed but the basic principles of Magna Carta were enshrined in the Statute Law of England in 1297. For a brief introduction see Claire Breay and Julian Harrison, 'Magna Carta; an Introduction', on the British Library website, and for its subsequent influence in North America see 'Magna Carta: Cornerstone of the US Constitution', on EDSITEment, the website of the National Endowment of the Humanities.

7 A notable exception was Jacques Godechot's *Histoire de l'Atlantique* (Paris: Bordas, 1947), and it is no surprise that Godechot worked closely with Palmer.

8 A largely forgotten pioneer in this area was Wesley Frank Craven, a colleague of Palmer at Princeton; see W. F. Craven, *White, Red and Black: The Seventeenth-Century Virginian* (Charlottesville: The University Press of Virginia, 1971).

9 J. P. Greene, *The Quest for Power: The Lower Houses of Assembly in the Southern Royal Colonies, 1689–1776* (Chapel Hill: University of North Carolina Press, 1963).

10 E. S. Morgan with H. Morgan, *The Stamp Act Crisis: Prologue to Revolution* (Chapel Hill: Collier, 1963).

11 For examples of this historiography see W. E. Washbourne, *The Governor and the Rebel: A History of Bacon's Rebellion* (Chapel Hill: University of North Carolina Press, 1957); E. S. Morgan, *American Slavery: American Freedom: The Ordeal of Colonial Virginia* (New York: Norton, 1975).

12 Indentured servants were usually recruited in Europe by ships' captains or their agents who covered the cost of their passage to America in return for indentures by which the servants contracted away their labour for a specified number of years (frequently seven). The captains recouped their investments by selling the labour that these servants had contracted away to employers in the colonies who frequently exploited these servants ruthlessly.

13 This was already adumbrated in Craven, *White, Red and Black* and in Morgan, *American Slavery*, but was developed in precise detail in a sequence of publications by a group of historians who dedicated themselves to the study of British colonial society in the Chesapeake in microscopic detail; this vast literature has been ably summarized and augmented in J. Horn, *Adapting to a New World: English Society*

in the Seventeenth-Century Chesapeake (Chapel Hill: University of North Carolina Press, 1994).

14 Perhaps the most influential of such publications was R. S. Dunn, *Sugar and Slaves: The Rise of the Planter Class in the English West Indies, 1624–1713* (New York: Norton, 1973).

15 H. Chaunu and P. Chaunu, *Séville et l'Atlantique* (8 vols, Paris: S. E. V. P. E. N, 1955–9).

16 R. Davis, *The Rise of the English Shipping Industry in the Seventeenth and Eighteenth Centuries* (London: David & Charles, 1962).

17 E. Williams, *Capitalism and Slavery* (Chapel Hill: University of Noth Carolina Press, 1944).

18 For examples of his work written in this vein see R. Pares, *A West India Fortune* (London: Longmans, 1950); R. Pares, 'Merchants and Planters', *Economic History Review*, Supplement 4 (Cambridge: Cambridge University Press, 1960); Pares had been writing on this subject ever before Eric Williams had published; see, for example, R. Pares, *War and Trade in the West Indies* (Oxford: Clarendon Press, 1936).

19 K. R. Andrews (ed.), *English Privateering Voyages to the West Indies, 1588–1595* (Hakluyt Society, Cambridge: Cambridge University Press, 1959).

20 K.R. Andrews, *Drake's Voyages: A Re-Assessment of their Place in Elizabethan Maritime Expansion* (London: Weidenfeld & Nicolson, 1970), p. 98.

21 For an appraisal of Quinn's work see N. Canny and K. Kupperman, 'The Scholarship and Legacy of David Beers Quinn, 1909–2002', *The William and Mary Quarterly*, 60 (2003), pp. 843–60; and for an appraisal of the work of Andrews see N. Canny, 'Kenneth Raymond Andrews, 1921–2012', *Biographical Memoirs of Fellows of the British Academy*, 8 (2014), pp. 2–15.

22 F. Braudel, *The Mediterranean and the Mediterranean World in the Age of Philip II* (Paris: Librairie Armand Colin, 1966) (2 vols., first English edition London, 1966 which was a translation of an updated French text that had first been published in France in 1949).

23 For Bailyn on Braudel see Bailyn, *Atlantic History*, pp. 4–5.

24 For an example of the conclusions being developed by the research team associated with the Harvard summer school see B. Bailyn and P. L. Denault (eds.), *Soundings in Atlantic History: Latent Structures and Intellectual Currents, 1500–1830* (Cambridge, MA: Harvard University Press, 2009).

25 Note the sequence of essays on various national Atlantics included both in J. P. Greene and P. D. Morgan (eds), *Atlantic History: A Critical Appraisal* (Oxford: Oxford University Press, 2009); and in N. Canny and P. Morgan (eds), *The Oxford Handbook of the Atlantic World, 1450–1850* (Oxford: Oxford University Press, 2011); each such essay makes reference to other work couched in a similar frame.

26 C. Schnurmann, *Europa trifft Amerika: Zwei alte Welten bilden eine neue Atlantische Welt, 1492–1783* (Berlin: LIT Verlag, 2009).

27 I. K. Steele, *The English Atlantic, 1675–1740: An Exploration of Communication and Community* (Oxford: Oxford University Press, 1986); N. A. M. Rodger, *The Command of the Ocean: A Naval History of Britain, 1649–1815* (London: W. W. Norton, 2004).

28 In this context I have found very persuasive S. D. Behrendt, 'Ecology, Seasonality, and the Transatlantic Slave Trade', in Bailyn and Denault, *Soundings in Atlantic History*, pp. 44–85.

29 The concept of re-peopling was developed by Bailyn himself in B. Bailyn, *The Peopling of British North America: An Introduction* (New York: Knopf, 1986).

30 B. Bailyn, *The Barbarous Years: The Peopling of British North America: The Conflict of Civilizations, 1600-1675* (New York: Knopf, 2012).

31 J. H. Elliott, *Empires of the Atlantic World: Britain and Spain in America, 1492-1830* (New Haven: Yale University Press 2006).

32 *Ibid.*

33 Bailyn, *Atlantic History*, p. 111.

34 See L. Dubois, *Avengers of the New World: The Story of the Haitian Revolution* (Cambridge, MA: Belknap Press of Havard University Press, 2004); D. Geggus, 'The Haitian Revolution in Atlantic Perspective', in Canny and Morgan, *The Oxford Handbook of the Atlantic World*, pp. 533-49.

35 This view is canvassed in P. A. Coclanis, 'Beyond Atlantic History', in Greene and Morgan, *Atlantic History*, pp. 337-56; in L. Colley, *The Ordeal of Elizabeth Marsh: A Woman in World History* (New York: HarperCollins, 2007); and in A. Games, *The Web of Empire: English Cosmopolitans in an Age of Expansion, 1560-1660* (Oxford: Oxford University Press, 2008); the responsibility of historians to address bigger topics is debated also in J. Guldi and D. Armitage, *The History Manifesto* (Cambridge: Cambridge University Press, 2014) although their principal concern is to encourage historians to identify change over long chronological spans rather than greater geographic spaces.

References

Andrews, K. R. *Drake's Voyages: A Re-Assessment of their Place in Elizabethan Maritime Expansion* (London: Weidenfeld & Nicolson, 1970).

Andrews, K. R. (ed.), *English Privateering Voyages to the West Indies, 1588-1595* (Hakluyt Society, Cambridge: Cambridge University Press, 1959).

Bailyn, B. *Atlantic History: Concept and Contours* (Cambridge, MA: Havard University Press, 2005).

Bailyn, B. *The Barbarous Years: The Peopling of British North America: The Conflict of Civilizations, 1600-1675* (New York: Knopf, 2012).

Bailyn, B. *The Peopling of British North America: An Introduction* (New York: Knopf, 1986).

Bailyn, B. and P. L. Denault (eds), *Soundings in Atlantic History: Latent Structures and Intellectual Currents, 1500-1830* (Cambridge, MA: Havard University Press, 2009).

Behrendt, S. D. 'Ecology, Seasonality, and the Transatlantic Slave Trade', in B. Bailyn and P. L. Denault (eds), *Soundings in Atlantic History: Latent Structures and Intellectual Currents, 1500-1830* (Cambridge, MA: Havard University Press, 2009), pp. 44-85.

Braudel, F. *The Mediterranean and the Mediterranean World in the Age of Philip II* (Paris: Librairie Armand Colin, 1966) (2 vols, first English edition London, 1966, which was a translation of an updated French text that had first been published in France in 1949).

Butterfield, H. *The Whig Interpretation of History* (Cambridge: Bell, 1931).

Canny, N. 'Kenneth Raymond Andrews, 1921-2012', *Biographical Memoirs of Fellows of the British Academy*, 8 (2014), pp. 2-15.

Canny, N. and K. Kupperman. 'The Scholarship and Legacy of David Beers Quinn, 1909–2002', *The William and Mary Quarterly*, 60 (2003), pp. 843–60.

Canny, N. and P. Morgan (eds), *The Oxford Handbook of the Atlantic World, 1450–1850* (Oxford: Oxford University Press, 2011).

Coclanis, P. A. 'Beyond Atlantic History', in J. P. Greene and P. D. Morgan (eds), *Atlantic History: A Critical Appraisal* (Oxford: Oxford University Press, 2009), pp. 337–56.

Colley, L. *The Ordeal of Elizabeth Marsh: A Woman in World History* (New York: Harper Collins, 2007).

Craven, W. F. *White, Red and Black: The Seventeenth-Century Virginian* (Charlottesville: The University Press of Virginia, 1971).

Davis, R. *The Rise of the English Shipping Industry in the Seventeenth and Eighteenth Centuries* (London: David & Charles, 1962).

Dubois, L. *Avengers of the New World: The Story of the Haitian Revolution* (Cambridge, MA: Belknap Press of Havard University Press, 2004).

Dunn, R. S. *Sugar and Slaves: The Rise of the Planter Class in the English West Indies, 1624–1713* (New York: Norton, 1973).

Elliott, J. H. *Empires of the Atlantic World: Britain and Spain in America, 1492–1830* (New Haven: Yale University Press, 2006).

Games, A. *The Web of Empire: English Cosmopolitans in an Age of Expansion, 1560–1660* (Oxford: Oxford University Press, 2008).

Geggus, D. 'The Haitian Revolution in Atlantic Perspective', in N. Canny and P. Morgan (eds), *The Oxford Handbook of the Atlantic World, 1450–1850* (Oxford: Oxford University Press, 2011), pp. 533–49.

Godechot, J. *Histoire de l'Atlantique* (Paris: Bordas, 1947).

Greene, J. P. *The Quest for Power: The Lower Houses of Assembly in the Southern Royal Colonies, 1689–1776* (Chapel Hill: University of North Carolina Press, 1963).

Greene, J. P. and P. D. Morgan (eds), *Atlantic History: A Critical Appraisal* (Oxford: Oxford University Press, 2009).

Guldi, J. and D. Armitage. *The History Manifesto* (Cambridge: Cambridge University Press, 2014).

Hofstadter, R. *The Progressive Historians, Turner, Beard and Parrington* (New York: Knopf, 1968).

Horn, J. *Adapting to a New World: English Society in the Seventeenth-Century Chesapeake* (Chapel Hill: University of North Carolina Press, 1994).

Morgan, E. S. *American Slavery: American Freedom: The Ordeal of Colonial Virginia* (New York: Norton, 1975).

Morgan, E. S. with H. Morgan. *The Stamp Act Crisis: Prologue to Revolution* (Chapel Hill: Collier, 1963).

O'Reilly, W. 'Genealogies of Atlantic History', *Atlantic Studies*, 1 (2004), pp. 66–84.

Palmer, R. *The Age of the Democratic Revolution: A Political History of Europe and America*, 2 vols: Vol. 1, *The Challenge* (Princeton: Princeton University Press, 1959), Vol. 2, *The Struggle* (Princeton: Princeton University Press, 1964).

Pares, R. 'Merchants and Planters', *Economic History Review*, Supplement 4 (Cambridge: Cambridge University Press, 1960).

Pares, R. *War and Trade in the West Indies* (Oxford: Clarendon Press, 1936).

Pares, R. *A West India Fortune* (London: Longmans, 1950).

Rodger, N. A. M. *The Command of the Ocean: A Naval History of Britain, 1649–1815* (London: W. W. Norton, 2004).

Schnurmann, C. *Europa trifft Amerika: Zwei alte Welten bilden eine neue Atlantische Welt, 1492–1783* (Berlin: LIT Verlag, 2009).

Steele, I. K. *The English Atlantic, 1675–1740: An Exploration of Communication and Community* (Oxford: Oxford University Press, 1986).

Washbourne, W. E. *The Governor and the Rebel: A History of Bacon's Rebellion* (Chapel Hill: University of North Carolina Press, 1957).

Williams, E. *Capitalism and Slavery* (Chapel Hill: University of North Carolina Press, 1944).

4

Atlantic Studies today

Philip D. Morgan

The study of the early modern Atlantic world has come of age in the twenty-first century. Books on the subject pour off the presses in dazzling – and dizzying – profusion. In recent years at least sixty books with the words 'Atlantic' or 'Atlantic World' in their titles have been published annually. A decade ago, the comparable number could be counted on the fingers of one hand.[1] This dramatic increase in such a short space of time is a testament to the cascading interest in the subject. Works that explore some aspect of the movement and interaction of people, commodities, microbes, cultural practices, and values across and around the Atlantic basin are now legion. Atlantic History runs the gamut from capacious to narrowly defined studies – from those employing broad-gauged transatlantic or circum-Atlantic frameworks to those taking a narrower, cis-Atlantic approach in which one corner of the Atlantic world is probed – but all are premised on the idea that such studies gain heightened meaning by being placed in an appropriately enlarged context. Thinking about a wider Atlantic world, it is assumed, enriches scholarship, whether large or small in scale.

Comparative oceanic studies or works with implicit oceanic comparisons are now beginning to appear. The collection of essays entitled *Pacific Histories* draws implicit contrasts with other oceans. Thus the editors of this volume claim that 'more than any similar oceanic region the Pacific has a fundamental physical unity'. The region's distinct hydrographic and climatic patterns make it 'a uniquely coherent oceanic space'. The Pacific 'suggests a whole globe in a way that other oceans do not'. The Pacific is clearly 'a sea of islands' in ways other oceans are not. Such statements invite comparisons with the Atlantic.[2] Another edited volume, entitled *Britain's Oceanic Empire*, pairs essays exploring oceanic contexts, law and governance, diplomatic and military relations, and commerce in both Atlantic and Indian Ocean worlds. There were obvious, glaring differences between the two – not least in the size of their indigenous populations – but those divergences should not, in the editors' words, 'mask the commonalities of regimes of legal and economic discipline that allowed Britain to project *imperium* globally and establish an oceanic empire'.[3]

Capacious approaches to the Atlantic or adjoining oceans are emerging, but they are swamped by the deluge of studies of particular locales (from a plantation to a colony to a region), various slices of the subject (whether by empire or by multi-coloured hues), events and processes, commodities, and singular individuals and groups, all set in Atlantic context. Sylvester Manor on Shelter Island, near the tip of Long Island, has merited two books that probe its Atlantic connections.[4] Located at the intersection of two models of French colonization, situated at the margin of three empires, linking Europe, North America, and the Caribbean, the colony of Louisiana has been depicted as a veritable crossroads of the Atlantic world.[5] Places as far removed as Nova Scotia and Curaçao have been studied for their Atlantic connections.[6] The Caribbean is one region that is attracting much interest for its Atlantic links.[7] The relationship of the American South and the Atlantic is the subject of a collection of essays.[8] Particular imperial Atlantics – whether Dutch, Spanish, Portuguese, or French – continue to be probed.[9] Wim Klooster acknowledges that the Dutch were 'ubiquitous as merchants, selling manufactures and slaves, buying produce, and extending loans across imperial boundaries', but emphasizes that 'the Dutch Atlantic empire was forged on the battle-field'; and Christopher Hodson and Brett Rushforth are at work on a narrative of the French Atlantic.[10] Other scholars prefer to dissect the Atlantic according to coloured hues.[11] Yet others turn to particular events and processes – whether banishment or impermanence or the Seven Years War – and place them in Atlantic context.[12] Commodity studies, ranging from indigo to cotton, from salt to cod, from mahogany to logwood, from silver to pearls invite attention to circum-Atlantic movements;[13] even the humble plantation hoe, a tool without north European precedent, is best seen as a quintessential Atlantic product.[14] Dress regimes and sartorial cultures have been explored on both large and small scales.[15] Notable individuals, such as Hans Staden or Olaudah Equiano, are archetypal Atlantic figures, around whom cottage industries have mushroomed.[16] Maroon groups and women – just to mention two segments of Atlantic societies – in various locales and empires have inspired recent books.[17]

It is impossible to keep pace with this torrent of scholarly endeavour, and any attempt to assess trends seems a brazen act of foolhardiness. Constraints of space dictate the singling out of just a few tendencies. The first is an increased attention to the ocean itself. Surprisingly, the first wave of Atlantic History paid little attention to the maritime world, but that is now changing. A second, a strong suit of Atlantic History from the beginning, is the search for interconnections and linkages of all kinds. Terms beloved in Atlantic History are currents, pathways, circuits, flows; the dominant metaphor, apt for this digital age, is the network.[18] Recovering the crucial linkages that connected regions is one of the rationales for Atlantic History. Finally, the supersized character of the Atlantic framework has threatened to eclipse singular actors and human agency, thereby generating a countervailing attention to individuals and families. These three trends hardly exhaust the riches of Atlantic History, but they showcase a few key lines of force.

As has been pointed out, Atlantic History is often 'history with a hole in the middle'. The Atlantic is viewed 'as a pre-defined, self-evident space, which serves as a rhetorical device to define the people living around its shores'. Much Atlantic History might be labelled 'history with the Atlantic left out'. Yet ships and seafaring were obviously fundamental to the construction of the Atlantic world and deserve much more attention than they have received.[19] Joyce Chaplin has suggested that the term Atlantic Ocean, which was hardly used at all at first, rose from the bottom up, from sailors, rather than the reverse, and became quite widespread in the late eighteenth century.[20] Much more needs to be known about the practicalities of seafaring, governing so much of life in this new world. Some advocate a 'new thalassography', emphasizing the differences between oceans and seas and the similarities among different seas; others call for more attention to maritime governance.[21] Be that as it may, a broad social history of Atlantic seafaring remains to be written.

One book that fills at least part of the gap is Stephen R. Berry's *A Path in the Mighty Waters*. It explores how many Europeans experienced the eighteenth-century crossing of the Atlantic Ocean. The ocean, in this telling, was more than a backdrop, but rather an active agent. The ocean journey was not just a transitory, fleeting period in people's lives but rather transformative. Cooped up in close quarters for months at a time, ships operated as compressed 'frontiers', where diverse groups encountered one another and established new patterns of social organization. Shipmates, for example, played a vital role. Experiences aboard ship can be likened to a conversion. Indeed, ships inspired travellers to express their faith in the midst of an environment usually thought hostile to organized religion. Berry's book focuses on the religious impact of the crossing, although it treats quotidian issues too, such as preparations for a voyage, coastal delays, the tedium of travel, terrifying storms, and the relief when land was sighted.[22]

Another popular genre is the study of a single voyage. One of the most successful such works is Robert Harms's use of the diary of a French mariner to illuminate the circum-Atlantic slave trading voyage of the *Diligent*, which left Vannes, Brittany in 1731, cruised the African coast from the Sestos River on the so-called Grain Coast to Whydah on the Bight of Benin, stopped at various Atlantic islands off the coast of Africa, before setting off on the infamous Middle Passage, and selling its slaves at Martinique, and returning to France over a year later.[23] A couple of years before the *Diligent* left Vannes, Marc-Antoine Caillot, an employee of the French Company of the Indies, departed for Louisiana. His *Relation du voyage*, which has recently come to light, has been described as possibly colonial Louisiana's 'most significant' manuscript discovery in well over a century, and is distinctive in beginning not with the ocean crossing, itself a riveting account 'marked in turn by wonder, horror, desperation, and hope', but rather with the author's overland journey from Paris to the coast.[24] Another voyage story concerns the *Hankey*, a British ship, which in 1792 first conveyed anti-slavery colonists to West Africa in a failed attempt to establish a free colony, before taking the remainder the following year to Grenada and then St Domingue in the West Indies, where supposedly it dramatically transformed the Atlantic world by sparking 'the first major pandemic of yellow fever in the Western Hemisphere'.[25] This claim is an exaggeration: many Atlantic voyages, not just one, created this pandemic, but yellow fever's toll throughout the Atlantic, which is captured well through the lens of a singular journey, was certainly real enough. One voyage of the *Amistad*, not transatlantic but inter-American in scope, has given rise to many books.[26]

Labour practices at sea have generated much interest. The role of impressment, for example, inspires contrasting opinions. The British naval historian N. A. M. Rodger is sanguine, seeing it as a well-accepted tradition; Marcus Rediker, the American social historian, considers Atlantic ships as sites of capitalist exploitation and proletarian resistance. Denver Brunsman, who has supplied the first comprehensive study of British naval impressment throughout the eighteenth-century Atlantic world, splits the difference. He recognizes the sacrifice and resistance caused by impressment; but also sees it as a remarkably efficient and productive way of securing forced labour. Of the major European naval powers, only the Dutch avoided some form of conscription. The French *inscription maritime* was a centralized and rationalized system but France (and Spain) 'sacrificed much of their merchant shipping to man their navies during war', whereas Britain 'could draw on a continuous reserve of skilled maritime labor in most wars long after more absolutist states had exhausted their supplies'.[27] The character of the seafaring experience was rooted as much in the terrestrial communities that launched mariners as in their working social relations, their shipboard communities.[28]

The ocean as an ecological space is getting its due. This is most evident in the work of Jeffrey Bolster. He focuses on the large marine ecosystem between Cape Cod and Newfoundland, which he terms 'an Atlantic crossroads, a hot spot of interaction between Natives, itinerant Europeans, and settlers in search of marine resources'.[29] One revelation is the impact of fishing on bird stocks, most particularly the use of seabirds as bait. Numerous rocky islands shifted from being sanctuaries to slaughterhouses. What happened to the great auk, the flightless North Atlantic 'penguins', extinct since 1844, casualties of overharvesting, is sobering. Edmund Burke's observation that the seas are 'vexed by their fisheries' is notably apt.[30] There is no getting around the declension story; there are no sunny outcomes. His is an unrelievedly grim tale, with commercial fishing depleting complex ecosystems rather rapidly. At the same time, Bolster makes the point that the ocean is an extremely changeable environment; and it is extraordinarily difficult to assess causation when human factors interact with natural environmental effects. His is an especially complicated and demanding narrative.[31] Other marine ecosystems in the Atlantic basin – rivers, creeks, estuaries, bays, and various intersections of land and sea – are now receiving attention.[32]

A venerable approach to the maritime world is a study of a port; and these have been multiplying of late. A number of recent books have focused on African coastal entrepôts, whether Ouidah (Whydah), Benguela, or Anomabu. Each of these were major centres of the slave trade, embarking overall more than 1,004,000, 764,000, and 466,000 captives respectively.[33] Law sees Ouidah as a community based on exchange, not just of commodities, but also mediating the transmission of cultural influences across the Atlantic.[34] Candido documents the profound transformation of Benguela by its deep involvement in the Atlantic economy; it became a Luso-African society, 'as creolized as any place in the Americas'.[35] Similarly, Sparks describes Annamaboe as 'a creolized society deeply embedded in the Atlantic world'.[36] One of the largest ports in the Americas, Havana, has received an excellent history of its sixteenth-century history; and more are in the offing concerning later centuries.[37] The origins of popular support for independence in Buenos Aires has been situated in the context of Atlantic History, particularly the city's growing integration in the Atlantic economy.[38] By the late eighteenth century, even a remote fur-trading centre such as Detroit was saturated with the same kind of transnational goods found around the Atlantic rim. It was incorporated into a broader Atlantic world.[39] Studies of port residents – ranging from slaves to women to Jews, just to take a few examples – are also mushrooming.[40] Collections of essays that bring together studies of individual ports and discussions of typologies and hierarchies now exist for the early modern period and its immediate successor.[41]

A second promising area is the elaboration of networks across the Atlantic – and beyond, in some cases. As with studies of ports, the history of commercial connections constitutes a classic Atlantic story.[42] David Hancock in his *Oceans of Wine* draws together European investors, island producers, syndicates of distributors, and consumers throughout the Atlantic world to tell the tale of a notable and distinctive Atlantic commodity, Madeira wine. He reveals a highly decentralized – what he terms self-organizing – mode of organization, far from dominated by any kind of top-down management or limited oligarchy. The core of the book focuses on the elaboration of distribution networks around the Atlantic. His work emphasizes the porousness of empire: it examines the flow of Madeira wine across imperial and political boundaries.[43] A very different kind of study, John Tutino's *Making a New World*, focuses on a fertile basin, the Bajío, extending northwest of Mexico City, a dynamic mining and agricultural region, its influences and connections radiating outward throughout the Atlantic and beyond. The site of an early commercial society, the Mexican Bajío 'fashioned a New World salient of capitalist social relations'.[44] It stood at the centre, rather than the margins, of not just Atlantic but global capitalism. Recent revisionist works on Spanish Atlantic trade have revealed significant risks and uncertainties, an emphasis on building trust, a competitive environment, a lack of monopoly practices in the fleet system, and a reliance in some settings on contraband.[45]

Much attention has recently been given to scientific, often specifically natural historical and medical, connections that span the Atlantic. Much of the work has been conducted within one or more imperial settings.[46] The hybridity that mixing produced – particularly the creative borrowings by Atlantic world residents from Native American, African, and European traditions – has been one focus. Practitioners of Atlantic science, as Kathleen Murphy has pointed out, now 'include enslaved and free Africans (as well as Native Americans and women) alongside more familiar figures such as Benjamin Franklin, Alexander von Humboldt, and Charles-Marie de La Condamine'.[47] Blacks and Amerindians had privileged knowledge; Euro-Americans sometimes valued – and at other times denigrated – that information. Euro-Americans conducted medical experiments on enslaved individuals and feared so-called African diseases.[48] Another theme has been the role of military and naval personnel in transforming knowledge about tropical medicine.[49] Yet another is the emergence of a contentious, far-flung, loosely knit, transnational intellectual or epistemic commu-nity, one that developed means of communication and rules of engagement to arrive at shared and fundamental understandings of the natural world.[50] A final theme is the attention to bodily health and healing practices, which in certain Atlantic colonies were especially experimental and in advance of Europe.[51]

Religious and ethnic groups – whether Quaker, Moravian, Huguenot, Jesuit, Kongo (just to mention a few that have merited recent work, too numerous to cite here) – also developed dense Atlantic ties. I would single out four groups for particular notice. Puritans seem the least likely religious group for further study, since so much is known about them, but considering southern New England and Bermuda in the same frame and exploring their relations with Native Americans and African Americans in the seventeenth century, Heather Miyano Kopelson highlights inclusiveness.[52] A number of essay collections have explored the role of Jews in the Atlantic.[53] One of the most intri-guing revelations has been the Jewish communities that emerged on the West African coast in the seventeenth century.[54] Relations between Jews and other groups attract interest.[55] Among Protestant missionaries, one of the more interesting findings has been that most evangelists were not white Anglo-Americans but members of the same groups that missionaries were trying to convert. Hundreds of African, Afro-American, and Native American missionaries evangelized blacks and Indians throughout the Atlantic world.[56] Finally, in the Catholic realm, perhaps the most stimulating recent book has been Stuart Schwartz's *All Can be Saved*. Who would have guessed that, at a time when Catholic orthodoxy was rampant, many common folk in the Iberian Atlantic world were either sceptical, indifferent, and/or believers in religious rela-tivism, freedom of conscience, and tolerance, as in the popular expression, 'each can be saved in his or her own faith'. Heterodox religious thinking flourished in the Iberian Atlantic, although more attention to its extent and distribution – employing network analysis, perhaps – will be necessary to chart its full contours.[57] Intriguingly, scholars in the Anglo-American tradition seem to have given Schwartz's findings a fairly wide berth.[58]

One final set of networks – intimate ones – deserve attention. Susannah Shaw Romney argues, in the case of seventeenth-century New Netherlands, that intimate networks rather than formal structures constituted empire (why the two could not be more symbiotic is a reasonable question). The process was bottom-up rather than top-down, she maintains. She is interested in the web of connections that arose from people's immediate, affective, and personal associations. These linkages could span large distances, but interpersonal interactions were crucial. Household, family, and neighbourhood formed the backbone of empire. Kin played an essential part in its creation; friends and colleagues helped stitch together a strong latticework of support. Women were key players, anchoring the system.[59] These arguments mesh well with a special issue of the *William and Mary Quarterly*, devoted to families in Atlantic History, with articles ranging from the early Spanish Caribbean to revolutionary France, from sixteenth-century Peru to the eighteenth-century African Gold Coast, from Montreal to Osu or present-day Accra. In this collection, 'the fungibility as well as the familiarity of family' is emphasized; and, as much as marriage mattered, so did other sources of trust, such as religion, ethnicity, law, and business customs.[60] Situating families at the centre of the French Atlantic world, Jennifer Palmer deploys the concept of intimacy to reveal the intersections of race, slavery, and gender.[61]

Given this interest in families and households, it is not surprising that a third tendency in Atlantic History is a focus on individuals and family groups. One aim is to capture some of the broad-scale processes that swept the Atlantic world in the interior lives of singular individuals. As one historian has put it, 'the Atlantic World has little meaning unless we can see it reflected in the lives of individuals'.[62] The 'biographical turn' embraced by many Atlantic historians is an appealing and manageable format to illuminate impersonal forces on a small scale. This is Atlantic History writ small – microhistory, in a word – or the 'examination of life stories that highlights personal trajectories and the ways people experienced everyday life'.[63] Rather than structures and abstractions, the emphasis is on human variability and idiosyncracy. Telling the story of an exceptional individual can disrupt sweeping generalizations, thereby emphasizing contingency and accident. Extraordinary lives enrich our understanding of what is possible – whether it is the forester from the Palatinate, Caspar Wistar, who became a wealthy Philadelphia merchant and manufacturer; or the transatlantic peregrinations of German Lutheran pastor, Henry Melchior Muhlenburg; or globe-trotting Elizabeth Marsh whose life was both Atlantic and global in scope; or seven-time Atlantic crossing Benjamin Franklin; or the Afro-Caribbean Moravian Rebecca Protten, a slave who became an evangelist; or the African healer Domingos Álvares who circumnavigated the Atlantic, from the interior of West Africa to Brazil and then to Portugal; or a sachem of the Niantics, Ninigret, who transformed himself into 'arguably the most influential Indian leader in southern New England'; or the slave trader and plantation owner, Zephaniah Kingsley, who married a Wolof woman with whom he had three children and to whom he eventually granted their freedom; or Alex Dumas, a mixed-race man born to an enslaved woman in St Domingue, who rose to become Napoleon's general-in-chief of the Army of the Alps; or Toussaint Louverture who laboured many decades as a slave before launching the only successful slave revolt in world history. Such works suggest the promise of connecting particular people and very specific locales to broader Atlantic developments.[64]

As a variation on the individual study, family sagas are also in vogue. The three generations of the Vincent/Tinchant family whose Atlantic journey began in Senegambia, taking in St Domingue, Cuba, New Orleans, France, and Belgium, are notable for their resort to documents in order to claim freedom and dignity. The two Robin Johns, slave traders, who were themselves sold into slavery in the Caribbean and the Chesapeake, finally reached England where they eventually won their freedom, before returning to Old Calabar where they resumed their old business of slave trading. The remarkably intertwined lives of white farmers the Hempsteads and black slaves the Jacksons in eighteenth-century New London, Connecticut reveals a thoroughly entangled world of alliances and betrayals, companionship and subjugation. The story of the Reyniers, a married couple, he of French Swiss extraction, she of German, who crossed the Atlantic several times as Moravian missionaries is at once a tale of a troubled union and of religious encounters ranging from Europe to North America to the Greater Caribbean. Another married couple, aristocratic southerners, who spent almost twenty years in West Africa, pursued a quixotic missionary odyssey that uncovers 'the mystery of good intentions and cruel consequences and the enigma of human freedom in the midst of slavery'.[65]

The Atlantic world encompassed more than travellers. Of late there has been a little flurry of attention to the landlocked and the sedentary, people who never ventured across the Atlantic but upon whose thought the Atlantic made an indelible impression. However restrictive their physical movements, their mind's eye surveyed the broad panorama of Atlantic life. John Locke never sailed on the Atlantic, saw the ocean only late in life, but, as David Armitage points out, his imperial vision was 'bounded by the Atlantic'.[66] Similarly, from his perch in the Scottish hills, David Hume, who at one time contemplated but never completed an Atlantic voyage, nevertheless lived in 'an uncertain and fleeting succession of Atlantic milieu'. His life, in Emma Rothschild's telling, illustrates 'the ways in which the Atlantic world of the eighteenth century extended far inland, into the interior of provinces and into the interior of individual existence'.[67] The same may be said of a number of German intellectuals and merchants residing a long way from the Atlantic in continental Europe.[68] It would be easy to multiply studies of particular individuals – Richard Hakluyt, the Marquis of Pombal, Pedro Rodriguez de Campomanes, Abbé Raynal, William Robertson – who never crossed the Atlantic but for whom the ocean loomed large in their thinking.

Attractive as these singular studies are, the question they obviously raise is: how typical or representative are the individuals or families on whom the spotlight falls? One solution is to group together individuals, to suggest some of the commonalities and variations. A group of radical reformers, cosmopolitan itinerants who crossed border to promote the cause of liberty, reveal the struggle for universal human rights that spanned the Atlantic.[69] A volume of essays on the Black Atlantic argues that by 'attaching names and faces to broad processes such as slaving, enslavement, identity formation, empire-building, migration, and emancipation, biography can illuminate the meanings of these large, impersonal forces for individuals'. Biography can, for example, 'reveal the contexts and decisions behind *slaving*, thus making explicitly historical a process that is often understood as static and structural'.[70] An eclectic volume entitled *Atlantic Biographies* brings together essays on individuals and small groups to illustrate larger themes – sojourning, exploitation, and identity formation.[71] A collection of eighteen Puritan biographies, drawn from the seventeenth century, is designed to illustrate the diversity of that religious faith and to outline the legacies these individuals collectively bequeathed to future Americans.[72]

A few years ago, one joke doing the rounds was that Atlantic History as a field would be dead when the first textbook appeared. The field must have experienced many deaths, because now there are a number of textbooks.[73] In addition, documentary collections and essay volumes have proliferated at a rapid clip.[74] A recent illustrated history touts the Atlantic as 'the ocean that changed the world'; while another popular history celebrates it as the centre of the world, 'a living thing', even with its own psychology and moods.[75]

As should be evident from this list of books alone, the field of Atlantic History is far from moribund; indeed it is vibrant, thriving, gathering momentum. Its promise outweighs its pitfalls.

True, the field has become so capacious that its limits and boundaries have become less detectable, more blurred and murky over time. True too, historians of the Atlantic world have focused much more on connections than on comparisons. There are few successors on the horizon to John Elliott's magisterial *Empires of the Atlantic World*.[76] True, also, there may be a retrospective imposition of 'Atlantic' onto experiences and events that were imagined and narrated differently by historical actors. Still, despite the problematic features of Atlantic History, the great virtue of thinking in Atlantic terms is that such an approach seeks to overcome the tyranny of the local; it encourages broad perspectives, transnational orientations, and expanded horizons, while offering the opportunity to overcome national and other parochialisms.

Notes

1 E. Slauter, 'History, Literature, and the Atlantic World', *William and Mary Quarterly*, 3d Ser., 65:1 (2008), pp. 135–66, p. 137.
2 D. Armitage and A. Bashford (eds), *Pacific Histories: Ocean, Land, People* (New York: Palgrave Macmillan, 2014), pp. 1, 5, 6, 8.
3 H. V. Bowen, E. Mancke, and J. G. Reid (eds), *Britain's Oceanic Empire: Atlantic and Indian Ocean Worlds, c.1650–1850* (New York: Cambridge University Press, 2012), p. 450.
4 M. Griswold, *The Manor: Three Centuries at a Slave Plantation on Long Island* (New York: Farrar, Straus, and Giroux, 2013); K. H. Hayes, *Slavery before Race: Europeans, Africans, and Indians at Long Island's Sylvester Manor Plantation 1651–1884* (New York: New York University Press, 2013).
5 C. Vidal (ed.), *Louisiana: Crossroads of the Atlantic World* (Philadelphia: University of Pennsylvania Press, 2014).
6 S. T. Henderson and W. G. Robicheau, *The Nova Scotia Planters in the Atlantic World, 1760–1830* (Fredericton: Acadiensis Press, 2012); L. Rupert, *Creolization and Contraband: Curaçao in the Early Modern Atlantic World* (Athens: University of Georgia Press, 2012).
7 E.g. J. R. McNeill, *Mosquito Empires: Ecology and War in the Greater Caribbean, 1620–1914* (New York: Cambridge University Press, 2010); D. Wheat, *Atlantic Africa and the Spanish Caribbean, 1570–1640* (Chapel Hill: University of North Carolina Press, 2016); E. Bassi, *An Aqueous Territory: Sailor Geographies and New Granada's Transimperial Greater Caribbean World* (Durham, NC: Duke University Press, 2016).
8 B. Ward, M. Bone, and W. A. Link (eds), *The American South and the Atlantic World* (Gainesville: University Press of Florida, 2013).
9 G. Oostindie and J. Vance Roitman, 'Repositioning the Dutch in the Atlantic, 1680–1800', *Itinerario. European Journal of Overseas History*, 32:2 (2012), pp. 129–60; A. J. Kuethe and K. J. Andrien (eds), *The Spanish Atlantic World in the Eighteenth Century: War and the Bourbon Reforms, 1713–1796* (New York: Cambridge University Press, 2014); H. Braun and L. Vollendorf (eds), *Theorising the Ibero-American*

Atlantic (Leiden: Brill, 2013); G. Paquette, *Imperial Portugal in the Age of Atlantic Revolutions: The Luso-Brazilian World, c. 1770–1850* (New York: Cambridge University Press, 2014).

10 W. Klooster, *The Dutch Moment: War, Trade, and Settlement in the Seventeenth-Century Atlantic World* (Ithaca: Cornell University Press, 2016), pp. 1, 3; C. Hodson and B. Rushforth, *Discovering Empire: France and the Atlantic World from the Crusades to the Age of Revolutions* (New York: Basic Books, forthcoming).

11 E.g. K. Wheland, 'The Green Atlantic: Radical Reciprocities between Ireland and America in the Long Eighteenth Century', in K. Wilson (ed.), *A New Imperial History: Culture, Identity, and Modernity in Britain and the Empire, 1660–1840* (Cambridge: Cambridge University Press, 2004), pp. 216–38; J. Weaver, *The Red Atlantic: American Indigenes and the Making of the Modern World, 1000–1927* (Chapel Hill: University of North Carolina Press, 2014).

12 G. Morgan and P. Rushton, *Banishment in the Early Atlantic World: Convicts, Rebels and Slaves* (London: Bloomsbury, 2013); P. Pope and S. Lewis-Simpson (eds), *Exploring Atlantic Transitions: Archaeologies of Transience and Permanence in New Found Lands* (Woodbridge: The Boydell Press, 2013); M. Schumann and K. Schweizer, *The Seven Years' War: A Transatlantic History* (London: Routledge, 2008); F. De Bruyn and S. Regan (ed.), *The Culture of the Seven Years' War: Empire, Identity, and the Arts in the Eighteenth-Century Atlantic World* (Toronto: University of Toronto Press, 2014).

13 For three examples see J. L. Anderson, *Mahogany: The Costs of Luxury in Early America* (Cambridge, MA: Harvard University Press, 2012); S. Beckert, *Empire of Cotton: A Global History* (New York: Alfred A. Knopf, 2014); M. Warsh, *American Baroque: Pearls and the Nature of Empire, 1492–1700* (Chapel Hill: University of North Carolina Press, 2018).

14 C. Evans, 'The Plantation Hoe: the Rise and Fall of an Atlantic Commodity, 1650–1850', *William and Mary Quarterly*, 3d Ser., 69:1 (2012), pp. 71–100.

15 R. S. DuPlessis, *The Material Atlantic: Clothing, Commerce, and Colonization in the Atlantic World, 1650–1800* (Cambridge: Cambridge University Press, 2016); Z. Anishanslin, *Portrait of a Woman in Silk: Hidden Histories of the British Atlantic World* (New Haven: Yale University Press, 2016).

16 E.g. H. Staden, *Hans Staden's True History: An Account of Cannibal Captivity in Brazil*, ed. and trans. N. L. Whitehead and M. Harbsmeier (Durham, NC: Duke University Press, 2008); E. M. Duffy and A. C. Metcalf, *The Return of Hans Staden: A Go-Between in the Atlantic World* (Baltimore: Johns Hopkins University Press, 2011); V. Carretta, *Equiano the African: Biography of a Self-Made Man* (Athens: University of Georgia Press, 2005).

17 E.g. K. M. Bilby, *True-Born Maroons* (Gainesville: University Press of Florida, 2005); N. Millett, *The Maroons of Prospect Bluff and their Quest for Freedom in the Atlantic World* (Gainesville: University Press of Florida, 2013); S. E. Owens and J. E. Mangan (eds), *Women of the Iberian Atlantic* (Baton Rouge: Louisiana State University Press, 2012); K. Candlin and C. Pybus (ed.), *Enterprising Women: Gender, Race, and Power in the Revolutionary Atlantic* (Athens: University of Georgia Press, 2015).

18 See, for example, K. Grandjean, *American Passage: The Communications Frontier in Early New England* (Cambridge, MA: Harvard University Press, 2015); A. Dubcovsky, *Informed Power: Communication in the Early American South* (Cambridge, MA: Harvard University Press, 2016).

19 N. A. M. Rodger, 'Atlantic Seafaring', in N. Canny and P. D. Morgan (eds), *Oxford Handbook of the Atlantic World, 1450–1850* (Oxford: Oxford University Press, 2011), pp. 71–86.

20 J. Chaplin, 'The Atlantic Ocean and Its Contemporary Meanings, 1492–1808', in J. P. Greene and P. D. Morgan (eds), *Atlantic History: A Critical Appraisal* (New York: Oxford University Press, 2009), pp. 35–51.

21 P. N. Miller (ed.), *The Sea: Thalassography and Historiography* (Ann Arbor: University of Michigan Press, 2013); P. C. Mancall and C. Shammas (eds), *Governing the Sea in the Early Modern Era: Essays in Honor of Robert C. Ritchie* (San Marino: Huntington Library, 2015).

22 S. R. Berry, *A Path in the Mighty Waters: Shipboard Life and Atlantic Crossings to the New World* (New Haven: Yale University Press, 2015); see also C. P. Magra, 'Faith at Sea: Exploring Maritime Religiosity in the Eighteenth Century', *International Journal of Maritime History*, 19:1 (2007), pp. 87–106.

23 R. Harms, *The Diligent: A Voyage through the Worlds of the Slave Trade* (New York: Basic Books, 2001); for another slaving voyage, see S. M. Kelly, *The Voyage of the Slave Ship Hare: A Journey into Captivity from Sierra Leone to South Carolina* (Chapel Hill: University of North Carolina Press, 2016).

24 M.-A. Caillot, *A Company Man: The Remarkable French-Atlantic Voyage of a Clerk for the Company of the Indies: A Memoir*, E. M. Greenwald (ed.) (New Orleans: The Historic New Orleans Collection, 2013), pp. xiii–xiv.

25 B. G. Smith, *Ship of Death: A Voyage that Changed the Atlantic World* (New Haven: Yale University Press, 2013), p. 168.

26 Most recently M. Rediker, *The Amistad Rebellion: An Atlantic Odyssey of Slavery and Freedom* (New York: Viking, 2012); B. N. Lawrance, *Amistad's Orphans: An Atlantic Story of Children, Slavery, and Smuggling* (New Haven: Yale University Press, 2015).

27 D. Brunsman, *The Evil Necessity: British Naval Impressment in the Eighteenth-Century Atlantic World* (Charlottesville: University of Virginia Press, 2013), p. 8; N. Rogers, *The Press Gang: Naval Impressment and its Opponents in Georgian Britain* (New York: Continuum, 2007).

28 See D. Vickers and V. Walsh, *Young Men and the Sea: Yankee Seafarers in the Age of Sail* (New Haven: Yale University Press, 2005); M. J. Jarvis, *In the Eye of All Trade: Bermuda, Bermudians, and the Maritime Atlantic World* (Chapel Hill: University of North Carolina Press, 2010); M. G. Hanna, *Pirate Nests and the Rise of the British Empire 1570–1740* (Chapel Hill: University of North Carolina Press, 2015); M. Rediker, *Outlaws of the Atlantic: Sailors, Pirates, and Motley Crews in the Age of Sail* (Boston: Beacon Press, 2014).

29 W. J. Bolster, 'Putting the Ocean in Atlantic History: Maritime Communities and Marine Ecology in the Northwest Atlantic, 1500–1800', *American Historical Review*, 113:1 (2008), pp. 9–47.

30 E. Burke, 'Speech in Conciliation with America, 22 March 1775', *The Works of Edmund Burke in nine volumes*, Vol. II (Boston: Little & Brown, 1839), p. 30.

31 W. J. Bolster, *The Mortal Sea: Fishing the Atlantic in the Age of Sail* (Cambridge, MA: Harvard University Press, 2012).

32 C. Pastore, *Between Land and Sea: The Atlantic Coast and the Transformation of New England* (Cambridge, MA: Harvard University Press, 2014); A. Lipman, *The Saltwater*

Frontier: Indians and the Contest for the American Coast (New Haven: Yale University Press, 2015).

33 D. Eltis and D. Richardson, *Atlas of the Transatlantic Slave Trade* (New Haven: Yale University Press, 2010), pp. 118, 121–2, 151.

34 R. Law, *Ouidah: The Social History of a West African Slaving 'Port' 1727–1892* (Athens: Ohio University Press, 2004).

35 M. P. Candido, *An African Slaving Port and the Atlantic World: Benguela and Its Hinterland* (New York: Cambridge University Press, 2013), pp. 122, 125.

36 R. J. Sparks, *Where the Negroes Are Masters: An African Port in the Era of the Slave Trade* (Cambridge, MA: Harvard University Press, 2014), p. 5.

37 A. De la Fuente, *Havana and the Atlantic in the Sixteenth Century* (Chapel Hill: University of North Carolina Press, 2008); E. Schneider, *The Occupation of Havana: Slavery, War, and Empire in the Eighteenth Century* (Chapel Hill: University of North Carolina Press, 2018).

38 L. L. Johnson, *Workshop of Revolution: Plebeian Buenos Aires and the Atlantic World, 1776–1810* (Durham, NC: Duke University Press, 2011).

39 C. Cangany, *Frontier Seaport: Detroit's Transformation into an Atlantic Entrepôt* (Chicago: University of Chicago Press, 2014).

40 J. Cañizares-Esguerra, M. D. Childs, and J. Sidbury (eds), *The Black Urban Atlantic in the Age of the Slave Trade* (Philadelphia: University of Pennsylvania Press, 2013); D. Catterall and J. Campbell (eds), *Women in Port: Gendering Communities, Economies, and Social Networks in Atlantic Port Cities, 1500–1800* (Leiden: Brill, 2012); D. Cesarani, *Port Jews: Jewish Communities in Cosmopolitan Maritime Trading Centres, 1550–1950* (Hoboken: Taylor & Francis, 2014); N. L. Gelfand, *To Live and to Trade: The Status of Sephardi Mercantile Communities in the Atlantic World during the Seventeenth and Eighteenth Centuries* (Oxford: The Littman Library of Jewish Civilization, 2014).

41 F. W. Knight and P. K. Liss (eds), *Atlantic Port Cities: Economy, Culture and Society in the Atlantic World, 1650–1850* (Knoxville: University of Tennessee Press, 1991); M. Suárez Bosa (ed.), *Atlantic Ports and the First Globalisation, c.1850–1930* (Basingstoke: Palgrave Macmillan, 2014).

42 N. Glaisyer, 'Networking: Trade and Exchange in the Eighteenth-Century British Empire', *Historical Journal*, 47:2 (2004), pp. 451–76; A. Graham, 'Mercantile Networks in the Early Modern World', *Historical Journal*, 56:1 (2013), pp. 279–95.

43 D. Hancock, *Oceans of Wine: Madeira and the Emergence of American Trade and Taste* (New Haven: Yale University Press, 2009).

44 J. Tutino, *Making a New World: Founding Capitalism in the Bajío and Spanish North America* (Durham: Duke University Press, 2011), p. 7.

45 X. Lamikiz, *Trade and Trust in the Eighteenth-Century Atlantic World: Spanish Merchants and their Overseas Networks* (Woodbridge: The Boydell Press for the Royal Historical Society, 2010); J. Cromwell, *Covert Commerce: A Social History of Contraband Trade in Venezuela, 1701–1789*, PhD dissertation (University of Texas at Austin, 2012); J. Baskes, *Staying Afloat: Risk and Uncertainty in Spanish Atlantic World Trade, 1760–1820* (Stanford: Stanford University Press, 2013).

46 S. S. Parrish, *American Curiosity: Cultures of Natural History in the British Atlantic World* (Chapel Hill: University of North Carolina Press, 2006); H. J. Cook, *Matters of Exchange: Commerce, Medicine, and Science in the Dutch Golden Age* (New Haven: Yale

University Press, 2007); A. López-Denis, *Disease and Society in Colonial Cuba, 1790–1840,* PhD dissertation (University of California, Los Angeles, 2007); J. cDelbourgo and N. Dew (eds), *Science and Empire in the Atlantic World* (New York: Routledge, 2008); N. Safier, *Measuring the New World: Enlightenment Science and South America* (Chicago: University of Chicago Press, 2008); D. Bleichmar, P. De Vos, K. Huffine, and K. Sheehan (eds), *Science in the Spanish and Portuguese Empires, 1500–1800* (Palo Alto: Stanford University Press, 2009); D. Bleichmar, *Visible Empire: Botanical Expeditions and Visual Culture in the Hispanic Enlightenment* (Chicago: University of Chicago Press, 2012); P. Chakrabarti, *Materials and Medicine: Trade, Conquest and Therapeutics in the Eighteenth Century* (Manchester: Manchester University Press, 2010); T. D. Walker, 'The Medicines Trade in the Portuguese Atlantic World: Acquisition and Dissemination of Healing Knowledge from Brazil (c. 1580–1800)', *Social History of Medicine,* 26:3 (2013), pp. 403–31; B. Breen, *Tropical Transplantations: Drugs, Nature, and Globalization in the Portuguese and British Empires, 1640–1755,* PhD dissertation (University of Texas at Austin, 2015).

47 K. S. Murphy, 'Collecting Slave Traders: James Petiver, Natural History, and the British Slave Trade', *William and Mary Quarterly,* 3d Ser., 70:4 (2013), pp. 637–70, p. 638; C. B. Strang, *Entangled Knowledge, Expanding Nation: Science and the United States Empire in the Southeast Borderlands, 1783–1842,* PhD dissertation (University of Texas at Austin, 2013); C. B. Strang, 'Indian Storytelling, Scientific Knowledge, and Power in the Florida Borderlands', *William and Mary Quarterly,* 3d Ser., 70:4 (2013), pp. 671–700; K. Rönnbäck, 'Enlightenment, Scientific Exploration and Abolitionism: Anders Sparrman's and Carl Bernhard Wadström's Colonial Encounters in Senegal, 1787–1788 and the British Abolitionist Movement', *Slavery and Abolition,* 34:3 (2013), pp. 425–55; L. Schiebinger, *Secret Cures of Slaves: People, Plants, and Medicine in the Eighteenth-Century Atlantic World* (Stanford: Stanford University Press, 2017); L. Schiebinger, 'Scientific Exchange in the Eighteenth-Century Atlantic World', in B. Bailyn and P. Denault (eds), *Soundings in Atlantic History: Latent Structures and Intellectual Currents, 1500–1830* (Cambridge, MA: Harvard University Press, 2009), pp. 294–328; and for a plea for more such work, see J. Cañizares-Esguerra and B. Breen, 'Hybrid Atlantics: Future Directions for the History of the Atlantic World', *History Compass,* 11:8 (2013), pp. 597–607.

48 K. S. Murphy, 'Translating the Vernacular: Indigenous and African Knowledge in the Eighteenth-Century British Atlantic', *Atlantic Studies,* 8:1 (2011), pp. 29–48; K. Paugh, 'Yaws, Syphilis, Sexuality, and the Circulation of Medical Knowledge in the British Caribbean and Atlantic World', *Bulletin of the History of Medicine,* 88:2 (2014), pp. 225–52; L. Schiebinger, 'Medical Experimentation and Race in the Eighteenth-Century Atlantic World', *Social History of Medicine,* 26:3 (2014), pp. 364–82; S. Snelders, 'Leprosy and Slavery in Suriname: Godfried Schilling and the Framing of a Racial Pathology in the Eighteenth Century', *Social History of Medicine,* 26:3 (2014), pp. 432–55.

49 M. Harrison, *Medicine in an Age of Commerce and Empire: Britain and its Tropical Colonies, 1660–1830* (Oxford: Oxford University Press, 2010); C. E. Kelly, *War and the Militarization of British Army Medicine, 1793–1830* (London: Pickering and Chatto, 2010); E. Charters, *Disease, War, and the Imperial State: The Welfare of the British Armed Forces during the Seven Years' War* (Chicago: University of Chicago Press, 2014).

50 K. Arner, *The Malady of Revolutions: Yellow Fever in the Atlantic World, 1793–1828*, PhD dissertation (Johns Hopkins University, 2014). See also T. Apel, *Feverish Bodies, Enlightened Minds: Yellow Fever and Common-Sense Natural Philosophy in the Early American Republic, 1793–1805*, PhD dissertation (Georgetown University, 2012).

51 P. Gómez, *The Experiential Caribbean: Creating Knowledge and Healing in the Early Modern Atlantic* (Chapel Hill: University of North Carolina Press, 2017); K. Johnston, 'The Constitution of Empire: Place and Bodily Health in the Eighteenth-Century Atlantic World', *Atlantic Studies*, 10:4 (2013), pp. 443–66; C. Gherini, '*Experiment and Good Sense Must Direct You': Managing Health and Sickness in the British Plantation Enlightenment, 1756–1815*, PhD dissertation (Johns Hopkins University, 2016).

52 H. M. Kopelson, *Faithful Bodies: Performing Religion and Race in the Puritan Atlantic* (New York: New York University Press, 2014).

53 P. Bernardini and N. Fiering (eds), *The Jews and the Expansion of Europe to the West, 1450–1800* (New York: Berghahn Books, 2001); R. L. Kagan and P. D. Morgan (eds), *Atlantic Diasporas: Jews, Conversos, and Crypto-Jews in the Age of Mercantilism, 1500–1800* (Baltimore: Johns Hopkins University Press, 2009); J. S. Gerber (ed.), *The Jews in the Caribbean* (Oxford: The Littman Library of Jewish Civilization, 2014).

54 P. Mark and J. da Silva Horta, *The Forgotten Diaspora: Jewish Communities in West Africa and the Making of the Atlantic World* (New York: Cambridge University Press, 2011).

55 E.g. J. Schorsch, *Swimming the Christian Atlantic: Judeoconverts, Afroiberians and Amerindians in the Seventeenth Century* (Leiden: Brill, 2009).

56 E. E. Andrews, *Native Apostles: Black and Indian Missionaries in the British Atlantic World* (Cambridge, MA: Harvard University Press, 2013).

57 S. Schwartz, *All Can Be Saved: Religious Tolerance and Salvation in the Iberian Atlantic World* (New Haven: Yale University Press, 2008).

58 'Critical Forum, featuring Lu Ann Homza, David D. Hall, Marcy Norton, Andrew R. Murphy, and Stuart B. Schwartz', *William and Mary Quarterly*, 3d Ser., 66:2 (2009), pp. 409–33; E. Glaser (ed.), *Religious Tolerance in the Atlantic World: Early Modern and Contemporary Perspectives* (Basingstoke: Palgrave Macmillan, 2014).

59 S. S. Romney, *New Netherland Connections: Intimate Networks and Atlantic Ties in Seventeenth-Century America* (Chapel Hill: University of North Carolina Press, 2014).

60 J. Hardwick, S. M. S. Pearsall, and K. Wulf (eds), 'Centering Families in Atlantic Histories', *William and Mary Quarterly*, 3d Ser., 70:3 (2013), pp. 205–424, p. 207.

61 J. L. Palmer, *Intimate Bonds: Family and Slavery in the French Atlantic* (Philadelphia: University of Pennsylvania Press, 2016).

62 Sparks, *Where the Negroes Are Masters*, p. 4; see also R. J. Sparks, *Africans in the Old South: Mapping Exceptional Lives across the Atlantic World* (Cambridge, MA: Harvard University Press, 2016).

63 R. Ferreira, *Cross-Cultural Exchange in the Atlantic World: Angola and Brazil during the Era of the Slave Trade* (New York: Cambridge University Press, 2012), p. 2.

64 R. Beiler, *Immigrant and Entrepreneur: The Atlantic World of Caspar Wistar, 1650–1750* (University Park, PA: The Pennsylvania State University Press, 2008); H. Wellenreuther, T. Müller-Bahlke, and A. G. Roeber (eds), *The Transatlantic World of Heinrich Melchior Mühlenberg in the Eighteenth Century* (Halle: Verlag der Franckeschen Stiftungen, 2013); L. Colley, *The Ordeal of Elizabeth Marsh: A Woman in World History* (New York: Pantheon Books, 2007); G. S. Wood,

The Americanization of Benjamin Franklin (New York: Penguin, 2004); J. F. Sensbach, *Rebecca's Revival: Creating Black Christianity in the Atlantic World* (Cambridge, MA: Harvard University Press, 2005); J. A. Fisher and D. J. Silverman, *Ninigret, Sachem of the Niantics and Narragansetts. Diplomacy, War, and the Balance of Power in Seventeenth-Century New England and Indian Country* (Ithaca: Cornell University Press, 2014), p. xi; D. L. Schafer, *Zephaniah Kingsley Jr. and the Atlantic World: Slave Trader, Plantation Owner, Emancipator* (Gainesville: University of Florida Press, 2013); T. Reiss, *Black Count: Glory, Revolution, Betrayal, and the Real Count of Monte Cristo* (New York: Broadway Books, 2012); P. Girard, *Toussaint Louverture: A Revolutionary Life* (New York: Basic Books, 2016).

65 R. J. Scott and J. Hébrard, *Freedom Papers: An Atlantic Odyssey in the Age of Emancipation* (Cambridge, MA: Harvard University Press, 2012); R. J. Sparks, *The Two Princes of Calabar: An Eighteenth-Century Atlantic Odyssey* (Cambridge, MA: Harvard University Press, 2004); A. Bonaventura, *For Adam's Sake: A Family Saga in Colonial New England* (New York: Liveright, 2013); A. S. Fogleman, *Two Troubled Souls: An Eighteenth-Century Couple's Spiritual Journey in the Atlantic World* (Chapel Hill: University of North Carolina Press, 2013); E. Clarke, *By the Rivers of Water: A Nineteenth-Century Atlantic Odyssey* (New York: Basic Books, 2013), p. xxii.

66 D. Armitage, 'John Locke: Theorist of Empire?', in S. Muthu (ed.), *Empire and Modern Political Thought* (New York: Cambridge University Press, 2012), pp. 84–111, p. 90.

67 E. Rothschild, 'The Atlantic Worlds of David Hume', in B. Bailyn and P. Denault (eds), *Soundings in Atlantic History: Latent Structures and Intellectual Currents, 1500–1830* (Cambridge, MA: Harvard University Press, 2009), pp. 405–48, pp. 429–30.

68 S. Lachenicht (ed.), *Europeans Engaging the Atlantic: Knowledge and Trade, 1500–1800* (Frankfurt and New York: Campus Verlag, University of Chicago Press, 2014).

69 J. Polasky, *Revolutions without Borders: The Call to Liberty in the Atlantic World* (New Haven: Yale University Press, 2015).

70 L. A. Lindsay and J. W. Sweet (eds), *Biography and the Black Atlantic* (Philadelphia: University of Pennsylvania Press, 2014), pp. 1, 3; see also B. G. Mamigonian and K. Racine (eds), *The Human Tradition in the Black Atlantic, 1500–2000* (Lanham: Rowman & Littlefield, 2010).

71 J. A. Fortin and M. Meuwese (eds), *Atlantic Biographies: Individuals and Peoples in the Atlantic World* (Leiden: Brill, 2014). See also K. Racine and B. G. Mamigonian (eds), *The Human Tradition in the Atlantic World, 1500–1850* (Lanham: Rowman & Littlefield, 2010).

72 F. J. Bremer, *First Founders: American Puritans and Puritanism in an Atlantic World* (Durham, NH: University of New Hampshire Press, 2012).

73 D. R. Egerton, A. Games, J. G. Landers, K. Lane, and D. R. Wright, *The Atlantic World: A History, 1400–1888* (Wheeling: Harlan Davidson, 2007); T. Benjamin, *The Atlantic World: Europeans, Africans, Indians and Their Shared History, 1400–1900* (New York: Cambridge University Press, 2009); K. O. Kupperman, *The Atlantic in World History* (New York: Oxford University Press, 2012); J. K. Thornton, *A Cultural History of the Atlantic World, 1250–1820* (New York: Cambridge University Press, 2012); A. Suranyi, *The Atlantic Connection: A History of the Atlantic World, 1450–1900* (New York: Routledge, 2014).

74 T. Benjamin, T. Hall, and D. Rutherford (eds), *The Atlantic World in the Age of Empire* (Boston: Houghton Mifflin, 2001); T. J. Shannon, *Atlantic Lives: A Comparative*

Approach to Early America (New York: Pearson, 2004); W. Klooster and A. Padula (eds), *The Atlantic World: Essays on Slavery, Migration, and Imagination* (Upper Saddle River: Pearson, 2005); J. Cañizares-Esguerra and E. R. Seeman (eds), *The Atlantic in Global History, 1500–2000* (Upper Saddle River: Pearson, 2007); A. Games and A. Rothman, *Major Problems in Atlantic History: Documents and Essays* (Major Problems in American History Series) (Belmont: Wadsworth, 2008); T. Falola and K. D. Roberts (eds), *The Atlantic World, 1450–2000* (Bloomington: Indiana University Press, 2008); B. Bailyn and P. Denault (ed.), *Soundings in Atlantic History: Latent Structures and Intellectual Currents, 1500–1830* (Cambridge, MA: Harvard University Press, 2009); J. P. Greene and P. D. Morgan (eds), *Atlantic History: A Critical Appraisal* (New York: Oxford University Press, 2009); N. Canny and P. D. Morgan (eds), *Oxford Handbook of the Atlantic World, 1450–1850* (Oxford: Oxford University Press, 2011); D. Coffman, A. Leonard, W. O'Reilly (eds), *The Atlantic World: 1400–1850* (London: Taylor & Francis, 2014); J. C. Miller, V. Brown, J. Cañizares-Esguerra, L. Dubois and K. Ordhal Kupperman (eds), *The Princeton Companion to Atlantic History* (Princeton: Princeton University Press, 2015).

75 M. W. Sandler, *Atlantic Ocean: The Illustrated History of the Ocean that Changed the World* (New York: Sterling, 2008); S. Winchester, *Atlantic: Great Sea Battles, Heroic Discoveries, Titanic Storms, and a Vast Ocean of a Million Stories* (New York: HarperCollins, 2011), pp. 21–2.

76 J. H. Elliott, *Empires of the Atlantic World: Britain and Spain in America, 1492–1830* (New Haven: Yale University Press, 2006).

References

Anderson, J. L. *Mahogany: The Costs of Luxury in Early America* (Cambridge, MA: Harvard University Press, 2012).

Andrews, E. E. *Native Apostles: Black and Indian Missionaries in the British Atlantic World* (Cambridge, MA: Harvard University Press, 2013).

Anishanslin, Z. *Portrait of a Woman in Silk: Hidden Histories of the British Atlantic World* (New Haven: Yale University Press, 2016).

Apel, T. *Feverish Bodies, Enlightened Minds: Yellow Fever and Common-Sense Natural Philosophy in the Early American Republic, 1793–1805*, PhD dissertation (Georgetown University, 2012).

Armitage, D. 'John Locke: Theorist of Empire?', in S. Muthu (ed.), *Empire and Modern Political Thought* (New York: Cambridge University Press, 2012), pp. 84–111.

Armitage, D. and A. Bashford (eds), *Pacific Histories: Ocean, Land, People* (New York: Palgrave Macmillan, 2014).

Arner, K. *The Malady of Revolutions: Yellow Fever in the Atlantic World, 1793–1828*, PhD dissertation (Johns Hopkins University, 2014).

Bailyn, B. and P. Denault (eds), *Soundings in Atlantic History: Latent Structures and Intellectual Currents, 1500–1830* (Cambridge, MA: Harvard University Press, 2009).

Baskes, J. *Staying Afloat: Risk and Uncertainty in Spanish Atlantic World Trade, 1760–1820* (Stanford: Stanford University Press, 2013).

Bassi, E. *An Aqueous Territory: Sailor Geographies and New Granada's Transimperial Greater Caribbean World* (Durham, NC: Duke University Press, 2016).

Beckert, S. *Empire of Cotton: A Global History* (New York: Alfred A. Knopf, 2014).

Beiler, R. *Immigrant and Entrepreneur: The Atlantic World of Caspar Wistar, 1650–1750* (University Park: The Pennsylvania State University Press, 2008).

Benjamin, T. *The Atlantic World: Europeans, Africans, Indians and Their Shared History, 1400–1900* (New York: Cambridge University Press, 2009).

Benjamin, T., T. Hall, and D. Rutherford (eds), *The Atlantic World in the Age of Empire* (Boston: Houghton Mifflin, 2001).

Bernardini, P. and N. Fiering (eds), *The Jews and the Expansion of Europe to the West, 1450–1800* (New York: Berghahn Books, 2001).

Berry, S. R. *A Path in the Mighty Waters: Shipboard Life and Atlantic Crossings to the New World* (New Haven: Yale University Press, 2015).

Bilby, K. M. *True-Born Maroons* (Gainesville: University Press of Florida, 2005).

Bleichmar, D. *Visible Empire: Botanical Expeditions and Visual Culture in the Hispanic Enlightenment* (Chicago: University of Chicago Press, 2012).

Bleichmar, D., P. De Vos, K. Huffine, and K. Sheehan (eds), *Science in the Spanish and Portuguese Empires, 1500–1800* (Palo Alto: Stanford University Press, 2009).

Bolster, W. J. *The Mortal Sea: Fishing the Atlantic in the Age of Sail* (Cambridge, MA: Harvard University Press, 2012).

Bolster, W. J. 'Putting the Ocean in Atlantic History: Maritime Communities and Marine Ecology in the Northwest Atlantic, 1500–1800', *American Historical Review*, 113:1 (2008), pp. 9–47.

Bonaventura, A. *For Adam's Sake: A Family Saga in Colonial New England* (New York: Liveright, 2013).

Bowen, H. V., E. Mancke, and J. G. Reid (eds), *Britain's Oceanic Empire: Atlantic and Indian Ocean Worlds, c.1650–1850* (New York: Cambridge University Press, 2012).

Braun, H. and L. Vollendorf (eds), *Theorising the Ibero-American Atlantic* (Leiden: Brill, 2013).

Breen, B. *Tropical Transplantations: Drugs, Nature, and Globalization in the Portuguese and British Empires, 1640–1755*, PhD dissertation (University of Texas at Austin, 2015).

Bremer, F. J. *First Founders: American Puritans and Puritanism in an Atlantic World* (Durham, NH: University of New Hampshire Press, 2012).

Brunsman, D. *The Evil Necessity: British Naval Impressment in the Eighteenth-Century Atlantic World* (Charlottesville: University of Virginia Press, 2013).

Burke, E. 'Speech in Conciliation with America, 22 March 1775', *The Works of Edmund Burke in nine volumes*, Vol. II (Boston: Little & Brown, 1839).

Caillot, M.-A. *A Company Man: The Remarkable French-Atlantic Voyage of a Clerk for the Company of the Indies: A Memoir*, E. M. Greenwald (ed.) (New Orleans: The Historic New Orleans Collection, 2013).

Candido, M. P. *An African Slaving Port and the Atlantic World: Benguela and Its Hinterland* (New York: Cambridge University Press, 2013).

Candlin, K. and C. Pybus (eds), *Enterprising Women: Gender, Race, and Power in the Revolutionary Atlantic* (Athens: University of Georgia Press, 2015).

Cangany, C. *Frontier Seaport: Detroit's Transformation into an Atlantic Entrepôt* (Chicago: University of Chicago Press, 2014).

Cañizares-Esguerra, J. and B. Breen. 'Hybrid Atlantics: Future Directions for the History of the Atlantic World', *History Compass*, 11:8 (2013), pp. 597–607.

Cañizares-Esguerra, J. and E. R. Seeman (eds), *The Atlantic in Global History, 1500–2000* (Upper Saddle River: Pearson, 2007).

Cañizares-Esguerra, J., M. D. Childs, and J. Sidbury (eds), *The Black Urban Atlantic in the Age of the Slave Trade* (Philadelphia: University of Pennsylvania Press, 2013).

Canny, N. and P. D. Morgan (eds), *Oxford Handbook of the Atlantic World, 1450–1850* (Oxford: Oxford University Press, 2011).

Carretta, V. *Equiano the African: Biography of a Self-Made Man* (Athens: University of Georgia Press, 2005).

Catterall, D. and J. Campbell (eds), *Women in Port: Gendering Communities, Economies, and Social Networks in Atlantic Port Cities, 1500–1800* (Leiden: Brill, 2012).

Cesarani, D. *Port Jews: Jewish Communities in Cosmopolitan Maritime Trading Centres, 1550–1950* (Hoboken: Taylor & Francis, 2014).

Chakrabarti, P. *Materials and Medicine: Trade, Conquest and Therapeutics in the Eighteenth Century* (Manchester: Manchester University Press, 2010).

Chaplin, J. 'The Atlantic Ocean and Its Contemporary Meanings, 1492–1808', in J. P. Greene and P. D. Morgan (eds), *Atlantic History: A Critical Appraisal* (New York: Oxford University Press, 2009), pp. 35–51.

Charters, E. *Disease, War, and the Imperial State: The Welfare of the British Armed Forces during the Seven Years' War* (Chicago: University of Chicago Press, 2014).

Clarke, E. *By the Rivers of Water: A Nineteenth-Century Atlantic Odyssey* (New York: Basic Books, 2013).

Coffman, D., A. Leonard, and W. O'Reilly (eds), *The Atlantic World: 1400–1850* (London: Taylor & Francis, 2014).

Colley, L. *The Ordeal of Elizabeth Marsh: A Woman in World History* (New York: Pantheon Books, 2007).

Cook, H. J. *Matters of Exchange: Commerce, Medicine, and Science in the Dutch Golden Age* (New Haven: Yale University Press, 2007).

'Critical Forum, featuring Lu Ann Homza, David D. Hall, Marcy Norton, Andrew R. Murphy, and Stuart B. Schwartz', *William and Mary Quarterly*, 3d Ser., 66:2 (2009), pp. 409–33.

Cromwell, J. *Covert Commerce: A Social History of Contraband Trade in Venezuela, 1701–1789*, PhD dissertation (University of Texas at Austin, 2012).

De Bruyn, F. and S. Regan (eds), *The Culture of the Seven Years' War: Empire, Identity, and the Arts in the Eighteenth-Century Atlantic World* (Toronto: University of Toronto Press, 2014).

De la Fuente, A. *Havana and the Atlantic in the Sixteenth Century* (Chapel Hill: University of North Carolina Press, 2008).

Delbourgo, J. and N. Dew (eds), *Science and Empire in the Atlantic World* (New York: Routledge, 2008).

Dubcovsky, A. *Informed Power: Communication in the Early American South* (Cambridge, MA: Harvard University Press, 2016).

Duffy, E. M. and A. C. Metcalf. *The Return of Hans Staden: A Go-Between in the Atlantic World* (Baltimore: Johns Hopkins University Press, 2011).

DuPlessis, R. S. *The Material Atlantic: Clothing, Commerce, and Colonization in the Atlantic World, 1650–1800* (Cambridge: Cambridge University Press, 2016).

Egerton, D. R., A. Games, J. G. Landers, K. Lane, and D. R. Wright. *The Atlantic World: A History, 1400–1888* (Wheeling: Harlan Davidson, 2007).

Elliott, J. H. *Empires of the Atlantic World: Britain and Spain in America, 1492–1830* (New Haven: Yale University Press, 2006).

Eltis, D. and D. Richardson. *Atlas of the Transatlantic Slave Trade* (New Haven: Yale University Press, 2010).

Evans, C. 'The Plantation Hoe: The Rise and Fall of an Atlantic Commodity, 1650–1850', *William and Mary Quarterly*, 3d Ser., 69:1 (2012), pp. 71–100.

Falola, T. and K. D. Roberts (eds), *The Atlantic World, 1450–2000* (Bloomington: Indiana University Press, 2008).

Ferreira, R. *Cross-Cultural Exchange in the Atlantic World: Angola and Brazil during the Era of the Slave Trade* (New York: Cambridge University Press, 2012).

Fisher, J. A. and D. J. Silverman. *Ninigret, Sachem of the Niantics and Narragansetts. Diplomacy, War, and the Balance of Power in Seventeenth-Century New England and Indian Country* (Ithaca: Cornell University Press, 2014).

Fogleman, A. S. *Two Troubled Souls: An Eighteenth-Century Couple's Spiritual Journey in the Atlantic World* (Chapel Hill: University of North Carolina Press, 2013).

Fortin, J. A. and M. Meuwese (eds), *Atlantic Biographies: Individuals and Peoples in the Atlantic World* (Leiden: Brill, 2014).

Games, A. and A. Rothman. *Major Problems in Atlantic History: Documents and Essays* (Major Problems in American History Series) (Belmont: Wadsworth, 2008).

Gelfand, N. L. *To Live and to Trade: The Status of Sephardi Mercantile Communities in the Atlantic World during the Seventeenth and Eighteenth Centuries* (Oxford: The Littman Library of Jewish Civilization, 2014).

Gerber, J. S. (ed.), *The Jews in the Caribbean* (Oxford: The Littman Library of Jewish Civilization, 2014).

Gherini, C. *'Experiment and Good Sense Must Direct You': Managing Health and Sickness in the British Plantation Enlightenment, 1756–1815*, PhD dissertation (Johns Hopkins University, 2016).

Girard, P. *Toussaint Louverture: A Revolutionary Life* (New York: Basic Books, 2016).

Glaisyer, N. 'Networking: Trade and Exchange in the Eighteenth-Century British Empire', *Historical Journal*, 47:2 (2004), pp. 451–76.

Glaser, E. (ed.), *Religious Tolerance in the Atlantic World: Early Modern and Contemporary Perspectives* (Basingstoke: Palgrave Macmillan, 2014).

Gómez, P. *The Experiential Caribbean: Creating Knowledge and Healing in the Early Modern Atlantic* (Chapel Hill: University of North Carolina Press, 2017).

Graham, A. 'Mercantile Networks in the Early Modern World', *Historical Journal*, 56:1 (2013), pp. 279–95.

Grandjean, K. *American Passage: The Communications Frontier in Early New England* (Cambridge, MA: Harvard University Press, 2015).

Greene, J. P. and P. D. Morgan (eds), *Atlantic History: A Critical Appraisal* (New York: Oxford University Press, 2009).

Griswold, M. *The Manor: Three Centuries at a Slave Plantation on Long Island* (New York: Farrar, Straus, and Giroux, 2013).

Hancock, D. *Oceans of Wine: Madeira and the Emergence of American Trade and Taste* (New Haven: Yale University Press, 2009).

Hanna, M. G. *Pirate Nests and the Rise of the British Empire 1570–1740* (Chapel Hill: University of North Carolina Press, 2015).

Hardwick, J., S. M. S. Pearsall, and K. Wulf (eds), 'Centering Families in Atlantic Histories', *William and Mary Quarterly*, 3d Ser., 70:3 (2013), pp. 205–424.

Harms, R. *The Diligent: A Voyage through the Worlds of the Slave Trade* (New York: Basic Books, 2001).

Harrison, M. *Medicine in an Age of Commerce and Empire: Britain and its Tropical Colonies, 1660–1830* (Oxford: Oxford University Press, 2010).

Hayes, K. H. *Slavery before Race: Europeans, Africans, and Indians at Long Island's Sylvester Manor Plantation 1651–1884* (New York: New York University Press, 2013).

Henderson, S. T. and W. G. Robicheau. *The Nova Scotia Planters in the Atlantic World, 1760–1830* (Fredericton: Acadiensis Press, 2012).

Hodson, C. and B. Rushforth. *Discovering Empire: France and the Atlantic World from the Crusades to the Age of Revolutions* (New York: Basic Books, forthcoming).

Jarvis, M. J. *In the Eye of All Trade: Bermuda, Bermudians, and the Maritime Atlantic World* (Chapel Hill: University of North Carolina Press, 2010).

Johnson, L. L. *Workshop of Revolution: Plebeian Buenos Aires and the Atlantic World, 1776–1810* (Durham, NC: Duke University Press, 2011).

Johnston, K. 'The Constitution of Empire: Place and Bodily Health in the Eighteenth-Century Atlantic World', *Atlantic Studies*, 10:4 (2013), pp. 443–66.

Kagan, R. L. and P. D. Morgan (eds), *Atlantic Diasporas: Jews, Conversos, and Crypto-Jews in the Age of Mercantilism, 1500–1800* (Baltimore: Johns Hopkins University Press, 2009).

Kelly, C. E. *War and the Militarization of British Army Medicine, 1793–1830* (London: Pickering and Chatto, 2010).

Kelly, S. M. *The Voyage of the Slave Ship Hare: A Journey into Captivity from Sierra Leone to South Carolina* (Chapel Hill: University of North Carolina Press, 2016).

Klooster, W. *The Dutch Moment: War, Trade, and Settlement in the Seventeenth-Century Atlantic World* (Ithaca: Cornell University Press, 2016).

Klooster, W. and A. Padula (eds), *The Atlantic World: Essays on Slavery, Migration, and Imagination* (Upper Saddle River: Pearson, 2005).

Knight, F. W. and P. K. Liss (eds), *Atlantic Port Cities: Economy, Culture and Society in the Atlantic World, 1650–1850* (Knoxville: University of Tennessee Press, 1991).

Kopelson, H. M. *Faithful Bodies: Performing Religion and Race in the Puritan Atlantic* (New York: New York University Press, 2014).

Kuethe, A. J. and K. J. Andrien (eds), *The Spanish Atlantic World in the Eighteenth Century: War and the Bourbon Reforms, 1713–1796* (New York: Cambridge University Press, 2014).

Kupperman, K. O. *The Atlantic in World History* (New York: Oxford University Press, 2012).

Lachenicht, S. (ed.), *Europeans Engaging the Atlantic: Knowledge and Trade, 1500–1800* (Frankfurt and New York: Campus Verlag, 2014).

Lamikiz, X. *Trade and Trust in the Eighteenth-Century Atlantic World: Spanish Merchants and their Overseas Networks* (Woodbridge: The Boydell Press for the Royal Historical Society, 2010).

Law, R. *Ouidah: The Social History of a West African Slaving 'Port' 1727–1892* (Athens: Ohio University Press, 2004).

Lawrance, B. N. *Amistad's Orphans: An Atlantic Story of Children, Slavery, and Smuggling* (New Haven: Yale University Press, 2015).

Lindsay, L. A. and J. W. Sweet (eds), *Biography and the Black Atlantic* (Philadelphia: University of Pennsylvania Press, 2014).

Lipman, A. *The Saltwater Frontier: Indians and the Contest for the American Coast* (New Haven: Yale University Press, 2015).

López-Denis, A. *Disease and Society in Colonial Cuba, 1790–1840*, PhD dissertation (University of California, Los Angeles, 2007).

Magra, C. P. 'Faith at Sea: Exploring Maritime Religiosity in the Eighteenth Century', *International Journal of Maritime History*, 19:1 (2007), pp. 87–106.

Mamigonian, B. G. and K. Racine (eds), *The Human Tradition in the Black Atlantic, 1500-2000* (Lanham: Rowman & Littlefield, 2010).

Mancall, P. C. and C. Shammas (eds), *Governing the Sea in the Early Modern Era: Essays in Honor of Robert C. Ritchie* (San Marino: Huntington Library, 2015).

Mark, P. and J. da Silva Horta, *The Forgotten Diaspora: Jewish Communities in West Africa and the Making of the Atlantic World* (New York: Cambridge University Press, 2011).

McNeill, J. R. *Mosquito Empires: Ecology and War in the Greater Caribbean, 1620-1914* (New York: Cambridge University Press, 2010).

Miller, J. C., V. Brown, J. Cañizares-Esguerra, L. Dubois and K. Ordhal Kupperman (eds), *The Princeton Companion to Atlantic History* (Princeton: Princeton University Press, 2015).

Miller, P. N. (ed.), *The Sea: Thalassography and Historiography* (Ann Arbor: University of Michigan Press, 2013).

Millett, N. *The Maroons of Prospect Bluff and their Quest for Freedom in the Atlantic World* (Gainesville: University Press of Florida, 2013).

Morgan, G. and P. Rushton. *Banishment in the Early Atlantic World: Convicts, Rebels and Slaves* (London: Bloomsbury, 2013).

Murphy, K. S. 'Translating the Vernacular: Indigenous and African Knowledge in the Eighteenth-Century British Atlantic', *Atlantic Studies*, 8:1 (2011), pp. 29–48.

Murphy, K. S. 'Collecting Slave Traders: James Petiver, Natural History, and the British Slave Trade', *William and Mary Quarterly*, 3d Ser., 70:4 (2013), pp. 637–70.

Oostindie, G. and J. Vance Roitman. 'Repositioning the Dutch in the Atlantic, 1680–1800', *Itinerario. European Journal of Overseas History*, 32:2 (2012), pp. 129–60.

Owens, S. E. and J. E. Mangan (eds), *Women of the Iberian Atlantic* (Baton Rouge: Louisiana State University Press, 2012).

Palmer, J. L. *Intimate Bonds: Family and Slavery in the French Atlantic* (Philadelphia: University of Pennsylvania Press, 2016).

Paquette, G. *Imperial Portugal in the Age of Atlantic Revolutions: The Luso-Brazilian World, c. 1770–1850* (New York: Cambridge University Press, 2014).

Parrish, S. S. *American Curiosity: Cultures of Natural History in the British Atlantic World* (Chapel Hill: University of North Carolina Press, 2006).

Pastore, C. *Between Land and Sea: The Atlantic Coast and the Transformation of New England* (Cambridge, MA: Harvard University Press, 2014).

Paugh, K. 'Yaws, Syphilis, Sexuality, and the Circulation of Medical Knowledge in the British Caribbean and Atlantic World', *Bulletin of the History of Medicine*, 88:2 (2014), pp. 225–52.

Polasky, J. *Revolutions without Borders: The Call to Liberty in the Atlantic World* (New Haven: Yale University Press, 2015).

Pope, P. and S. Lewis-Simpson (eds), *Exploring Atlantic Transitions: Archaeologies of Transience and Permanence in New Found Lands* (Woodbridge: The Boydell Press, 2013).

Racine, K. and B. G. Mamigonian (eds), *The Human Tradition in the Atlantic World, 1500-1850* (Lanham: Rowman & Littlefield, 2010).

Rediker, M. *The Amistad Rebellion: An Atlantic Odyssey of Slavery and Freedom* (New York: Viking, 2012).

Rediker, M. *Outlaws of the Atlantic: Sailors, Pirates, and Motley Crews in the Age of Sail* (Boston: Beacon Press, 2014).

Reiss, T. *Black Count: Glory, Revolution, Betrayal, and the Real Count of Monte Cristo* (New York: Broadway Books, 2012).

Rodger, N. A. M. 'Atlantic Seafaring', in N. Canny and P. D. Morgan (eds), *Oxford Handbook of the Atlantic World, 1450–1850* (Oxford: Oxford University Press, 2011), pp. 71–86.

Rogers, N. *The Press Gang: Naval Impressment and its Opponents in Georgian Britain* (New York: Continuum, 2007).

Romney, S. S. *New Netherland Connections: Intimate Networks and Atlantic Ties in Seventeenth-Century America* (Chapel Hill: University of North Carolina Press, 2014).

Rönnbäck, K. 'Enlightenment, Scientific Exploration and Abolitionism: Anders Sparrman's and Carl Bernhard Wadström's Colonial Encounters in Senegal, 1787–1788 and the British Abolitionist Movement', *Slavery and Abolition*, 34:3 (2013), pp. 425–55.

Rothschild, E. 'The Atlantic Worlds of David Hume', in B. Bailyn and P. Denault (eds), *Soundings in Atlantic History: Latent Structures and Intellectual Currents, 1500–1830* (Cambridge, MA: Harvard University Press, 2009), pp. 405–48.

Rupert, L. *Creolization and Contraband: Curaçao in the Early Modern Atlantic World* (Athens: University of Georgia Press, 2012).

Safier, N. *Measuring the New World: Enlightenment Science and South America* (Chicago: University of Chicago Press, 2008).

Sandler, M. W. *Atlantic Ocean: The Illustrated History of the Ocean that Changed the World* (New York: Sterling, 2008).

Schafer, D. L. *Zephaniah Kingsley Jr. and the Atlantic World: Slave Trader, Plantation Owner, Emancipator* (Gainesville: University of Florida Press, 2013).

Schiebinger, L. 'Medical Experimentation and Race in the Eighteenth-Century Atlantic World', *Social History of Medicine*, 26:3 (2014), pp. 364–82.

Schiebinger, L. 'Scientific Exchange in the Eighteenth-Century Atlantic World', in B. Bailyn and P. Denault (eds), *Soundings in Atlantic History: Latent Structures and Intellectual Currents, 1500–1830* (Cambridge, MA: Harvard University Press, 2009), pp. 294–328.

Schiebinger, L. *Secret Cures of Slaves: People, Plants, and Medicine in the Eighteenth-Century Atlantic World* (Stanford: Stanford University Press, 2017).

Schneider, E. *The Occupation of Havana: Slavery, War, and Empire in the Eighteenth Century* (Chapel Hill: University of North Carolina Press, 2018).

Schorsch, J. *Swimming the Christian Atlantic: Judeoconverts, Afroiberians and Amerindians in the Seventeenth Century* (Leiden: Brill, 2009).

Schumann, M. and K. Schweizer. *The Seven Years' War: A Transatlantic History* (London: Routledge, 2008).

Schwartz, S. *All Can Be Saved: Religious Tolerance and Salvation in the Iberian Atlantic World* (New Haven: Yale University Press, 2008).

Scott, R. J. and J. Hébrard. *Freedom Papers: An Atlantic Odyssey in the Age of Emancipation* (Cambridge, MA: Harvard University Press, 2012).

Sensbach, J. F. *Rebecca's Revival: Creating Black Christianity in the Atlantic World* (Cambridge, MA: Harvard University Press, 2005).

Shannon, T. J. *Atlantic Lives: A Comparative Approach to Early America* (New York: Pearson, 2004).

Slauter, E. 'History, Literature, and the Atlantic World', *William and Mary Quarterly*, 3d Ser., 65:1 (2008), pp. 135–66.

Smith, B. G. *Ship of Death: A Voyage that Changed the Atlantic World* (New Haven: Yale University Press, 2013).

Snelders, S. 'Leprosy and Slavery in Suriname: Godfried Schilling and the Framing of a Racial Pathology in the Eighteenth Century', *Social History of Medicine*, 26:3 (2014), pp. 432–55.

Sparks, R. J. *Africans in the Old South: Mapping Exceptional Lives across the Atlantic World* (Cambridge, MA: Harvard University Press, 2016).

Sparks, R. J. *The Two Princes of Calabar: An Eighteenth-Century Atlantic Odyssey* (Cambridge, MA: Harvard University Press, 2004).

Sparks, R. J. *Where the Negroes Are Masters: An African Port in the Era of the Slave Trade* (Cambridge, MA: Harvard University Press, 2014).

Staden, H. *Hans Staden's True History: An Account of Cannibal Captivity in Brazil*, ed. and trans. N. L. Whitehead and M. Harbsmeier (Durham, NC: Duke University Press, 2008).

Strang, C. B. *Entangled Knowledge, Expanding Nation: Science and the United States Empire in the Southeast Borderlands, 1783–1842*, PhD dissertation (University of Texas at Austin, 2013).

Strang, C. B. 'Indian Storytelling, Scientific Knowledge, and Power in the Florida Borderlands', *William and Mary Quarterly*, 3d Ser., 70:4 (2013), pp. 671–700.

Suárez Bosa, M. (ed.), *Atlantic Ports and the First Globalisation, c.1850–1930* (Basingstoke: Palgrave Macmillan, 2014).

Suranyi, A. *The Atlantic Connection: A History of the Atlantic World, 1450–1900* (New York: Routledge, 2014).

Thornton, J. K. *A Cultural History of the Atlantic World, 1250–1820* (New York: Cambridge University Press, 2012).

Tutino, J. *Making a New World: Founding Capitalism in the Bajío and Spanish North America* (Durham, NC: Duke University Press, 2011).

Vickers, D. and V. Walsh. *Young Men and the Sea: Yankee Seafarers in the Age of Sail* (New Haven: Yale University Press, 2005).

Vidal, C. (ed.), *Louisiana: Crossroads of the Atlantic World* (Philadelphia: University of Pennsylvania Press, 2014).

Walker, T. D. 'The Medicines Trade in the Portuguese Atlantic World: Acquisition and Dissemination of Healing Knowledge from Brazil (c. 1580–1800)', *Social History of Medicine*, 26:3 (2013), pp. 403–31.

Ward, B., M. Bone, and W. A. Link (eds), *The American South and the Atlantic World* (Gainesville: University Press of Florida, 2013).

Warsh, M. *American Baroque: Pearls and the Nature of Empire, 1492–1700* (Chapel Hill: University of North Carolina Press, 2018).

Weaver, J. *The Red Atlantic: American Indigenes and the Making of the Modern World, 1000–1927* (Chapel Hill: University of North Carolina Press, 2014).

Wellenreuther, H., T. Müller-Bahlke, and A. G. Roeber (eds), *The Transatlantic World of Heinrich Melchior Mühlenberg in the Eighteenth Century* (Halle: Verlag der Franckeschen Stiftungen, 2013).

Wheat, D. *Atlantic Africa and the Spanish Caribbean, 1570–1640* (Chapel Hill: University of North Carolina Press, 2016).

Wheland, K. 'The Green Atlantic: Radical Reciprocities between Ireland and America in the Long Eighteenth Century', in K. Wilson (ed.), *A New Imperial History: Culture, Identity, and Modernity in Britain and the Empire, 1660–1840* (Cambridge: Cambridge University Press, 2004), pp. 216–38.

Winchester, S. *Atlantic: Great Sea Battles, Heroic Discoveries, Titanic Storms, and a Vast Ocean of a Million Stories* (New York: HarperCollins, 2011).

Wood, G. S. *The Americanization of Benjamin Franklin* (New York: Penguin, 2004).

5

The Transnational Transatlantic: Private organizations and governmentality[1]

Giles Scott-Smith

There is no doubt that a particular transatlantic era is now drawing to a close. Levels of trade and investment are greater than any other inter-regional economic space, and NATO continues to function as a unique common security organization. Yet the conditions that led to the transatlantic era's dominance in global affairs are fading out. Other areas of the world – the Asia-Pacific, Latin America – are taking on greater significance, politically, economically, financially, and in terms of global governance. US–European relations are being marked now not so much by discord as by gradually diverging interests, and a creeping indifference coloured with disappointment.[2] Various Atlanticist commentators see the negotiations for a Transatlantic Trade and Investment Partnership (TTIP) as a kind of 'last chance saloon' to redress the decline.[3] It is not just the American Century that is winding down, but the Transatlantic Century as well.[4] Mary Nolan has phrased it succinctly with reference to the widening divide in economics, values, and foreign policy:

> This situation is unlikely to change, for the Atlantic has continued to widen and the market gap, the God gap, and the war gap show no signs of disappearing. The American Century in Europe is over.[5]

Yet the end of the transatlantic era does not mean the end of the relevance of the transatlantic as a field of investigation. It is, in fact, its beginning. If one can talk of a distinctly transatlantic era, it must surely fall within the bounds of the twentieth century, taking in not only the rise (and relative decline) of the United States as a great power but also the unique collective power of the Atlantic region in terms of politics, economics, and security. Through the late nineteenth and early twentieth centuries, US political, economic, and security interests expanded so that the balance of power on the European continent became of vital importance. This realist orientation was complemented by deeper social and cultural ties, and by the expanding commercial reach of US business.[6] Woodrow Wilson's desire to make the world safe for democracy and economic exchange was primarily aimed at Europe, and that desire resonated throughout transatlantic relations – and the rest of the world – through the century.[7]

The focus on the twentieth century differs from the acknowledged subject-area of Atlantic Studies, which examines the interchanges of the era of the great revolutions and the slave trade, and peters out some time in the early 1800s.[8] What sets this transatlantic era apart is the scale and depth of US–European interactions, ranging from large-scale migration, to the transfer of political causes and scientific innovation, to the commitments to enduring security alliances, to the embeddedness of mutual economic and financial interests on both sides of the Atlantic. It became of vital interest to the United States to play a role in securing the economic and political stability of the European continent, out of desire for great power prestige, out of concerns that a powerful rival could emerge to challenge it, and out of an idealist drive to re-shape global politics. It was this that took the United States into both world wars against Germany and led it to 'contain' the Soviet Union during the Cold War. The close ties were exemplified by the North Atlantic Treaty Organization (NATO), tying both the United States and Canada to the security of Europe for the first time since their establishment as independent nation states.

This chapter attempts to move beyond this orthodox interpretation. The point made here is that this identifiable transatlantic era should not be taken for granted as simply the logical result of economic growth, governmental decisions, and security concerns. It was, throughout the twentieth century (and into the twenty-first), the construction and *deliberate projection* of overlapping networks of public figures, intellectuals, academics, and media personalities, who believed in the need to cement the ties between the United States and Europe by presenting and promoting them as much as possible as a rational fait accompli. The hypothesis is that US–European relations were established and maintained as a given in the public arena not by national security policies or the threat of common enemies, but by the consistent efforts of a host of private organizations, institutions, and professional networks that voluntarily took on this role. In doing so, they fulfilled a role that governments could not, and they acted in the name of vital governmental interests. These groups form what we can call the Transnational Transatlantic. Their efforts were behind the creation and perpetuation of a unique political space, an Atlantic Community, as a guiding sign of consensus with which both sides of the ocean could identify. It was also the nucleus for what many perceived to be the future of global governance[9] – the transatlantic core for efficient and effective public policy management, and the basis for a normative system of democratic values worldwide. The use of transnational historical approaches now recognizes the significance of these linkages. As Patricia Clavin remarked, 'transnationalism, despite its early identification with the transfer or movement of money and goods, is first and foremost about people: the social space that they inhabit, the networks they form and the ideas they exchange.'[10] One can also add: the worldviews that they configured, promoted, and perpetuated.

Studies of the kinds of individuals and connections that concern us here have often drawn on theories of the power of elites and elite networks, much of it critically examining the influence of these groups (often based on economic/financial power) from their positions 'outside' the official realms of government (although many key figures obviously occupied positions in both worlds).[11] Being able to place these groups within a cartography of 'transnational power lines' has proved awkward due to the diffuse nature of public–private identities in these settings, and the lack of conclusive 'evidence of effectiveness'. This lay behind Scott Lucas's assertion of 'the caricature of the private dimension in the state-private network either as an autonomous element in liberal democracy or as co-opted and controlled servants of the state'.[12] Some groups are not only part of the foreign policy establishment but also embedded into the wider foreign policy apparatus, as think tanks and research centres (such as Chatham House or the International Institute for Strategic Studies). Others are still part of the Atlanticist elite firmament but more directed towards public opinion and education (such as the Atlantic Treaty Association). As a result there are major issues concerning scale, dimension, and limit if one wants to address the Transnational Transatlantic as a coherent focus for research.

This does not assume that all notions of the Atlantic Community fitted together neatly, or that there were no contradictions between the various standpoints. On the contrary – the debate enhanced the fact that this was something that motivated people to act, and gave politics a wider meaning. As Ken Weisbrode has put it, 'in reality there were multiple Atlanticisms' possessing 'just the right degree of ambiguity' to avoid fundamental clashes and to foster a sense of common destiny, however much the details still needed to be worked out.[13] Neither does it assume that all the figures involved were private citizens. The Transnational Transatlantic involved many who stepped easily between state and non-state positions of influence, whether to do with careers, public calling, or changes in leadership and access to power. This terrain was as much assembled through the political imagery of diplomats as it was through the determination of private proselytisers. It was perhaps the epitome of the imagined community – a self-fulfilling, dense collection of overlapping networks of elites who collectively formed, associated with, and acted in the name of the Atlantic Community of peoples and states they hoped to nurture. The promotion of Atlantic unity through multiple designs fits the identification in Charles Maier's chapter of a collective political passion mobilizing the 'public mind' and shaping political consciousness beyond the mere processes of governmental decision-making.

It may well be possible to investigate the Transnational Transatlantic as a habitus, referring in Bourdieu's sense to the characteristics of a specific field within which worldviews, social practices, and hierarchies are reproduced, in so doing reinforcing the field's self-understanding. Stefano Guzzini applied this approach to studying the 'international power elite', and there are definitely useful elements such as Bourdieu's notion of an 'act of social magic' whereby entities are given a certain status ('nominated') and then imposed as a part of social reality. In contrast to speech acts, whereby language has a performative function, it is exactly the particular social conditions that determine whether this process will succeed. Guzzini himself sees the value, but also the difficulties, 'not least of which the question whether such an elite can ever be circumscribed in the first place'.[14] To bypass the limitations identified by Guzzini, an alternative perspective can be outlined that draws on Foucault's concept of governmentality. Foucault outlined this as a set of techniques used to govern ('mentalities of government' that encompass the who, how, and why of governing) and the subjectivities that are produced as a result ('mentalities of government' that refers to the internalization of the required identity and behaviour). In an early definition of governmentality's scope, Foucault clarified three dimensions at work, two of which are relevant here:

The ensemble formed by the institutions, procedures, analyses, and reflections, the calculations and tactics that allow the exercise of this very specific albeit complex form of power, which has as its target population, as its principal form of knowledge political economy, and as its essential technical means apparatuses of security.

The tendency which, over a long period and throughout the West, has steadily led towards the pre-eminence over all other forms (sovereignty, discipline, etc) of this type of power which may be termed government, resulting, on the one hand, in the formation of a whole series of specific governmental apparatuses, and, on the other, in the development of a whole complex of *savoirs*.[15]

Foucault points to a particular kind of knowledge being needed in order for a particular kind of power to be exercised. Rejecting a reductionist definition, the above quotation indicates that the important historically specific processes involved are not so much 'the *étatisation* of society, as the "governmentalization" of the state' – the 'overflow' of the state's role into new spaces of political activity, resulting in the adoption of novel techniques of governance by a wider array of institutions.[16] Mitchell Dean has pointed out that governmentality also refers to a specifically historical moment, when 'the modern art of government' sought the optimal organization and realization of a given population through 'apparatuses of security': 'all the practices and institutions that ensure the optimal and proper functioning of the economic, vital and social processes that are found to exist within that population and would thus also include health, welfare and education systems'.[17]

Transatlantic governmentality therefore represents a distinct historical, transnational phase in the 'mentalities of government', looking beyond the embedding of national structures. For the transatlantic region to become pre-eminent in the public sphere, techniques of government were required that framed the Atlantic Community as a designated population (civilization),[18] source of legitimacy (being), and goal to be realized (becoming). To undertake this, the field is divided up into three main sections: the English-speaking world; Atlantic federalism; Cold War elites. The focus on an Anglo-America core is used as a deliberate means to structure this initial investigation and provide the base for further probing, and should not be taken as a prejudice against alternative conceptions.

The English-speaking world

A useful starting point would be the initial moves in the late nineteenth century to re-incorporate the United States within a global Anglo-Saxon community as exemplified by the British empire. 'Greater Britain' was a flexible moniker put forward as a tool to configure how to perpetuate the influence of British colonial power beyond the era of gunboats and consuls.[19] This was a predominantly racial, hierarchical interpretation of international relations disguised as the promotion of civilization for the benefit of all.[20] Cecil Rhodes, the archetypal 'race patriot', became its most pronounced exponent, providing the first practical tool to foster a future Anglo-American condominium. Heavily influenced by John Ruskin at Oxford, Rhodes, alongside Alfred Milner, Philip Kerr, and Lionel Curtis, looked to transform British global influence from a reliance on imperial rule to a more cosmopolitan, federal, networked framework. These ideas soon spawned Milner's Round Table, the Rhodes Trust, and the associated Rhodes Scholarships.[21] Intended to bring quality students to Oxford University, the scholarships were open to a select group of applicant regions as specified in Rhodes's will (Australia, Bermuda, Canada, Jamaica, Rhodesia, Newfoundland, New Zealand, Southern Africa, and the United States) but have always possessed a heavy bias towards American participants. Of the fifty-two original scholarships allocated for the programme's first year, thirty-two were allocated to the United States, evidence of 'how much importance [Rhodes] still attached to the Anglo-American partnership. He never wholly abandoned the hope that the United States might one day rejoin the Empire'.[22] In 1925 the Rhodes Scholarships were reciprocated when the New York-based Commonwealth Fund initiated a fellowship programme for British scholars to study in the United States. These were extended to Australia, New Zealand, Canada, and South Africa in 1927, and were renamed the Harkness fellowships in 1961.

Similar ideas lay behind the creation of the English-Speaking Union (ESU) in 1918, the brainchild of Ulsterman Sir John Evelyn Wrench. Wrench had already formed the Royal Overseas League in 1910 as a means to unite the peoples of the dominions, and his experience in the First World War (particularly with the Ministry of Information with responsibility for the United States) led him to establish the Union. Its mission was clear: 'Believing that the peace of the world and the progress of mankind can be largely helped by the unity in purpose of the English-Speaking Democracies, we pledge ourselves to promote by every means in our power a good understanding between the peoples of the USA and the British Commonwealth.'[23]

Rhodes's initiative laid down a marker for transatlantic intellectual interchanges through the twentieth century. Many influential figures would subsequently benefit from his philanthropy. William Fulbright's experience in 1925 led him to promote the value of international exchanges for fostering peaceful relations with his own initiative twenty years later. Major figures of US politics who studied in Oxford thanks to Rhodes include Bill Clinton, Dean Rusk, and Strobe Talbott. Remarkably, Rhodes's original conception of an Anglo-Saxon community with global reach has been resuscitated in recent years in the form of the 'Anglosphere', most notably by the Australian prime minister (2013–15) and former Rhodes scholar Tony Abbott, and the appointment of Canadian Mark Carney as Governor of the Bank of England only reinforced this perception. In the words of James Bennett, 'To be part of the Anglosphere requires adherence to the fundamental customs and values that form the core of English speaking cultures. These include individualism, rule of law, honoring contracts and covenants, and the elevation of freedom to the first rank of political and cultural values'. In contrast to Rhodes's more traditional imperial perceptions, its twenty-first-century incarnation represents 'a network civilization without a corresponding political form'.[24]

The overtones of imperial legacies and racial hierarchies evident in these positions should not obscure the fact that a powerful model for global governance was being put forward, indeed one that resonated throughout the rest of the century. Mark Mazower has chronicled how the League of Nations came about not from any universal *angst* for further war, but from 'a fusion of American missionary zeal and British imperial calculation' – a necessary development to prevent further anarchy at the hands of abso-lutist chauvinism.[25] This was deeply nineteenth century in conception: it was deemed as evolutionary in development, led by an Anglo-American sense of superiority that was firmly rooted in a hierarchical understanding of race and racial characteristics. Only such a background can explain the key role played by Jan Smuts and his understanding of the League and the United Nations as promoting the standards of civilization as set out – according to him – by the white settler communities of the British Commonwealth. Smuts's initiatives therefore built in the Anglo-American core as a foundation stone for international organization on a global scale, with peace and prosperity the desired result.[26] But this 'global turn' was a balance-of-power move writ large, geared as it was towards balancing whatever power bases might arise on the European continent. The result was potentially the exclusion of European states from the emerging Anglo-American condominium. It would take two major wars to shift the boundaries of this vision for world order.

It was the First World War that exposed the limitations of the Anglo-American ideal and pushed forward the need for a truly Atlantic alternative – an Atlantic Community.[27] The key protagonist in its initial articulation was journalist Walter Lippmann. Lippmann's conceptualization of an 'Atlantic Community' is important for three principal reasons. First, he was one of the first to pitch the idea of commu-nity – not alliance, or treaty, but community – as the common ground that united both sides, thereby designating a transatlantic *population* to be governed. Second, he re-framed the Atlantic Ocean not as an obstacle or security shield but as a two-way *highway* – for people, commerce, and ideas. Third, he played a key role in keeping the concept alive by bridging the gap between the First and Second World Wars. In 1917 the *New Republic* journalist first articulated the necessity of the transatlantic frame for US security interests, but did so in a way that went beyond mere questions of arms:

The safety of the Atlantic highway is something for which America should fight. Why? Because on the two shores of the Atlantic ocean there has grown up a pro-found web of interest which joins together the western world. Britain, France, Italy, even Spain, Belgium, Holland, the Scandinavian countries, and Pan-America are in the main one community in their deepest needs and their deepest purposes. They have a common interest in the ocean that unites them. They are to-day more inextricably bound together than most even as yet realize.[28]

Ronald Steel correctly identifies this rhetorical move as 'a new concept of geopolitics', and Lippmann would revive it following the Nazi *blitzkrieg* and continental dominance in 1940–1. The context of the Second World War saw Lippmann expand his notion, transforming the 'highway' into an 'inland sea' and membership to also include the British Commonwealth, Denmark, and Norway. British–American relations, for strategic as well as value-laden reasons, necessarily lay at its core – the 'nucleus of force around which the security of the whole region must necessarily be organized'.[29] British diplomacy invested a lot to make this a taken-for-granted cause.[30] For Lippmann, the Atlantic Community must be used to define US national interest: it both focused the energies of US foreign policy in the most productive and effective way, and it countered idealist presumptions of unlimited hegemony such as the Wilsonian dream of global 'orderly progress' and the 'American Century' pomposity of Henry Luce.[31] One might call Lippmann's interventions as gambits in governmentality, since they were claims to speak for and frame the US national interest in the terms of a transatlantic security apparatus. This would be more fully tested after the Second World War.

Atlantic federalism

Lippmann was the one who crystallized the cause of an Atlantic Community, but his silence on the matter in between the wars (and his support for US neutrality prior to May 1940) illustrated the weakness of the concept in times when security interests were not directly attached to it. The question therefore remained to what extent the Atlantic Community had value as a framework for developing and guaranteeing peaceful and prosperous relations between its members over the longer term. The person who did the most to promote this particular cause was Clarence Streit.

Streit had come to prominence in 1938 with the publication of *Union Now!* A Rhodes scholar and journalist with the *New York Times* covering Europe during the late 1920s and early 1930s, Streit's book was a call for a 'Union of Democracies' as the most effective way to pool resources, protect liberal values, and oppose the rising threat of totalitarian regimes. Streit's importance comes from his blending of the values and hierarchies of the Anglo-American condominium but making it open to other nations of the Transatlantic World on the basis not of race but of efficiency. Streit's Union was intended 'to provide effective common government in our democratic world in those fields where such common government will clearly serve man's freedom better than separate governments', thereby creating 'a nucleus world government capable of growing into universal world government peacefully and as rapidly as such growth will serve man's freedom'.[32] Streit's call met with praise from the Round Table's Philip Kerr, by 1939 Lord Lothian and holding the post of British Ambassador in Washington, DC, but was chastised by George Orwell who saw through the presumptions of another international project looking to obfuscate the realities of white rule around the globe.[33] With the Second World War as the catalyst, Streit looked to expand the proposal's leverage through founding Federal Union Incorporated. Renamed the Association to Unite the Democracies, it was this that provided the platform for supporting the North Atlantic Treaty after the war. An Atlantic Union Committee was formed in 1949 to act as an interest group for the federalist cause, and this eventually merged into what became the Atlantic Council in 1962.

Streit is important for our narrative because he was far more consistent in his promotion of the Atlantic Community ideal than Lippmann ever was. Both could count many among the high and mighty of the US foreign policy establishment as their personal friends, but of the two it was undoubtedly Streit who possessed more of the businessman's acumen to organize and market a good idea, and more of the willingness to try and turn opinion into reality. Others were also struck by the same cause. George Catlin, professor of politics at Cornell, co-founder of the American British Commonwealth Association (later part of the ESU), and also close to Lord Lothian, produced the pamphlet Anglo-American Union as a Nucleus of World Federation in 1943 and continued to proselytize after the war. Catlin rightly observed in 1959: 'that approach would be too narrow which confined itself to Anglo-American or, for that matter, to Anglo-French (or even Anglo-European) integration. We speak rather of the Atlantic Community or Organic Union of the Commonwealth of Free Nations'.[34]

In the late 1950s these ideas would be further formulated by Karl Deutsch and others under the guise of a 'security community'. Part of a project investigating the elimination of war run by Princeton's Center for Research on World Political Institutions, the 1957 study that defined this phenomenon regarded it as 'a group of people which has become "integrated"', whereby a 'sense of community' and 'institutions and practices' are strong enough to ensure that 'social problems' would be resolved 'by institutionalized procedures, without resort to large-scale physical force'.[35] The move of Deutsch *et al.* was significant because it maintained the uniqueness of the transatlantic realm while shifting the debate on that uniqueness into the 'value-free' space of post-war US political science. Although it faded out largely due to the declining influence of the Atlantic Community idea through the 1960s and into the 1970s, Deutsch's perspective has since been revived, albeit in a broader, global setting.[36] It is perhaps the clearest example of the Transnational Transatlantic as governmentality, encompassing as it does population, political economy, and security.

At the heart of all of these schemes remained the assumption of Anglo-American predominance and leadership, if not in practice then at least as catalyst. As Duncan Bell has outlined, the majority of proposals for 'supra-national unions' through the twentieth century 'were descended, in part or wholly, from the earlier Anglo-world projects' and 'placed the transatlantic British-American connection at the core of global order'.[37] Streit's proposals have lived on, both in terms of the notion of a 'democratic peace' (again embodying the broader transatlantic realm as a 'more evolved' example of civilization) and through attempts to organize and unite democratic nations around a benign vision of world order.[38] The Community of Democracies is the best example of the latter, founded as it was in 2000 with the Warsaw Declaration and the first ministerial meeting attended by representatives of Poland, Portugal, the United States, Chile, the Czech Republic, India, Mali, Mexico, the Republic of Korea, and South Africa (still at the forefront a century after Smuts, but now with its racial politics turned upside down). Perhaps the 'messianic impulse' of earlier versions has died away, as have hopes of transcending the state system, but the sense of being at the vanguard of the good side of history remains. While many in the disillusioned 'centre' regard these efforts as either empty posturing or the ravings of the right-wing, for those on the frontlines of the 'periphery' these kinds of networks represent something of deep significance.[39]

There were alternative conceptions of transatlantic governmentality that transgressed the established centre–periphery dynamic, as outlined in the chapter by Giuliana Chamedes in this volume on the role of Catholic Atlanticism. In contrast to the Anglo-American secular liberal political and economic order so far discussed, a Catholic vision of Western value-based solidarity opposed to godless communism arose out of the Second World War. The two perspectives merged around anti-communism, but the Catholic worldview was grounded on the Vatican and expanded its reach due to the existence of Catholic communities outside of the conceived Anglo-American space for Atlanticism. American elites such as C. D. Jackson played key roles in organizing these anti-communist networks via Rome, but the centre of gravity was definitely European.[40]

These Atlantic Community dreams were challenged on many fronts in terms of actual realization. There was also the emergence of a challenger within their midst, partly brought into being by the drive for transatlantic governmentality itself: European integration. The European institutions created after the Second World War were based from the very beginning on a legal foundation out of which mentalities of government were pursued in a more profound manner than the Atlanticism so far discussed. The attempt to co-opt the European subjectivities generated by these developments within a broader Atlantic population (in the Foucauldian sense) was a flexible response, but indicated clearly that the transatlantic framework was, outside of the formalities of the North Atlantic Treaty, built on discourse, custom, and wealth-generation. Jean Monnet's personal networks, formalized in the Action Committee for a United Europe, traversed the Atlantic and during the 1950s and early 1960s gave him direct access to the White House, and many like him would find the Atlantic and European frames easily compatible, if moving at different speeds and with different means.[41]

But principal among the weaknesses was the fact that these Atlantic dreams were tied too much to an external threat. Deutsch had highlighted the endogenous characteristics of creating a peaceful form of international relations on a regional basis, but even before that had been put forward there was a strong sense that no progress could be made without decisive exogenous pressure. Thus one observer stated in 1955: 'With an apparent slackening or absence of this threat some people may be lulled to a sense of false security relaxing their guard and allowing cooperation to diminish … There is now a greater need than ever for cooperation upon non-military matters.'[42] The missed opportunities and lack of commitment to Article II of the North Atlantic Treaty, pushed by the Canadians to allay domestic political opposition to the North Atlantic Treaty and overcome the dominant influence of the United States in the alliance.[43] Article II asked the commitment of the parties to 'the further development of peaceful and friendly international relations by strengthening their free institutions, by bringing about a better understanding of the principles upon which these institutions are founded, and by promoting conditions of stability and well-being'. Yet it ultimately illustrated well the problem of turning well-meaning rhetoric into effective activity.[44] Where was the interface between dreams and reality?

Cold War elites

The Cold War obviously intensified the need for a strong transatlantic alliance, with NATO at its core. The Atlantic Community idea was most strongly promoted by a range of organizations from the late 1940s to the late 1960s, with a high point being the Kennedy administration of 1961–3 and President Kennedy's 'Declaration of Interdependence' speech of 4 July 1962.[45] Some simple statistics would suggest that the term had far less currency in successive presidential administrations. Whereas a search for 'Atlantic Community' and 'Kennedy' in the *New York Times* database reveals 105 hits between 1960 and 1963, the same combination search with President Johnson for 1964–8 produces 78, for Nixon in 1969–73 46, for Ford during 1974–6 only 4, and for Carter in 1977–80 a mere 8. Diplomatic historians have continued to focus on the interactions of the governments in the transatlantic region, although the public sphere has begun to attract more attention. In 2002 Vojtech Mastny pointed out that 'the subject of "soft power" – the economic, cultural, moral, and other non-military assets that, in their own way, shaped interactions between and within the alliances' of NATO and the Warsaw Pact deserved more attention.[46] Article II has since received further scrutiny from Valerie Aubourg, John Milloy, and Linda Risso, including its value as a justification for private organizations to mobilize and organize support, something that NATO itself could not agree on.[47] The importance of these organizations comes from their collective creation of an informal transatlantic network of cultural affinity. The failure to construct new levels of decision-making – to successfully transform the Atlantic Community from ideology to policy-making reality – should not deflect attention for this phenomenon. Scepticism still remains paramount amongst historians, as with Jeffrey Giauque's comment:

> By the end of 1963 the Atlantic Community had largely ground to a halt. Common values and interests had proved strong enough to hold the alliance together and preserve existing institutions and a modicum of cooperation, but were insufficient to overcome divergent national goals and enable the construction of a new Atlantic architecture.[48]

Yet in many ways, these organizations, with their overlapping (elite) memberships, comparable agendas, and closeness to policy circles were *themselves* the embodiment of the Atlantic Community. Certainly their outreach into public information and education contributed to the normalization of the transatlantic alliance across Western societies, but focusing on this alone misses how they represented 'a new Atlantic architecture' in their own right.

Aubourg provides a very useful genealogy of the groups that arose in the early 1950s. The first group, the Atlantic Treaty Association (ATA), was British in orientation, offering a 'restrained vision of loosely federated national, private bodies aiming at popular education and support for NATO'. ATA, formally established in 1955, was the umbrella organization for national bodies such as the British Atlantic Committee, a body close to the Foreign Office and internationalist groups such as the ESU and the United Nations Association.[49] The second centred on the activities of, and was inspired by, Clarence Streit, as his Atlantic Union Committee generated offshoots such as the Atlantic Citizens Congress and the Declaration of Atlantic Unity. In line with Streit's federal cause, these directed their attention more to the democratic infrastructure (in particular the US Congress) and sought to facilitate the fulfilment of Article II's aims by overcoming national obstacles to greater economic and cultural cohesion. The third was the NATO Parliamentarians Conference (after 1956 an Assembly) that was driven largely by Canadian and Norwegian concerns over democratic input into NATO's governance, role, and purpose, drawing support from Streit's Declaration of Atlantic Unity.[50]

In terms of governmentality, the introduction of secrecy is an important extra ingredient. Elite conclaves necessarily maintain an air of aloofness out of the public eye, this adding to the sensation that they operate as hidden power-brokers in public affairs. The advent of the Bilderberg meetings in 1954 took this to a new level. Conceived as an informal means to overcome the mutual fall-out from divisions over security (the demise of the European Defence Community plans) and ideology (European anti-Americanism as a result of McCarthyism and suspicions of US hegemonic power), the annual Bilderberg meetings continue to this day as the doyen of the clandestine Transnational Transatlantic. Conspiracy theories abound, often maintained by no more than the combination of guest lists of prominent figures and a continuing media black-out. Thanks to the opening up of various public and private archives – including that of the Bilderberg secretariat itself, albeit under a fifty-year rule – historical fact has gradually been emerging out of hysterical fiction over the past decade.[51] The value of this work comes not just from its historical groundedness but also its appreciation for structure and agency, assessing not just the who and the how and the why, but also the relevance of Bilderberg for the transactions of political economy and security in the transatlantic region.[52]

Bilderberg is not alone in this regard, it being followed up – or 'paralleled' – by other significant elite networks, in particular the Trilateral Commission, which extended transatlantic governmentality by seeking to incorporate Japan in the early 1970s. The rise of Japanese economic and financial power made such a move understandable, and there is no doubt that the 'TriCom' was *not* a blending or meeting of equal cultures but an attempt to co-opt Japanese elites within a Western mindset on global organiza-tion.[53] This had already been presaged by Henry Kissinger in his infamous first speech as Secretary of State in May 1973. That Kissinger included Japan in the Year of Europe did raise an eyebrow or two. On one level there is nothing but sensible politics at work here. The United States was ready to engage Japan on a new level, just as it was looking for a new arrangement with Europe. It fitted the end of the post-Second World War paradigm and the forging of a new one. Yet there is also something striking about the words 'the Atlantic community cannot be an exclusive club. Japan must be a principal partner in our common enterprise'.[54] The implications are worth picking out. The com-munity is not defined by territory but by an idea. This returns partly to Lippmann's original formulations from both 1917 and 1944, since in each case, according to extenuating circumstances, he altered the list of member nations.[55] As some obser-vers saw, networks of capital were being reconfigured in the 1970s, resulting in the re-mapping of elite politics.[56] At the same time, the uniqueness of the US–European relationship was coming into question, although Cold War dynamics can also be traced in the transformations of the EC.[57] Kissinger wanted to revive the idea, but precisely because the world had changed, its original assumptions were increasingly irrelevant. This was also the logic behind the Trilateral Commission, and the incorporation of Japan within a new transnational elite network did meet resistance from the transat-lantic 'traditionalists' of Bilderberg.

In short, this is the moment when the Atlantic Community shifted from the *Gemeinschaft* of kinship to the *Gesellschaft* of rational contract[58] – it exchanged the traditional image of civilizational unity for the realities of a modern nego-tiable partnership. As stated above, the Atlantic Community was from its very beginnings an 'excess', since the Anglo-American core was placed at the centre of an English-speaking globe. The inclusion of Japan in the 1970s continued the excess and maintained the importance of democratic values, but it shifted the emphasis away from identity and race towards exchange and GDP. As Arianne Leendertz has argued in her chapter in this volume, the changed international environment of the 1970s, in terms of shifting power hierarchies, the onset of détente, and challenges to the established post-Second World War order in the West, brought with it an inev-itable re-framing of the transatlantic, and with it new forms of governmentality. In this sense, the epitome of the 'new' Transnational Transatlantic became the Organisation for Economic Cooperation and Development (OECD). This built-in excess is partly the cause of the continuous declarations of 'crisis' in the lit-erature produced on the Atlantic Community, although these calls for renewed vigour to achieve unity are certainly also declarations of self-importance.[59] These forces would reconfigure one final time, during the 'Successor Generation' period of the late 1970s and early 1980s when the 'security community' ideal was revived by a renewed campaign orchestrated by state-led public diplomacy and private organizations in tandem. The United States Information Agency (USIA) took a lead role, but it could achieve little without the input of well-endowed allies such as the Atlantic Council, the Atlantic Institute, and the Ford Foundation. Further research is required to identify to what extent they were actually the driving forces behind it.[60]

One can mark the end of this version of the Transnational Transatlantic as the closure of the Atlantic Institute in Paris in 1991.[61] Established in the early 1960s to function as *the* policy-relevant think tank on Atlantic affairs and lavishly funded by the Ford Foundation, the Institute followed the *Gemeinschaft-Gesellschaft* turn and shifted more into security-related research that, by the late 1980s, was becoming redundant. Since then, private organizations continue proselytizing the transatlantic framework – transatlantic governmentality does not simply end because an institute closes, after all – but they have become one voice among many. Collective memory has been a key factor in maintaining the cohesiveness of the transatlantic, as with Second World War and D-Day memorials, and this was partly reinforced in the aftermath of 9/11. Yet in a world made fluid by global connections, and both the United States and Europe considering the Asia-Pacific to be the site of the future, there is a strong sense that the transatlantic governmentality that arose in the twentieth century as a response to certain specific conditions (population – political economy – security) has now passed, because the conditions no longer require it.[62] The transatlantic is now no more than one of many regions. In this context, the attempted revival of a 'transatlantic imperative' with the TTIP is an interesting phenomenon, its advocates stressing not just the strengths of the past but also the need for a new era of economic discipline to ensure victory. This gives it, appropriately enough, a distinctly Foucauldian ring.[63]

Conclusion

Does Foucault's notion of governmentality open up possibilities for investigating the relevance of the Transnational Transatlantic as a structure of power that shaped political subjectivities and possibilities? What has been presented here is obviously no more than a sketch. Framing this field of activity as a collective exercise in governmentality glides over the multiple levels of functionality that these individual organizations contributed. This goes beyond assessing their relative proximity to government – the formal and informal links, be they personal and/or role-based – and the access and involvement this provided in policy-making fields (for instance, as epistemic communities).[64] It also requires addressing how these organizations were created and operated as necessary extensions of government, or rather of a particular configuration of transatlantic government that arose in the United States and Great Britain in the early twentieth century in response to a combination of historical factors and that spread further by the impact of revolution and world war. Where this approach does offer new research vistas is in the contribution of the Transnational Transatlantic towards promoting and sustaining particular subjectivities over time, using a variety of methods (education, propaganda, training, networks). A dual approach, taking in the mentalities of government and the government of mentalities, could open up new fields of investigation that confirm the Transnational Transatlantic as a unique historical phenomenon, and one that continues to have a profound impact on our interpretation of political realities today.

Notes

1 Governmentality is a term first used by Michel Foucault to refer to the many techniques used to regulate and shape the subjectivities and behaviours of others. Governmentality therefore functions to establish governable subjects in a given space.

2 J. Anderson, G. J. Ikenberry, and T. Risse (eds), *The End of the West? Crisis and Change in the Atlantic Order* (Ithaca: Cornell University Press, 2008); G. Scott-Smith (ed.), *Obama, US Politics, and Transatlantic Relations: Change or Continuity?* (Brussels: Peter Lang, 2012).

3 D. Hamilton, *Winning the Trade Peace: How to Make the Most of the EU-US Trade and Investment Partnership* (New Direction Foundation, May 2013).

4 A. Bacevich, *The Short American Century: A Postmortem* (Cambridge, MA: Harvard University Press, 2012).

5 M. Nolan, *The Transatlantic Century: Europe and America, 1890–2010* (Cambridge: Cambridge University Press, 2012), p. 373.

6 V. de Grazia, *Irresistible Empire: America's Advance through the Twentieth Century* (Cambridge, MA: Belknap Press, 2006).

7 R. L. Moore and M. Vaudagna (eds), *The American Century in Europe* (Ithaca: Cornell University Press, 2003).

8 B. Bailyn, *Atlantic History: Concept and Contours* (Cambridge, MA: Harvard University Press, 2005).

9 Governance refers to the broad apparatus of institutions, including but more extensive than government, that form and maintain social rules and norms for a given community.

10 P. Clavin, 'Defining Transnationalism', *Central European History*, 14:4 (2005), p. 422.

11 See for instance K. van der Pijl, *The Making of an Atlantic Ruling Class* (London: Verso, 1984); L. Sklair, *The Transnational Capitalist Class* (Oxford: Blackwell, 2001).

12 S. Lucas, 'Mobilizing Culture: The State-Private Network and the CIA in the Early Cold War', in D. Carter and R. Clifton (eds), *War and Cold War in American Foreign Policy 1942–1962* (Basingstoke: Palgrave, 2002), pp. 85–6.

13 K. Weisbrode, *The Atlantic Century* (Cambridge: DaCapo Press, 2009), p. 8.

14 See S. Guzzini, 'Applying Bourdieu's Framework of Power Analysis to IR: Opportunities and Limits', paper given to the 47th annual convention of the International Studies Association, Chicago, 2006. Online, available at http://pendientedemigracion.ucm.es/info/sdrelint/ficheros_materiales/materiales051.pdf (accessed 29 August 2014).

15 M. Foucault, 'Governmentality', in G. Burchell, C. Gordon, and P. Miller (eds), *The Foucault Effect: Studies in Governmentality* (Chicago: University of Chicago Press, 1991), pp. 102–3. 'Savoirs' refers to the conditions existing in a given period that enable an object to be understood and explained.

16 *Ibid.*, p. 103.

17 M. Dean, *Governmentality: Power and Rule in Modern Society* (London: Sage, 2014), p. 25, 29.

18 Civilization here refers to the ideologically loaded late nineteenth-century notion of Western cultural superiority in a hierarchical worldview, such that 'Western civilization' represents historical progress compared to others.

19 D. Bell, *The Idea of Greater Britain: Empire and the Future of World Order, 1860–1900* (Princeton: Princeton University Press, 2007).

20 S. Vucetic, *The Anglosphere: A Genealogy of a Racialized identity in International Relations* (Stanford: Stanford University Press, 2011).

21 For the background to these developments see C. Quigley, *Tragedy and Hope* (New York: Macmillan, 1966), pp. 130–1; D. Bell, 'The Project for a New Anglo Century: Race, Space, and Global Order', in P. Katzenstein (ed.), *Anglo-America and its Discontents: Civilisational Identities beyond West and East* (London: Routledge, 2012), p. 42.

22 P. Ziegler, *Legacy: Cecil Rhodes, the Rhodes Trust and Rhodes Scholarships* (New Haven: Yale University Press, 2008).

23 See W. V. Griffin, *Sir Evelyn Wrench and His Continuing Vision of International Relations during 40 Years* (New York: Newcomen Society in North America, 1950).

24 J. C. Bennett, 'An Anglosphere Primer', Foreign Policy Research Institute, 2002. Online, available at http://explorersfoundation.org/archive/anglosphere_primer.pdf (accessed 6 November 2013).

25 M. Mazower, *Governing the World: The History of an Idea* (New York: Penguin, 2012), p. 119.

26 M. Mazower, *No Enchanted Palace: The End of Empire and the Ideological Origins of the United Nations* (Princeton: Princeton University Press, 2009), pp. 40–2.

27 On the development of the Round Table's federalist worldview see A. Bosco, *The Round Table Movement and the Fall of the 'Second' British Empire, 1909–1919* (Newcastle upon Tyne: Cambridge Scholars Publishing, 2017).

28 W. Lippmann, 'Defense of the Atlantic World', *The New Republic*, 17 February 1917, p. 73; R. Steel, *Walter Lippmann and the American Century* (Boston: Little, Brown, 1980).

29 W. Lippmann, *US Foreign Policy: Shield of the Republic* (Boston: Little, Brown, 1943), pp. 114–36.

30 H. Butterfield Ryan, *The Vision of Anglo-America: The US-UK Alliance and the Emerging Cold War 1943–1946* (Cambridge: Cambridge University Press, 1987).

31 R. Steel, 'Walter Lippmann and the Invention of the Atlantic Community', in V. Aubourg, G. Bossuat, and G. Scott-Smith (eds), *European Community, Atlantic Community?* (Paris: Soleb, 2008), pp. 31, 33–4; L. Ambrosius, 'Woodrow Wilson and the Quest for Orderly Progress', in L. Ambrosius, *Wilsonianism: Woodrow Wilson and His Legacy in American Foreign Relations* (New York: Palgrave Macmillan, 2002), pp. 31–48.

32 C. Streit, *Union Now! A Proposal for an Atlantic Federal Union of the Free* (New York: Harpers & Bros., 1949), p. 4.

33 N. N., 'New Peace Plan Hailed by Lothian', *New York Times*, 6 March 1939, p. 3; G. Orwell, 'Not Counting Niggers', *Adelphi* (July 1939).

34 G. Catlin, *The Atlantic Community* (Wakefield: Coram, 1959), pp. 4–5.

35 K. Deutsch, S. A. Burrell, R. A. Kann, M. Lee, M. Lichtermann, R. E. Lindgren, F. L. Loewenheim and R. W. Van Wagenen, *Political Community and the North Atlantic Area: International Organization in the Light of Historical Experience* (Princeton: Princeton University Press, 1957), p. 5.

36 'There is emerging a transnational community of Deutschian policy-makers, if you will, who are challenging the once nearly hegemonic position of relativist-inspired policy-makers and offering an alternative understanding of what is possible in global politics and a map to get there', in E. Adler and M. Barnett (eds), *Security Communities* (Cambridge: Cambridge University Press, 1998), p. 4.

37 Bell, 'The Project for a New Anglo Century', p. 44.

38 *Ibid.*, p. 51. See also I. Parmar, 'American Power and Philanthropic Warfare: From the War to End All Wars to the Democratic Peace', *Global Society*, 28 (January 2014), pp. 54–69, esp. pp. 65–6.

39 See for instance Z. Pavilionis, 'The Community of Democracies: A New Instrument of Transatlantic Efforts to Enhance Democracy Building?' *Lithuanian Foreign Policy Review*, 23 (2010), pp. 113–22; R. Pastor, 'A Community of Democracies in the Americas: Instilling Substance into a Wondrous Phrase', *Canadian Foreign Policy Journal*, 10 (2003), pp. 15–29.

40 V. Aubourg, '"A Philosophy of Democracy under God": C.D. Jackson, Henry Luce and the Pro Deo Movement (1946–1964)', *Revue Francaise d'Etudes Americaines*, 107 (2006), pp. 29–46; J. Grossmann, *Die Internationale der Konservativen: Transnationale Elitenzirkel und private Außenpolitik in Westeuropa seit 1945* (Munich: De Gruyter, Oldenbourg, 2014).

41 W. Yondorf, 'Monnet and the Action Committee: The Formative Period of the European Communities', *International Organization*, 19 (1965), pp. 885–912; I. Wall and P.-E. Raviart, 'Jean Monnet, les États-Unis et le plan français', *Vingtième Siècle*, 30 (1991) pp. 3–21; B. Szele 'The European Lobby: The Action Committee for a United States of Europe', *European Integration Studies*, 4 (2005), pp. 109–19.

42 N. Padelford, 'Political Cooperation in the North Atlantic Community', *International Organization*, 9 (August 1955), p. 355.

43 See L. Pearson, *The International Years: Memoirs 1948–1957, Vol. 2* (London: Victor Gollancz, 1974), pp. 37–60; E. Reid, *Time of Fear and Hope: The Making of the North Atlantic Treaty 1947–1949* (Toronto: McClelland & Stewart, 1977), pp. 167–84.

44 See J. Milloy, *The North Atlantic Treaty Organization 1948–1957: Community or Alliance?* (Montreal: McGill-Queens University Press, 2006).

45 The Atlantic Community project of the Roosevelt Study Center and the University of Cergy-Pontoise attempted to unite research on the broad spectrum of activities in the private sphere with the focus on foreign policies as pursued by diplomatic history. For the results see V. Aubourg, G. Bossuat, and G. Scott-Smith (eds), *European Community, Atlantic Community?* (Paris: Soleb, 2008); G. Scott-Smith and V. Aubourg (eds), *Atlantic, Euratlantic, or Europe-America? The Atlantic Community and the European Idea from Kennedy to Nixon* (Paris: Solbe, 2011).

46 V. Mastny, 'The New History of Cold War Alliances', *Journal of Cold War Studies*, 4:2 (2002), p. 84.

47 Aubourg recounts that the NATO Information Service had no real policy or purpose towards the private organizations – it appreciated their importance, but did not initiate

them. See V. Aubourg, 'Creating the Texture of the Atlantic Community: The NATO Information Service, Private Atlantic Networks and the Atlantic Community in the 1950s', in Aubourg *et al.*, *European Community, Atlantic Community?* pp. 390–415. See also L. Risso, *Propaganda and Intelligence in the Cold War: The NATO Information Service* (London: Routledge, 2014).

48   J. Giauque, *Grand Designs and Visions of Unity: The Atlantic Powers and the Reorganization of Western Europe, 1955–1963* (Chapel Hill: University of North Carolina Press, 2002), p. 123.

49   J. Jenks, *British Propaganda and the News Media in the Cold War* (Edinburgh: Edinburgh University Press, 2006), p. 104.

50   Aubourg, 'Creating the Texture', pp. 404–7. For more detail see V. Aubourg, 'The Atlantic Congress of 1959: An Ambiguous Celebration of the Atlantic Community', in G. Schmidt (ed.), *A History of NATO: The First Fifty Years*, Vol. 2 (Basingstoke: Palgrave, 2001), pp. 341–58.

51   For the best of this recent research see T. Gijswijt, *Uniting the West: The Bilderberg Group, the Cold War and European Integration, 1952–1966*, PhD thesis (Heidelberg, 2008); I. Philipsen, *Diplomacy with Ambiguity: The History of the Bilderberg Organisation 1952–1977*, PhD thesis (Copenhagen University, 2009).

52   See V. Aubourg, 'The Bilderberg Group: Promoting European Governance Inside an Atlantic Community of Values', in W. Kaiser, B. Leucht, and Michael G. (eds), *Transnational Networks in Regional Integration: Governing Europe 1945–1983* (Basingstoke: Palgrave, 2010), pp. 38–60; I. Richardson, A. Kakabadse, and N. Kakabadse, *Bilderberg People: Elite Power and Consensus in World Affairs* (London: Routledge, 2011).

53   D. Knudsen, *The Trilateral Commission: The Global Dawn of Informal Elite Governance and Diplomacy 1972–1981*, PhD thesis (Copenhagen University, 2013).

54   N. N., 'The Year of Europe', *Department of State Bulletin*, 14 May 1973, p. 598.

55   See W. Lippmann, 'The Defense of the Atlantic World', *New Republic*, 17 November 1917; W. Lippmann, *US War Aims* (London: Hamilton, 1944).

56   See H. Sklar (ed.), *Trilateralism: The Trilateral Commission and Elite Planning for World Management* (Montreal: Black Rose Books, 1980).

57   N. Piers Ludlow, 'The New Cold War and the Expansion of the EC – A Nexus?', in J. Laursen (ed.), *The Institutions and Dynamics of the European Community, 1973–83* (Baden-Baden: Nomos, 2015).

58   This distinction comes from Ferdinand Tönnies and was developed further by Max Weber. It contrasts social groups based on personal interactions (*Gemeinschaft*) with those organised according to more impersonal ties and rational agreements (*Gesellschaft*).

59   See for example H. Kissinger, *Troubled Partnership: A Re-appraisal of the Atlantic Alliance* (New York: McGraw-Hill, 1965); H. van B. Cleveland, *The Atlantic Idea and its European Rival* (New York: McGraw-Hill, 1966); D. Calleo, *The Atlantic Fantasy: The US, NATO, and Europe* (Washington, DC: Johns Hopkins University Press, 1970); D. Middleton, *A Study in Unity and Disunity* (New York: David McKay, 1965); R. Kleinman, *Atlantic Crisis: American Diplomacy Confronts a Resurgent Europe* (New York: Norton, 1964); R. Steel, *The End of Alliance: America and the Future of Europe* (New York: The Viking Press, 1964); R. L. Pfaltzgraff, *The Atlantic Community, a Complex Imbalance* (New York: Van Nortrand Reinhold, 1969); J.

Chace and E. C. Ravenal (eds), *Atlantis Lost: US-European Relations after the Cold War* (New York: New York University Press, 1976); W. F. Hahn and R. L. Pfaltzgraff, *Atlantic Community in Crisis: A Redefinition of the Transatlantic Relationship* (New York: Pergamon Press, 1979); R. Dahrendorf, A. J. Pierre, and T. Sorensen (eds), *A Widening Atlantic? Domestic Change and Foreign Policy* (New York: Council on Foreign Relations, 1986).

60 G. Scott-Smith, 'Maintaining Transatlantic Community: US Public Diplomacy, the Ford Foundation and the Successor Generation Concept in US Foreign Affairs, 1960s-1980s', *Global Society*, 28:1 (January 2014), pp. 90–103.

61 There is still no full account of the Atlantic Institute, although Nancy Collins's forthcoming study of the Atlantic Council may cover some of this gap. On its origins see V. Aubourg, 'Organizing Atlanticism: The Bilderberg Group and the Atlantic Institute, 1952-1962', in G. Scott-Smith and H. Krabbendam (eds), *The Cultural Cold War in Western Europe, 1945-1970* (London: Frank Cass, 2003), pp. 92–105.

62 See for instance P. Isernia and L. Basile, 'To Agree or Disagree? Elite Opinion and Future Prospets of the Transatlantic Partnership', *Transworld* WP 34 (June 2014).

63 Hamilton, *Winning the Trade Peace*; P. van Ham, 'TTIP and the Renaissance of Transatlanticism: Regulatory Power in the Age of Rising Regions', *Clingendael Report* (July 2014).

64 Epsitemic communities are groups of experts who play policy-relevant roles as advisers in identifying public policy problems and then offering solutions.

References

Adler, E. and M. Barnett (eds), *Security Communities* (Cambridge: Cambridge University Press, 1998).

Ambrosius, L. 'Woodrow Wilson and the Quest for Orderly Progress', in L. Ambrosius, *Wilsonianism: Woodrow Wilson and His Legacy in American Foreign Relations* (New York: Palgrave Macmillan, 2002), pp. 31–48.

Anderson, J., G. J. Ikenberry, and T. Risse (eds), *The End of the West? Crisis and Change in the Atlantic Order* (Ithaca: Cornell University Press, 2008).

Aubourg, V. 'The Atlantic Congress of 1959: An Ambiguous Celebration of the Atlantic Community', in G. Schmidt (ed.), *A History of NATO: The First Fifty Years*, Vol. 2 (Basingstoke: Palgrave, 2001), pp. 341–58.

Aubourg, V. 'The Bilderberg Group: Promoting European Governance inside an Atlantic Community of Values', in W. Kaiser, B. Leucht, and Michael G. (eds), *Transnational Networks in Regional Integration: Governing Europe 1945-1983* (Basingstoke: Palgrave, 2010), pp. 38–60.

Aubourg, V. 'Creating the Texture of the Atlantic Community: The NATO Information Service, Private Atlantic Networks and the Atlantic Community in the 1950s', in V. Aubourg, G. Bossuat, and G. Scott-Smith (eds), *European Community, Atlantic Community?* (Paris: Soleb, 2008), pp. 390–415.

Aubourg, V. 'Organizing Atlanticism: The Bilderberg Group and the Atlantic Institute, 1952-1962', in G. Scott-Smith and H. Krabbendam (eds), *The Cultural Cold War in Western Europe, 1945-1970* (London: Frank Cass, 2003), pp. 92–105.

Aubourg, V. '"A Philosophy of Democracy under God": C.D. Jackson, Henry Luce and the Pro Deo Movement (1946–1964)', *Revue Francaise d'Etudes Americaines*, 107 (2006), pp. 29–46.

Aubourg, V., G. Bossuat, and G. Scott-Smith (eds), *European Community, Atlantic Community?* (Paris: Soleb, 2008).

Bacevich, A. *The Short American Century: A Postmortem* (Cambridge, MA: Harvard University Press, 2012).

Bailyn, B. *Atlantic History: Concept and Contours* (Cambridge, MA: Harvard University Press, 2005).

Bell, D. *The Idea of Greater Britain: Empire and the Future of World Order, 1860–1900* (Princeton: Princeton University Press, 2007).

Bell, D. 'The Project for a New Anglo Century: Race, Space, and Global Order', in P. Katzenstein (ed.), *Anglo-America and its Discontents: Civilisational Identities beyond West and East* (London: Routledge, 2012), pp. 33–55.

Bennett, J. C. 'An Anglosphere Primer', Foreign Policy Research Institute, 2002. Online, available at http://explorersfoundation.org/archive/anglosphere_primer.pdf (accessed 6 November 2013).

Bosco, A. *The Round Table Movement and the Fall of the 'Second' British Empire, 1909–1919* (Newcastle upon Tyne: Cambridge Scholars Publishing, 2017).

Butterfield Ryan, H. *The Vision of Anglo-America: The US-UK Alliance and the Emerging Cold War 1943–1946* (Cambridge: Cambridge University Press, 1987).

Calleo, D. *The Atlantic Fantasy. The US, NATO, and Europe* (Washington, DC: Johns Hopkins University Press, 1970).

Catlin, G. *The Atlantic Community* (Wakefield: Coram, 1959).

Chace, J. and E. C. Ravenal (eds), *Atlantis Lost: US-European Relations after the Cold War* (New York: New York University Press, 1976).

Clavin, P. 'Defining Transnationalism', *Central European History*, 14:4 (2005), pp. 421–39.

Dahrendorf, R., A. J. Pierre, and T. Sorensen (eds), *A Widening Atlantic? Domestic Change and Foreign Policy* (New York: Council on Foreign Relations, 1986).

Dean, M. *Governmentality: Power and Rule in Modern Society* (London: Sage, 2014).

Deutsch, K., S. A. Burrell, R. A. Kann, M. Lee, M. Lichtermann, R. E. Lindgren, F. L. Loewenheim and R. W. Van Wagenen. *Political Community and the North Atlantic Area: International Organization in the Light of Historical Experience* (Princeton: Princeton University Press, 1957).

Foucault, M. 'Governmentality', in G. Burchell, C. Gordon, and P. Miller (eds), *The Foucault Effect: Studies in Governmentality* (Chicago: University of Chicago Press, 1991), pp. 87–104.

Giauque, J. *Grand Designs and Visions of Unity: The Atlantic Powers and the Reorganization of Western Europe, 1955–1963* (Chapel Hill: University of North Carolina Press, 2002).

Gijswijt, T. *Uniting the West: The Bilderberg Group, the Cold War and European Integration, 1952–1966*, PhD thesis (Heidelberg, 2008).

de Grazia, V. *Irresistible Empire: America's Advance through the Twentieth Century* (Cambridge, MA: Belknap Press, 2006).

Griffin, W. V. *Sir Evelyn Wrench and His Continuing Vision of International Relations during 40 Years* (New York: Newcomen Society in North America, 1950).

Grossmann, J. *Die Internationale der Konservativen: Transnationale Elitenzirkel und private Außenpolitiek in Westeuropa seit 1945* (Munich: De Gruyter, Oldenbourg, 2014).

Guzzini, S. 'Applying Bourdieu's Framework of Power Analysis to IR: Opportunities and Limits', paper given to the 47th annual convention of the International Studies Association, Chicago, 2006. Online, available at http://pendientedemigracion.ucm.es/info/sdrelint/ficheros_materiales/materiales051.pdf (accessed 29 August 2014).

Hahn, W. F. and R. L. Pfaltzgraff. *Atlantic Community in Crisis: A Redefinition of the Transatlantic Relationship* (New York: Pergamon Press, 1979).

Hamilton, D. *Winning the Trade Peace: How to Make the Most of the EU-US Trade and Investment Partnership* (New Direction Foundation, May 2013).

Isernia, P. and L. Basile. 'To Agree or Disagree? Elite Opinion and Future Prospets of the Transatlantic Partnership', *Transworld* WP 34 (June 2014).

Jenks, J. *British Propaganda and the News Media in the Cold War* (Edinburgh: Edinburgh University Press, 2006).

Kissinger, H. *Troubled Partnership: A Re-appraisal of the Atlantic Alliance* (New York: McGraw-Hill, 1965).

Kleinman, R. *Atlantic Crisis: American Diplomacy Confronts a Resurgent Europe* (New York: Norton, 1964).

Knudsen, D. *The Trilateral Commission: The Global Dawn of Informal Elite Governance and Diplomacy 1972-1981*, PhD thesis (Copenhagen University, 2013).

Lippmann, W. 'Defense of the Atlantic World', *The New Republic*, 17 February 1917.

Lippmann, W. 'The Defense of the Atlantic World', *New Republic*, 17 November 1917.

Lippmann, W. *US Foreign Policy: Shield of the Republic* (Boston: Little, Brown, 1943).

Lippmann, W. *US War Aims* (London: Hamilton, 1944).

Lucas, S. 'Mobilizing Culture: The State-Private Network and the CIA in the Early Cold War', in D. Carter and R. Clifton (eds), *War and Cold War in American Foreign Policy 1942-1962* (Basingstoke: Palgrave, 2002), pp. 83–107.

Mastny, V. 'The New History of Cold War Alliances', *Journal of Cold War Studies*, 4:2 (2002), pp. 55–84.

Mazower, M. *Governing the World: The History of an Idea* (New York: Penguin, 2012).

Mazower, M. *No Enchanted Palace: The End of Empire and the Ideological Origins of the United Nations* (Princeton: Princeton University Press, 2009).

Middleton, D. *A Study in Unity and Disunity* (New York: David McKay, 1965).

Milloy, J. *The North Atlantic Treaty Organization 1948-1957: Community or Alliance?* (Montreal: McGill-Queens University Press, 2006).

Moore, R. L. and M. Vaudagna (eds), *The American Century in Europe* (Ithaca: Cornell University Press, 2003).

N. N. 'The Year of Europe', *Department of State Bulletin*, 14 May 1973, p. 598.

N. N. 'New Peace Plan Hailed by Lothian', *New York Times*, 6 March 1939.

Nolan, M. *The Transatlantic Century: Europe and America, 1890-2010* (Cambridge: Cambridge University Press, 2012).

Orwell, G. 'Not Counting Niggers', *Adelphi* (July 1939).

Padelford, N. 'Political Cooperation in the North Atlantic Community', *International Organization*, 9 (August 1955).

Parmar, I. 'American Power and Philanthropic Warfare: From the War to End All Wars to the Democratic Peace', *Global Society*, 28 (January 2014), pp. 54–69.

Pastor, R. 'A Community of Democracies in the Americas: Instilling Substance into a Wondrous Phrase', *Canadian Foreign Policy Journal*, 10 (2003), pp. 15–29.

Pavilionis, Z. 'The Community of Democracies: A New Instrument of Transatlantic Efforts to Enhance Democracy Building?' *Lithuanian Foreign Policy Review*, 23 (2010), pp. 113–22.

Pearson, L. *The International Years: Memoirs 1948–1957, Vol. 2* (London: Victor Gollancz, 1974).

Pfaltzgraff, R. L. *The Atlantic Community, a Complex Imbalance* (New York: Van Nortrand Reinhold, 1969).

Philipsen, I. *Diplomacy with Ambiguity: The History of the Bilderberg Organisation 1952–1977*, PhD thesis (Copenhagen University, 2009).

Piers Ludlow, N. 'The New Cold War and the Expansion of the EC – A Nexus?', in J. Laursen (ed.), *The Institutions and Dynamics of the European Community, 1973–83* (Baden-Baden: Nomos, 2015), pp. 131–49.

Quigley, C. *Tragedy and Hope* (New York: Macmillan, 1966).

Reid, E. *Time of Fear and Hope: The Making of the North Atlantic Treaty 1947–1949* (Toronto: McClelland & Stewart, 1977).

Richardson, I., A. Kakabadse, and N. Kakabadse. *Bilderberg People: Elite Power and Consensus in World Affairs* (London: Routledge, 2011).

Risso, L. *Propaganda and Intelligence in the Cold War: The NATO Information Service* (London: Routledge, 2014).

Scott-Smith, G. 'Maintaining Transatlantic Community: US Public Diplomacy, the Ford Foundation and the Successor Generation Concept in US Foreign Affairs, 1960s-1980s', *Global Society*, 28:1 (January 2014), pp. 90–103.

Scott-Smith, G. (ed.), *Obama, US Politics, and Transatlantic Relations: Change or Continuity?* (Brussels: Peter Lang, 2012).

Scott-Smith, G. and V. Aubourg (eds), *Atlantic, Euratlantic, or Europe-America? The Atlantic Community and the European Idea from Kennedy to Nixon* (Paris: Solbe, 2011).

Sklair, L. *The Transnational Capitalist Class* (Oxford: Blackwell, 2001).

Sklar, H. (ed.), *Trilateralism: The Trilateral Commission and Elite Planning for World Management* (Montreal: Black Rose Books, 1980).

Steel, R. *The End of Alliance: America and the Future of Europe* (New York: The Viking Press, 1964).

Steel, R. *Walter Lippmann and the American Century* (Boston: Little, Brown, 1980).

Steel, R. 'Walter Lippmann and the Invention of the Atlantic Community', in V. Aubourg, G. Bossuat, and G. Scott-Smith (eds), *European Community, Atlantic Community?* (Paris: Soleb, 2008), pp. 28–36.

Streit, C. *Union Now! A Proposal for an Atlantic Federal Union of the Free* (New York: Harpers & Bros., 1949).

Szele, B. 'The European Lobby: The Action Committee for a United States of Europe', *European Integration Studies*, 4 (2005), pp. 109–19.

van B. Cleveland, H. *The Atlantic Idea and its European Rival* (New York: McGraw-Hill, 1966).

van der Pijl, K. *The Making of an Atlantic Ruling Class* (London: Verso, 1984).

van Ham, P. 'TTIP and the Renaissance of Transatlanticism: Regulatory Power in the Age of Rising Regions', *Clingendael Report* (July 2014).

Vucetic, S. *The Anglosphere: A Genealogy of a Racialized identity in International Relations* (Stanford: Stanford University Press, 2011).

Wall, I. and P.-E. Raviart. 'Jean Monnet, les Etats-Unis et le plan francais', *Vingtieme Siecle*, 30 (1991), pp. 3–21.

Weisbrode, K. *The Atlantic Century* (Cambridge: DaCapo Press, 2009).

Yondorf, W. 'Monnet and the Action Committee: The Formative Period of the European Communities', *International Organization* 19 (1965), pp. 885–912.

Ziegler, P. *Legacy: Cecil Rhodes, the Rhodes Trust and Rhodes Scholarships* (New Haven: Yale University Press, 2008).

6

Contemporary history as critical perspective: Transatlantic debates about the Nazi past

Konrad H. Jarausch

Compared to other problematic countries, the Germans have developed a surprisingly critical understanding of their own recent past. This achievement is all the more surprising, since in 1945 the majority of the population rejected all responsibility for the Nazi crimes, wallowing in self-pity and struggling to assure its own survival. Whether as old-style Prussians or newer ethno-nationalists, professional historians had contributed significantly to spreading that spirit of nationalism which had helped precipitate the catastrophe of the Second World War and mass murder. Yet half a century later German politicians readily apologized for Nazi crimes, and intellectuals had embraced a veritable Holocaust-sensibility as their enthusiasm for Daniel Goldhagen's exaggerated indictment of eliminationist anti-Semitism showed.[1] Resisting efforts to relativize this terrible legacy, scholars wrote probing accounts of the failure of democracy, the rise of National Socialism and the terrible crimes of genocide. While this difficult reversal was never complete, it was more extensive than in post-militarist Japan, post-fascist Italy, or post-communist Russia.[2]

One partial explanation that has assigned most of the credit to the positive influence of the United States is the 'proconsul-view'. Memoirs of 'old German hands' in the military or among diplomats tend to stress that the Western effort at reorientation eventually helped revise popular stereotypes.[3] Scholarly analyses of occupation policy point to the three 'd's' of demilitarization, denazification, and decartelization in preparing the ground for the recovery of democracy.[4] Cultural investigations put more emphasis on the salutary example of the America-Houses and on the impact of exchange movements that brought young Germans to the United States, while other studies focus instead on the pervasive process of Americanization in the younger generation through Hollywood and rock-and-roll.[5] Yet the impact of external intervention should not be exaggerated, since forcing the defeated to witness the effects of German crimes in Buchenwald or Dachau sometimes had the opposite effect of hardening obduracy. Moreover, many historians, shielded by their craft, were often impervious to such outside pressures.

Equally problematic is the internal version that primarily focuses on the domestic conversion to explain the process of distancing from the Third Reich. The shock of the second defeat and of the Nazi crimes forced even national-conservative historians like Gerhard Ritter into soul-searching about 'a total revision of German historical thinking', though he wanted to salvage whatever he could from the national tradition. More self-critical was the liberal Friedrich Meinecke who saw the excesses of Prussian militarism as the root-cause of the 'German catastrophe' that made it deviate from Western development. Similarly, the part-Jewish archivist Ludwig Dehio asserted that the continuity of hegemonic striving which led from William II to Hitler was responsible for unleashing both world wars.[6] These attempts at critical reflection during the post-war period reveal a lively debate among German historians and intellectuals about the reasons for the Third Reich, but they remained largely within the confines of a 'politically and morally tamed historicism'. At best they were a first step towards repudiating nationalism.[7]

A more complete interpretation of the critical turn of German historiography therefore needs to focus on the interaction between outside pressures and internal rethinking. Due to the ideological support of the war effort on both sides, it was not at all a foregone conclusion that historians in the Anglo-American world and West Germany would be able to overcome their mutual suspicion and actually work together. And yet during the post-war decades former enemy scholars succeeded in developing a substantive and methodological cooperation which has been extraordinarily intense and fruitful.[8] Though East German historians also attempted to follow the Marxist lead of their Soviet colleagues, their communication remained more superficial and reluctant than among their western counterparts.[9] In the West, the joint transatlantic effort to confront the historical reasons and consequences of the Nazi dictatorship produced an entirely new subspecialty – German contemporary history.[10] How did this surprising disciplinary innovation that supported the critical turn come about?

Beginning separately

In 1945 the situation was hardly propitious for the development of a critical approach to the recent past, since neither the victorious allies nor the defeated Germans were ready for such an endeavour. After years of debate about the aftermath of victory, Anglo-American opinion remained divided between advocates of a punitive policy towards National Socialism and spokesmen of a rehabilitative approach that would try to change German behaviour.[11] Moreover, intellectuals were also caught up in the stereotypes of their own war propaganda, treating the Germans as the 'near other' which had rejected Western democracy by insisting on a separate development that led straight from Luther to Hitler.[12] The liberation of the concentration camps from Buchenwald to Dachau hardened such historical clichés through the discovery of the shocking atrocities committed within them. Finally, professional historians on both sides of the Atlantic remained deeply suspicious of the 'presentism' involved in addressing the recent past without the proper temporal distance or access to official documents.[13]

Humiliated by defeat and uneasy about their collaboration with the Third Reich, most German scholars also resented being lectured about their own transgressions by outsiders. The conservative Gerhard Ritter polemicized against the blanket condemnation of the German past, which he called 'Vansittartism' according to the condemnatory attitude of the British Foreign Office.[14] Similarly, one of the founders of contemporary history, Paul Kluke, argued that true understanding of the Third Reich 'is perhaps granted only to those people who have had the dubious honor of personally living and suffering through the events'.[15] As a result of such reluctance, the self-cleansing of the German historical profession remained rather limited, excluding only those colleagues like Ernst Anrich or Günter Franz who had most vociferously supported National Socialism. The majority of the conservative or ethnic nationalists was left in office to ponder its political misjudgements – and only a few, like Johannes Haller or Hermann Heimpel, were willing to distance themselves publicly from their prior errors.[16]

Part of the problem in Britain and the United States was the paucity of first-rate historians who had concerned themselves with recent German history before 1939. Most American scholars interested in Europe explored the common cultural heritage with Great Britain or worked on the impulses of the Enlightenment and the revolution emanating from France. In contrast to such a shared heritage, Germany seemed rather problematic, attracting only the interest of diplomatic historians like Sidney Fay or Bernadotte Schmitt in the revisionist controversy about the responsibility for the outbreak of the First World War.[17] During the Second World War, the Office of Strategic Services (OSS) did gather a highly talented group of scholars, often with other temporal or subject area specialties, in order to work on intelligence regarding German opinion and fighting power. As a result German historians who had emigrated to the United States, such as Hajo Holborn or Hans Rosenberg, gained a good deal of influence, but they were themselves politically divided and their position in American academe remained somewhat marginal.[18] In contrast to keen public interest, academic research remained therefore rather limited.

In Germany there were also few internationalized historians ready to examine their own contribution to the national catastrophe in critical terms. By their resolute defence of their country's policy in the First World War, many scholars had made themselves unwelcome in international circles even before the Second World War cut them entirely off from such contacts. Institutionally, most resisted the efforts of interested Americans like Edward Hartshorne to reform their universities, since they thought them uncorrupted in their core and still leading in the world.[19] Sympathetic US visitors like the medievalist Walter Dorn found hardly any colleagues like Franz Schnabel with whom they could exchange ideas about what needed to be changed to democratize German intellectual life. As a result, few emigrated historians were invited to return, and even fewer, like Hans Rothfels or Golo Mann, actually followed the call and became cultural intermediaries.[20] While Anglo-American colleagues watched out for signs of dangerous revisionism, the reconstruction of the historical profession was largely left to German scholars themselves.

In spite of these differences, most Anglo-American observers and a minority of German historians found common ground in agreeing on the need for a critical approach to National Socialism. Since the 'stab-in-the back' legend as well as the campaign against the 'war guilt lie' had fed that chauvinist revisionism which helped the Nazis to seize power, both agreed that the repetition of nationalist mythmaking had to be prevented at all costs. While general reflection on the cultural causes for the catastrophe was important, only a critical, document-based scholarship could provide a reliable underpinning for the democratization of historical consciousness. Meeting this challenge required overcoming the academic disdain for recent events by systematic research in order to discredit popular propaganda myths. Since the Nazi crimes extended all over Europe, the study of their causes and effects had to be a transnational enterprise from the beginning. In spite of much hostile stereotyping, it became gradually clear that a joint effort between the victors and defeated was needed in order to address the horrors of the recent past.[21]

Working in parallel

One important impulse for confronting the recent past was the Nuremberg Trial of the chief Nazis, German elites, and leading organizations of the Third Reich. Unlike after 1918, the Allies insisted on formal legal proceedings in order to obtain a measure of justice for Hitler's crimes and to educate the defeated country about the enormity of its complicity. No doubt, the judicial basis of the charges of conspiracy to unleash war, of classical war crimes, and of a new category of crimes against humanity was somewhat problematic, since it was unprecedented. But even if the transgressions of the victors, like the Katyn massacre, were not discussed, the procedure was adversarial, providing chances for defence, and the ultimate judgment differentiated between various degrees of culpability. For historians, the key consequence was the collection of a vast amount of documentary material on the inhumane policies of the Third Reich. Even if part of the German public resented such 'victors' justice', the various trials provided an enormous impetus for historical research so as to prove respective guilt or innocence.[22]

Since the victors did not trust the defeated, they insisted on safeguarding the 'captured German documents' themselves, allowing only their own researchers access. The paper detritus of the Third Reich was divided into locations in the Berlin Document Centre for individual prosecution, Whaddon Hall in the UK, Alexandria in the United States, and Moscow. Ironically, this seizure of the German records made it rather difficult for German historians to research the brutal Nazi policies, privileging instead scholars from the victorious countries which left them open to charges of producing allied history. In response to pressures from Bonn, the British and Americans eventually agreed to undertake a huge microfilming project – only to run up against military secrecy that required constant efforts at declassification. While the microfilms and their guides provided an important resource for the first wave of post-war research, allied distrust hampered German access to this documentation and therefore postponed the development of a critical internal approach to Nazi crimes until the records were returned in the second half of the 1950s.[23]

In Anglo-American academe the great public interest in explanations of the Nazi riddle led to the emergence of the field of German history as a specialty within European History. During the 1950s a cohort of talented students crowded into the seminars, learning from *émigrés* and war participants about what had gone wrong with the German past. Many of the new PhDs like Peter Gay, Theodore Hamerow, Georg Iggers, George Mosse, Fritz Stern, Gerhard Weinberg, and others were second-generation refugees who had escaped the Third Reich as children and now sought to understand the reasons for their fate, serving as intermediaries between their birthplace that had expelled them and their country of residence which offered them academic careers.[24] As a result of the captured documents, an odd group of microfilm specialists also emerged who knew the Nazi records, but could hardly speak any German and had never been to the continent. By the late 1950s these newly minted specialists founded a German Documents committee, created a Conference Group for Central European History and also a journal of the same name.[25]

Within Germany, historians sought to revive their institutions and to resume academic work during the restoration climate of the Adenauer years. The first challenge was to reopen the universities and recover libraries and archives in order to return to professional teaching and research without ideological pressure. Limited as it was, denazification also created some space for rehabilitated Weimar democrats who then became the new spokesmen of the profession. Due to his ties to the resistance and willingness to distance himself from some Nazi excesses, Gerhard Ritter was elected president of the reconstituted Association of German Historians, even if more liberal colleagues criticized his national-conservative views. The appointment of the half-Jewish Ludwig Dehio as editor of the prestigious journal *Historische Zeitschrift* signalled a somewhat greater openness to criticism. Among the younger generation erstwhile partisans of ethnic approaches such as Werner Conze or Theodor Schieder gradually changed their vocabulary to structural history.[26] But on the whole, the Nazi past was so overwhelming that most historians still shied away from openly engaging it.

More promising was the founding of an Institute for Contemporary History (*Institut für Zeitgeschichte*) in Munich in 1950, since it sought to address the failure of German democracy and the success of National Socialism head on. Though the collection of documents started immediately after the war, it took three years of complicated negotiations from 1947 on to develop the conception of a new 'research institute on the history of the Third Reich'. The basic question was whether to focus on popular anti-fascist propaganda or to concentrate on impartial scholarship as the best method to counter nationalist myths. An advisory council of prominent democratic politicians like Theodor Heuss, publicists such as Eugen Kogon, and historians like Franz Schnabel pushed for the establishment of a scholarly institute and mediated between the Bavarian politician Gerhard Kroll and his academic critic Gerhard Ritter. With the 1953 founding of a new journal, called *Vierteljahrshefte für Zeitgeschichte*, under the aegis of Hans Rothfels who had just returned from the University of

Chicago, the institute shed its Catholic conservatism and allowed Germany to catch up to the international debate by becoming a centre of critical research on the recent Nazi past.[27]

Out of these separate beginnings, a degree of communication gradually developed among contemporary historians on both sides of the Atlantic. During the Cold War even conservative scholars could find counterparts in defence of a common 'Western Civilization', called occident or *Abendland* in contrast to the Soviet East.[28] An example of more progressive cooperation was the founding of the Free University of Berlin (FU) in 1948 which not only sought to combat the communist menace but also spread critical perspectives on the German past through innovations like the Otto Suhr Institute for political science, in which scholars returning from emigration like Ernst Fraenkel and Richard Löwenthal played a central role. One of its professors was the young Karl Dietrich Bracher, who had just come back from a year at Harvard, and who was working on the reasons for the collapse of the Weimar Republic. Among the historians the formerly nationalist, part-Jewish Hans Herzfeld also tried to provide a more critical outlook on the Third Reich.[29] A further platform for transatlantic debate was Walter Laqueur's and Georg Mosse's founding of the *Journal of Contemporary History* in 1966.[30]

The gradual emergence of a transatlantic dialogue was supported by a systematic policy of academic exchange which created a personal network of relationships. While efforts at reorientation began already in the American prisoner-of-war camps, it took several years before young Germans were included in various exchange programmes sponsored by civil society groups like the Quakers or by the government-run Fulbright Program. As the personal recollections of scholars such as Hans-Ulrich Wehler or Jürgen Kocka show, it was less the formal training in a different view of German history than the experience of a vibrant democracy that left deep traces in their subsequent work.[31] At the same time specialists from the United States like Peter Gay were invited to German universities, allowing them to work in archives and to overcome some of their war-time resentment by viewing a more democratic and cosmopolitan Federal Republic. The German Academic Exchange Service (DAAD) and other foundations systematically sponsored such transatlantic movement, while the founding of the German Historical Institute (GHI) in Washington, DC provided an institutional bracket.[32]

Developing cooperation

Even if perspectives remained different, personal encounters and intellectual debates facilitated the shared project of creating a critical contemporary history of Germany. In the Anglo-American realm a lively discussion had developed that inverted the positive claims of a special German path, called *Sonderweg*, into a negative perspective of deviation from the Western norm.[33] While some scholars emphasized deep cultural roots such as the Reformation or Romanticism, others stressed more recent social developments like the revolution of 1848 or the weakness of social democracy.[34] Rather resentful of facile generalizations from the outside, German traditionalists tended to blame transnational developments like the rise of modern mass politics for the catastrophe; but even they could not deny that such trends had rather more disastrous consequences in Germany and that explanations were needed why Central European development had led to war and genocide.[35] Through exchanges of lectures, journal articles, and reviews a transatlantic debate developed that wrestled with the same fundamental question of what had gone wrong.

A first test of the emerging cooperation was the discussion of the origins of the Second World War that caused a firestorm of controversy in the early 1960s. On the one hand the Germanophile US historian David Hoggan accused Polish leader Colonel Beck and British politician Lord Halifax of a conspiracy to block Hitler's legitimate claims in the West Prussian Corridor in order to unleash a second carnage.[36] On the other hand the Germanophobe British gadfly A. J. P. Taylor argued provocatively that Hitler was just an opportunist, no worse than any other German statesman, who did not really want to fight Britain and therefore blamed inept diplomacy for the war. Interestingly enough, the scholarly response to such claims was as devastating as it was unanimous.[37] From Gerhard Weinberg in the United States to Andreas Hillgruber in the Federal Republic, historians dismissed Hoggan's scholarship as slipshod and Taylor's theses as irresponsible grandstanding. This largely forgotten incident demonstrates, however, that a consensus on the main political interpretations was gradually emerging on both sides of the Atlantic.

Another *cause célèbre* that reinforced critical cooperation was the Fischer controversy about German responsibility for the outbreak of the First World War. Starting as a Protestant nationalist, Fischer had recanted his errors after learning of SS crimes and spending time in the United Kingdom and United States. He was so shocked by the extent of the annexationist aims in the First World War that he attributed more responsibility to the imperial government for its outbreak than any German scholar had done previously. Conservative colleagues were outraged over this violation of the war guilt taboo, and blocked his lecture tour to the United States. But American scholars then came to Fischer's aid, financing his trip, and Fritz Stern defended him during the stormy meeting of the Association of German Historians in 1964. Though not agreeing in all details with Fischer's rather moralistic assertions, most Anglo-American historians praised his political courage and defended him against his domestic critics. This spontaneous support showed a typical mechanism of transatlantic cooperation during the 1960s in which US scholars intervened to strengthen self-critical tendencies in the German profession.[38]

In the methodological struggle to break with the traditional primacy of grand politics, Anglo-American scholars also generally supported the development of the new social history. Inspired by New Left intellectuals like Eric Hobsbawm, researchers in the United States were themselves shifting their topical interests from international issues to domestic questions. Since the conception of a new history of society, called *Gesellschaftsgeschichte*, by younger historians such as Hans-Ulrich Wehler and Jürgen Kocka rested on social science theories of German deviation from Western modernization, US historians found many of their structural arguments familiar. Moreover, the explicit democratic commitment of the turn to the history of society appeared welcome to international observers who advocated a further distancing from German authoritarian traditions.[39] In the debate about historical methods during the early 1970s with defenders of diplomatic history like Klaus Hildebrand, Anglo-American historians like Gerald Feldman, Vernon Lidtke, or James Sheehan sided with their German colleagues who were proclaiming a new 'primacy of domestic politics'.[40]

The introduction of quantitative methods in the 1970s was another step towards transatlantic cooperation in spreading new approaches to the past. Since most of the hardware and software was developed in the United States, social scientists in the Interuniversity Consortium for Political and Social Research at Michigan were also quick to make use of the potential of computers. While Americans focused on a new political history of voting analysis, British demographers worked on family reconstitution and French economic historians, clustered around the journal *Annales*, compiled long time series. A younger group of historians and sociologists both in the United States and in the Federal Republic of Germany quickly adapted such methods to German subjects, seeking numerical proof for impressionistic assertions from parliamentary politics to university history. In Cologne Wilhelm Schroeder and Heinrich Best founded the QUANTUM group that published a new journal and established itself as part of social science infrastructure. In the international commission INTERQUANT, co-founded with the Social Science History Association and the American Historical Association, German and American scholars worked together on equal terms.[41]

In the infamous *Historikerstreit* Anglo-American scholars once again intervened on the side of the supporters of a critical view of the German past. In the second half of the 1980s conservative commentators began to argue that enough contrition was enough and that Germans ought to cease blaming themselves for the Holocaust. When the traditional historian of ideas Ernst Nolte argued in the conservative newspaper *Frankfurter Allgemeine Zeitung* that Hitler had learned from Stalin, since Soviet crimes pre-dated Nazi atrocities, the leftist sociologist Jürgen Habermas accused him of relativizing German guilt. Similarly, when the military historian Andreas Hillgruber showed more sympathy for the German flight and expulsion on the Eastern front than for the suffering of the Jews, Hans-Ulrich Wehler polemicized against such an apologetic stance.[42] Carried on in the pages of newspapers and magazines this 'historians' quarrel' provoked much commentary from Anglo-American scholars, ranging from Richard Evans to Charles Maier, all of whom were defending a critical consensus on the German past.[43]

German and American historians also cooperated in combating oversimplifications regarding sensitive issues, as the Goldhagen controversy showed. The author was the son of a Romanian Holocaust survivor who was trained at Harvard as a political scientist and created a stir with his published dissertation on *Hitler's Willing Executioners*. In this book, he vigorously argued that Germans collaborated in the genocide of Jews due to a deep-seated 'eliminationist anti-Semitism' that pervaded the entire culture. Promoted by the *New York Times* and the liberal weekly *Die Zeit*, Goldhagen's thesis became a 'publishing phenomenon', selling hundreds of thousands of copies to a general public eager to embrace a simplistic explanation. But among most historians the reception was devastating. Leading scholars like Christopher Browning and Hans Mommsen savaged the book for its many errors and its exaggerated generalization that accused Germans of anti-Semitism and failed to explain their democratic conversion after 1945.[44] This time the front-line ran between amateurs and professionals on both sides of the Atlantic.

Even for such highly charged issues as the overdue compensation of former slave labourers, the transatlantic collaboration of historians helped lay the groundwork through research. The final settlement was a political achievement, compelling German industry as well as the government to create a new foundation called 'Remembrance, Responsibility and Future' to compensate the 1.665 million survivors by paying out 4.4 billion euro.[45] But much of the research behind it was produced by international teams of historians. When giant companies such as the Allianz insurance group and the Deutsche Bank finally decided to open their records, scholarly commissions were comprised both of American and German historians, involving Gerald Feldman as well as Harold James as chief authors of the studies.[46] In the most recent effort to research the National Socialist history and post-war memory of the German Foreign Office, Germans like Eckhart Conze and Norbert Frei worked together with the American Peter Hayes and the Israeli Moshe Zimmermann.[47] In contrast to the tensions of the early post-war years, this cooperation had now become a matter of course.

Debating interpretations

Such collaboration did not mean that views on the German past were becoming identical – they rather continued to diverge due to different cultural settings and intellectual agendas. Historical outlooks between a worldwide English language discourse and a more limited continental German speaking discussion continued to differ fundamentally, since for the United States the Third Reich was a defeated enemy, but for the Germans the direct antecedent of the present. Moreover, both academic systems remained largely separate with distinctive job and reward pyramids, especially since the Central European universities were still more highly structured and exclusive. In the German case, dealing with the Third Reich involved ambivalent feelings of guilt as well as painful memories of suffering among one's own family members. Moreover, it continually raised issues of crimes committed towards neighbours who resented the resurgence of the Federal Republic. Because the second democracy was founded on a clear rejection of Nazi and communist dictatorships, German history was by necessity more ideologically politicized.

For Americans and especially the British, defeating the Nazis remained an important validation of their own version of capitalist democracy, since it was the last really 'good war'. Yet the continent was much further away and fewer family members suffered either absolutely or relatively. Moreover, studying Nazi history required not just learning 'the awful German language', but also immersing oneself in a strange culture. Since Anglo-American assumptions remained a point of departure, dealing with Germany was always implicitly comparative, sometimes even explicitly so when juxtaposing it to France or other continental states. As a result, scholars in the United States or United Kingdom were more directly driven by the intellectual interests and methodological fashions of their non-German colleagues, for instance exploring the potential of post-modern approaches which remained unpopular in Germany.[48] Even if their research interests overlapped and their critical assessments converged, Germans and Americans approached the recent past from different directions, leading to contrasting interpretations.

These underlying differences ironically surfaced in the *Sonderweg* debate that revolved around the German deviation from the Western model of development. Breaking with nationalist apologias, this inversion of the imperial claim to superiority was a considerable achievement in the continental context. Yet from Geoff Eley's and David Blackbourn's perspective, the normative use of Anglo-American development seemed superficial, because it ignored the Western legacy of racism, imperialism, and exploitation. Compared to the role of the middle class in other countries, the German educated and propertied bourgeoisie did not look nearly as weak as the refeudalization thesis suggested. Since the British critics were also ideologically on the Left, the historians of society, often called the Bielefeld school due to their principal location, felt betrayed by their attack which reversed the tradition of Anglo-American support for progressive views in Germany. Instead of reinforcing the charge of an especially problematic German development, the Eley–Blackbourn critique ultimately dissolved the thesis of a special German path into many distinctive patterns of national development.[49]

Although the German discussion about responsibility for Nazi crimes began immediately after the war, its eventual form as Holocaust sensibility was largely an American import. Initially this topic was largely ignored, since scholars tried to explain the Third Reich with concepts such as intentionalism or functionalism. But between the Eichmann trial in 1961 and the Holocaust TV series in 1979 a cultural shift moved the genocide of the Jews from the margins to the centre of Second World War remembrance. In the United States there were many more Jewish refugees; the issue of political support for Israel was more important; and among intellectuals the Nazis' systematic mass murder became emblematic of man's propensity for evil as such.[50] Prodded by such transatlantic impulses, Germans intensified their own research into the genocide of Jews, the public debated the complicity of the armed forces in atrocities, and local concentration camps were transformed into a network of memorial sites. The Washington Holocaust Museum even inspired the building of a central memorial in Berlin next to the Brandenburg Gate.[51] Now a dense network of memory institutions links both sides of the Atlantic.

Other methodological advances like Everyday-History were, instead, developed in Germany and spread to the United States from there. Following Scandinavian and British impulses, in the early 1980s Alf Luedtke and Hans Medick began to elaborate a microhistorical approach which they called *Alltagsgeschichte*, because it departed from the grand narratives by looking at the daily lives of ordinary people. As a scholarly counterpart to the grassroots movement of the Greens, History Workshops formed in order to investigate the local history of the working class or of the Nazi dictatorship. Since it involved 'digging where you stand' and collecting oral testimony, this history from below also attracted a lay public, interested in uncovering traces of the past in its own community. This bottom-up perspective rejected the Historical Social Science approach of the *Bielefelders*, since it focused on small-scale events rather than on broad generalizations.[52] In the United States, this everyday approach attracted the interest of diverse social historians such as Geoff Eley or David Crew.[53]

In the debate about cultural history, most impulses came once again from the American side, since 'cultural studies' had made stronger inroads there. In the United States the tradition of intellectual history, engaging grand thinkers, had survived more strongly than in Germany. Also the example of anthropologists such as Clifford Geertz who studied symbolic cultural practices via fieldwork and 'thick description' attracted the attention of historians. But most pervasive was the impact of the 'linguistic turn', promoted by French theorists such as Lyotard, Derrida, and Foucault, since it provided various minority movements with a critique of white and male power beyond Marxism. When some US scholars of modern Germany like Michael Geyer and I tried to explore the potential of pluralizing narratives, the leaders of the Bielefeld school admitted that they had underestimated the importance of experience, but drew a line at Max Weber's sociological conception of culture.[54] Only a minority of younger colleagues like Martina Kessel or Christoph Conrad was willing to engage cultural topics in a more open-minded way.[55]

Though gender history stemmed from similar feminist impulses, this new approach also made more rapid gains in the United States than in the Federal Republic of Germany. According to Karen Hagemann, the American movement from the 1960s on followed a liberal 'integrationist' strategy of trying to incorporate women's topics into existing departments of history. In contrast, the somewhat later German effort was more radical in its rejection of the maternalist tradition, first creating independent institutions and only then establishing university research centres. While there was also considerable patriarchical resistance in the United States, the greater size, diversity and responsiveness of the academic system to student demands made it possible to achieve quicker gains than in the state-dominated university structures of the Federal Republic. One of the resulting interpretative controversies was the transatlantic debate among female historians in which Gisela Bock of the Free University of Berlin saw women primarily as Nazi victims while Claudia Koonz of Duke University stressed their perpetrator role instead. But during the last decades the transition from women's to gender history has helped to bridge the Atlantic divide.[56]

Regarding communist dictatorship, Germans took the lead, since they had to wrestle with the legacy of the German Democratic Republic on a daily basis. In order to delegitimize the East German system, historians worked as expert witnesses for the commission of inquiry, sponsored by the federal parliament.[57] At the same time, many scholars also served on evaluation boards that decided which of their East German colleagues would be clean and competent enough to retain their positions in united

Germany. On the one hand, Cold Warriors denounced the defeated enemy through 'totalitarianism theory' that equated the dictatorial features of National Socialism with communism, while on the other Marxist historians sought to rescue its emancipatory utopia from the debris of 'real existing socialism'. More moderate scholars like this author, attuned to the tension between repression and everyday life, coined concepts like 'welfare dictatorship'.[58] While some Western leftists mourned the loss of a socialist alternative, other colleagues like Mary Fulbrook and Charles Maier rather supported the nuanced approach, elaborated by the Centre for Research in Contemporary History (ZZF) of Potsdam.[59]

The transatlantic response to the most recent challenge of a transnational widening of perspective towards a global history also shows commonalities and differences. On both sides historians are gradually beginning to investigate the dynamics of globalization which have transformed trade, financing, communication, and culture, investigating such issues as migration, terrorism, and the environment that transcend traditional frontiers. In the United States the demand of global leadership, the call for ethnic heritage history, and the breadth of regional specialization in history departments have replaced the teaching of Western Civilization with courses on World History.[60] Instead, in Germany the dependence on international trade, the question of welfare state competitiveness, and the progress of integration have drawn more attention to the writing of European history.[61] In both contexts, younger scholars are exploring transnational economic and cultural connections or cross-cutting problems that have been neglected by national narratives, though the exact shape which a new global history will take still remains somewhat indistinct.

The differing institutional settings and contrasting intellectual priorities have made for lively and productive exchanges between German specialists on both sides of the Atlantic. Initially many of the critical impulses emanated from the United States, but from the 1960s on a new generation of self-critical and innovative German scholars emancipated itself from such tutelage and developed independent approaches such as the *Gesellschaftsgeschichte* of the Bielefeld school. Nonetheless, the more open academic structures in the United States facilitated more methodological experimentation with quantitative methods, the linguistic turn, or global history. Yet in transferring some approaches like the Holocaust sensibility to the continent, they have assumed a different accent and a more theoretical outlook. In Germany, epochal changes like the overthrow of communism have forced contemporary historians to reorient their priorities, since the public demanded explanations for such unexpected events. While the fundamental asymmetry of the setting has occasionally led to unnecessary polemics, on the whole the exchanges between inside and outside perspectives have been quite fruitful.

Thinking transatlantically

Compared with other transnational efforts, the degree of cooperation between German historians on both sides of the Atlantic has been truly extraordinary. While

US colleagues such as Robert Paxton have provided some critical impulses, by and large the debate about the French past has been dominated by Parisian scholars.[62] In contrast, trying to explain the paradoxes of Central European development, historians from the Anglo-American victors have come to work in a shared enterprise with scholars from the defeated country in frankly confronting the crimes of the recent past. That development required the cultural outsiders to get beyond merely supplying basic information about the defeated enemy country, while it demanded from the insiders that they transcend the impulse towards defensive apologia of their nation's problematic policies. Though the progression from parallel research to shared interpretations also involved some misunderstandings and conflicts, in the end this transatlantic dialogue has contributed to the development of a surprisingly critical perspective on contemporary German history.

This international collaboration was the result of the resolve to avoid another world war by creating a better infrastructure for intellectual communication. In charge of rehabilitating the occupied country, American academics sought to understand the reasons for the defeat of democracy and the aggressive policy of their erstwhile enemy. Trying to survive the collapse of the National Socialist dictatorship, the shocked German intellectuals also wanted to find out what had gone wrong in their politics and culture to devastate Europe and destroy their own nation. To continental academics the wealthy and democratic United States appeared as an example to be emulated, whereas American scholars found at least some thoughtful Germans willing to break with their nationalist heritage.[63] To facilitate such communication, an array of enlightened exchange programmes from Fulbright and the Ford Foundation to the German Academic Exchange Service (DAAD) and the Humboldt Stiftung made personal encounters possible that helped reduce mutual prejudices through direct conversation. The key to learning from each other was therefore bringing thousands of Americans to Europe and thousands of Germans to the United States.[64]

Different styles of contemporary history, nonetheless, continued to create distinctive perspectives and interpretations on both sides. Most English-speaking scholars approached the recent past pragmatically, while German historians developed a complex theoretical justification of *Zeitgeschichte* as the study of the 'epoch of the contemporaries'.[65] Due to their wider context, Anglo-American academics were more methodologically innovative, whereas continental scholars were more involved in the politics of the past, striving to shape public memory culture. In the United States researchers tended to work individually, but in Germany contemporary historians were involved in collective work via the thematic groups of the German Research Council (SFBs), the Institute for Contemporary History in Munich or the Centre for Research in Contemporary History in Potsdam.[66] Anglo-American dissertations usually asked broader questions, not always grounded sufficiently in the evidence, while German *Doktoranden* (PhD students) preferred to investigate more narrow issues, smothering the problem in empirical detail. These distinctions made for some ritual jousting, but have also kept the debate lively and productive.

The future of transatlantic cooperation in contemporary history remains, however, rather uncertain, since the founding constellation of confronting the Nazi legacy is disappearing. In the United States, interest in Germany is waning, language teaching is eroding, and European history is being overshadowed by questions of race and global concerns. In Germany, there is surprisingly little scholarly work on the United States, political differences with Washington are looming larger, and integration is moving the frame of reference to Europe. Moreover, the relevant caesuras of structuring the recent past diverge between the peaceful revolution of 1989/90 on the continent and the terrorist attack of 9/11 in the United States.[67] Finally, the history of the present is shifting interest away from the Holocaust to new issues of structural transformation since the 1970s such as the IT revolution, the rise of international terrorism, the effects of migration, or environmental degradation.[68] Hence the exceptional transatlantic bond will only survive if the successor generation understands its intellectual importance and reaffirms its basic values of human rights and social solidarity.

Notes

1 D. J. Goldhagen, *Hitler's Willing Executioners: Ordinary Germans and the Holocaust* (London: Little Brown, 1996); see also G. Eley, *The 'Goldhagen Effect': History, Memory, Nazism – Facing the German Past* (Ann Arbor: University of Michigan Press, 2000).

2 S. Conrad, *The Quest for the Lost Nation: Writing History in Germany and Japan in the American Century* (Berkeley: University of California Press, 2010); and D. Satter, *It Was a Long Time Ago and it Never Happened Anyway: Russia and the Communist Past* (New Haven: Yale University Press, 2012).

3 L. D. Clay, *Decision in Germany* (Garden City: Doubleday, 1950); and D. Acheson, *Present at the Creation: My Years in the State Department* (New York: Norton, 1969).

4 K. D. Henke, *Die amerikanische Besetzung Deutschlands* (Munich: Oldenbourg, 1995); and K. H. Jarausch, *After Hitler: Recivilizing Germans, 1945–1995* (New York: Oxford University Press, 2006).

5 R. Wagnleitner, *Coca-Colonization and the Cold War: The Cultural Mission of the US in Austria after the Second World War* (Chapel Hill: University of North Carolina Press, 1994); and U. Poiger, *Jazz, Rock and Rebels: Cold War Politics and American Culture in a Divided Germany* (Berkeley: University of California Press, 2000).

6 G. Ritter, *Europa und die Deutsche Frage: Betrachtungen über die geschichtliche Eigenart des deutschen Staatsdenkens* (Munich: Münchner Verlag, 1948); F. Meinecke, *Die deutsche Katastrophe: Betrachtungen und Erinnerungen* (Wiesbaden: Brockhaus, 1949); and L. Dehio, *Gleichgewicht oder Hegemonie* (Krefeld: Scherpe, 1948).

7 W. Schulze, *Deutsche Geschichtswissenschaft nach 1945* (Munich: Dt. Taschenbuch-Verlag, 1989); and E. Schulin, *Traditionskritik und Rekonstruktionsversuch: Studien zur Entwicklung von Geschichtswissenschaft und historischem Denken* (Göttingen: Vandenhoeck & Ruprecht, 1979).

8 C. Epstein, 'German Historians at the Back of the Pack: Hiring Patterns in Modern European History, 1945–2010', *Central European History*, 46 (2013), pp. 599–639.

9 G. Iggers, K. H. Jarausch, M. Middell, and M. Sabrow (eds), *Die DDR-Geschichtswissenschaft als Forschungsproblem* (Munich: Oldenbourg, 1998), Beiheft 27 of the *Historische Zeitschrift*.

10 T. Lindenberger and M. Sabrow (eds), *German Zeitgeschichte: Konturen eines Forschungsfeldes* (Göttingen: Wallenstein Verlag, 2016).

11 M. Hoenicke-Moore, *Know Your Enemy: The American Debate on Nazism 1933–1945* (Cambridge: Cambridge University Press, 2010).

12 S. Berger, P. Lambert, and P. Schumann (eds), *Historikerdialoge: Geschichte, Mythos und Gedächtnis im deutsch-britischen kulturellen Austausch, 1750–2000* (Göttingen: Vandenhoeck & Ruprecht, 2003), pp. 9–61.

13 A. Eckert, *Der Kampf um die Akten: Die Westalliierten und die Rückgabe von deutschem Archivgut nach dem zweiten Weltkrieg* (Stuttgart: Franz Steiner Verlag, 2004).

14 K. Schwabe and R. Reichardt (eds), *Gerhard Ritter: Ein politischer Historiker in seinen Briefen* (Boppard: Boldt, 1984).

15 P. Kluke cited in A. Eckert, 'The Transnational Beginnings of West German Zeitgeschichte in the 1950s', *Central European History*, 40 (2007), pp. 63–87.

16 R. Hohls and K. H. Jarausch, *Versäumte Fragen: Deutsche Historiker im Schatten des Nationalsozialismus* (Stuttgart: Deutsche Verlags-Anstalt, 2000). See also A. D. Moses, *German Intellectuals and the Nazi Past* (Cambridge: Cambridge University Press, 2007).

17 Epstein, 'At the Back of the Pack', *passim*.

18 H. Lehmann and J. J. Sheehan (eds), *An Interrupted Past: German-Speaking Refugee Historians in the US after 1933* (Washington, DC: Cambridge University Press, 1991).

19 E. Y. Hartshorne, *Academic Proconsul: Harvard Sociologist Edward Y. Hartshorne and the Reopening of German Universities: His Personal Account* (Trier: Wissenschaftlicher Verlag Trier, 1998).

20 S. P. Remy, *The Heidelberg Myth: The Nazification and Denazification of a German University* (Cambridge, MA: Harvard University Press, 2002); and K. H. Jarausch, '"Wo man die stärksten Bindungen fühlt": Zur Remigration von Historikern nach 1945', in I. Löhr (ed.), *Kultur und Beruf in Europa* (Stuttgart: Steiner, 2012).

21 G. A. Ritter (ed.), *Friedrich Meinecke: Akademischer Lehrer und emigrierte Schüler: Briefe und Aufzeichnungen 1910–1977* (Munich: Oldenbourg, 2006).

22 E. Davidson, *The Trial of the Germans: An Account of the Twenty-Two Defendants Before the International Military Tribunal at Nuremberg* (New York: Macmillan, 1966); and T. Taylor, *The Anatomy of the Nuremberg Trials: A Personal Memoir* (New York: Little Brown, 1992).

23 Eckert, *Kampf um die Akten*, *passim*.

24 A. Daum, H. Lehmann, and J. J. Sheehan (eds), *The Second Generation: Émigrés from Nazi Germany as Historians* (New York: Berghahn, 2016).

25 K. H. Jarausch, 'German Social History – American Style', *Journal of Social History*, 19 (1985), pp. 349–60.

26 Schulze, *Deutsche Geschichtswissenschaft*, pp. 46ff.

27 H. Auerbach, 'Die Gründung des Instituts für Zeitgeschichte', *Vierteljahrshefte für Zeitgeschichte*, 18 (1970), pp. 529–54; and H. Rothfels, 'Zeitgeschichte als Aufgabe', *Vierteljahrshefte für Zeitgeschichte*, 1 (1953), pp. 1–8.

28 A. Schildt, *Zwischen Abendland und Amerika: Studien zur westdeutschen Ideenlandschaft der 50er Jahre* (Munich: Oldenbourg, 1999).

29 J. Tent, *The Free University of Berlin: A Political History* (Bloomington: Indiana University Press, 1988). See also K.-D. Bracher, *Die Auflösung der Weimarer Republik: Eine Studie zum Machtverfall einer Demokratie* (Villingen: Ring-Verlag, 1971).

30 G. Mosse and W. Laqueur, 'Editorial Note', *Journal of Contemporary History*, 1 (1966), pp. iii–vi.

31 P. Stelzel, *Rethinking Modern German History: Critical Social History as a Transatlantic Enterprise*, dissertation (Chapel Hill, 2010).

32 Often underestimated in its crucial significance, the financial commitment of the German government to this exchange is much higher than of any comparable country.

33 B. Faulenbach, *Die Ideologie des deutschen Weges: Die deutsche Geschichte in der Historiographie zwischen Kaiserreich und Nationalsozialismus* (Munich: Beck, 1980).

34 For instance T. S. Hamerow, *Restoration, Revolution and Reaction: Economics and Politics in Germany, 1815–1871* (Princeton: Princeton University Press, 1958); and C. E. Schorske, *German Social Democracy, 1905–1917: The Development of the Great Schism* (Cambridge: Harper & Row, 1955).

35 See changes in successive editions of B. Gebhardt, *Handbuch der deutschen Geschichte*, Vol. IV (Stuttgart: Klett-Cotta, 1959).

36 D. L. Hoggan, *Der erzwungene Krieg: Ursachen und Urheber des zweiten Weltkriegs* (Tübingen: Grabert, 1961).

37 A. J. P. Taylor, *The Origins of the Second World War* (New York: Hamilton, 1961).

38 K. H. Jarausch, 'Der nationale Tabubruch: Wissenschaft, Öffentlichkeit und Politik in der Fischer-Kontroverse', in M. Sabrow, R. Jessen, and K. Große Kracht (eds), *Zeitgeschichte als Streitgeschichte: Große Kontroversen seit 1945* (Munich: Beck, 2003).

39 J. Kocka, *Sozialgeschichte: Begriff – Entwicklung – Probleme* (Göttingen: Vandenhoeck & Ruprecht, 1977); and T. Welskopp, 'Identität *ex negativo*: Der "deutsche Sonderweg" als Metaerzählung in der bundesdeutschen Geschichtswissenschaft der siebziger und achtziger Jahre', in K. H. Jarausch and M. Sabrow (eds), *Die historische Meistererzählung: Deutungslinien deutscher Nationalgeschichte nach 1945* (Göttingen: Vandenhoeck & Ruprecht, 2002), pp. 109–39.

40 H. Heffter, 'Vom Primat der Außenpolitik', *Historische Zeitschrift*, 171 (1951), pp. 1–20, versus H.-U. Wehler (ed.), *Der Primat der Innenpolitik. Gesammelte Aufsätze zur preußisch-deutschen Sozialgeschichte im 19. und 20. Jahrhundert von Eckart Kehr* (Berlin: de Gruyter, 1965).

41 K. H. Jarausch and K. Hardy, *Quantitative Methods for Historians: A Guide to Research, Data and Statistics* (Chapel Hill: University of North Carolina, 1991). See also K. H. Jarausch, 'Contemporary History as Transatlantic Project: The German Problem, 1960–2010', *Historical Social Research*, Supplement 24 (2012).

42 R. Augstein, K. D. Bracher, and M. Broszat, *Historikerstreit: Die Dokumentation der Kontroverse um die Einzigartigkeit der nationalsozialistischen Judenvernichtung* (Munich: Piper, 1987).

43 C. S. Maier, *The Unmasterable Past: History: Holocaust and German National Identity* (Cambridge, MA: Harvard University Press, 1988); and R. Evans, *In Hitler's Shadow: West German Historians and the Attempt to Escape from the Nazi Past* (New York: Pantheon Books, 1989).

44 See Note 1. See R. A. Shandley, *Unwilling Germans? The Goldhagen Debate* (Minneapolis: University of Minnesota Press, 1998) and the review by D. Moses in *The Journal of Modern History*, 75 (2003), pp. 994–1000.

45 http://www.stiftung-evz.de/ (accessed 3 April 2018).

46 H. James, *The Nazi Dictatorship and the Deutsche Bank* (Cambridge: Cambridge University Press, 2004); G. D. Feldman, *Allianz and the German Insurance Business, 1933–1945* (New York: Cambridge University Press, 2001).

47 E. Conze, N. Frei, P. Hayes, and M. Zimmermann, *Das Amt und die Vergangenheit: Deutsche Diplomaten im Dritten Reich und in der Bundesrepublik* (Munich: Blessing, 2010).

48 See the introduction to K. H. Jarausch, H. Wenzel, and K. Goihl (eds), *Different Germans, Many Germanies* (New York: Berghahn, 2017).

49 G. Eley and D. Blackbourn, *Peculiarities of German History: Bourgeois Society and Politics in Nineteenth Century Germany* (Oxford: Oxford University Press, 1984), versus J. Kocka, 'German History before Hitler: The Debate about the German Sonderweg', *Journal of Contemporary History*, 23 (1988), pp. 3–16.

50 P. Novick, *The Holocaust in American Life* (Boston: Houghton Mifflin, 1999); D. van Laak, 'Der Platz des Holocaust im deutschen Geschichtsbild', in K. H. Jarausch and M. Sabrow (eds), *Die historische Meistererzählung: Deutungslinien deutscher Nationalgeschichte nach 1945* (Göttingen: Vandenhoeck & Ruprecht, 2002), pp. 163–93.

51 J.-H. Kirsch, *Nationaler Mythos oder historische Trauer? Der Streit um ein zentrales 'Holocaust-Mahnmal' für die Berliner Republik* (Cologne: Böhlau, 2003).

52 A. Luedtke (ed.), *Alltagsgeschichte: Zur Rekonstruktion historischer Erfahrungen und Lebensweisen* (Frankfurt: Campus-Verlag, 1989). See also the journal *Werkstatt Geschichte*.

53 D. Crew, '*Alltagsgeschichte*: A New Social History from Below?', *Central European History*, 22 (1989), pp. 394–407; and G. Eley, 'Labor History, Social History, "*Alltagsgeschichte*:" Experience, Culture and the Politics of the Everyday – A New Direction for German Social History', *Journal of Modern History*, 61 (1989), pp. 297–343.

54 K. H. Jarausch and M. Geyer, *Shattered Past: Reconstructing German Histories* (Princeton: Princeton University Press, 2003), versus H.-U. Wehler, *Die Herausforderung der Kulturgeschichte* (Munich: Beck, 1998).

55 C. Conrad and M. Kessel (eds), *Kultur und Geschichte: Neue Einblicke in eine alte Beziehung* (Stuttgart: Reclam, 1998).

56 K. Hagemann and J. Quaetert, 'Geschichte und Geschlechter: Geschichtsschreibung und akademische Kultur in Westdeutschland und den USA im Vergleich', in K. Hagemann and J. Quaetert (eds), *Geschichte und Geschlechter: Revisionen der neueren deutschen Geschichte* (Frankfurt a. M.: Campus-Verlag, 2008), pp. 11–63.

57 A. Beattie, *Playing Politics with History: The Bundestag Inquiries into East Germany* (New York: Berghahn, 2008).

58 K. H. Jarausch (ed.), *Dictatorship as Experience: Towards a Socio-Cultural History of the GDR* (Oxford: Berghahn, 1999).

59 C. Ross, *The East German Dictatorship: Problems and Perspectives in the Interpretation of the GDR* (London: Arnold, 2002).

60 J. Osterhammel, *Globalization: A Short History* (Princeton: Princeton University Press, 2005); and M. Geyer and C. Bright, 'World History in a Global Age', *American Historical Review*, 100 (1995), pp. 1034–60.

61 K. H. Jarausch and T. Lindenberger (eds), *Conflicted Memories: Europeanizing Contemporary Histories* (New York: Berghahn, 2007).

62 R. Paxton, *Vichy France: Old Guard, New Order* (New York: Barrie & Jenkins, 1972); and H. Rousso, *The Vichy Syndrome: History and Memory in France since 1944* (New York: Harvard University Press, 1991).

63 F. Stern, *Five Germanys I Have Known* (New York: Farrar, Straus and Giroux, 2006), pp. 199ff.; and H.-U. Wehler, *'Eine lebhafte Kampfsituation:' Ein Gespräch mit Manfred Hettling und Cornelius Thorp* (Munich: Beck, 2006).

64 E. Latzin, *Lernen von Amerika? Das US-Kulturaustauschprogramm und seine Absolventen in Bayern* (Stuttgart: Steiner, 2005); and P. Alter (ed.), *Spuren in die Zukunft: Deutscher Akademischer Austauschdienst 1925–2000* (Bonn: DAAD, 2000), 3 vols.

65 Rothfels, 'Zeitgeschichte als Aufgabe' versus Mosse and Laqueur, 'Editorial Note'. See also C. Klessmann, *Zeitgeschichte in Deutschland nach dem Ende des Ost-West-Konflikts* (Essen: Klartext, 1998).

66 www.ifz-muenchen.de/; www.zzf-pdm.de/ (accessed 3 April 2018). See also the Hannah Arendt Institut in Dresden as well as the Forschungsstelle für Zeitgeschichte in Hamburg.

67 M. Sabrow, 'Writing Contemporary German History in the Present', in Lindenberger and Sabrow, *German Zeitgeschichte*, pp. 13–27; and A. Wirsching, *Preis der Freiheit: Geschichte Europas in unserer Zeit* (Munich: Beck, 2012).

68 K. H. Jarausch, 'Demokratie in der Globalisierung', *Francia*, 38 (2011), pp. 311–20; and K. H. Jarausch, *Out of Ashes: A New History of Europe in the 20th Century* (Princeton: Princeton University Press, 2015).

References

Acheson, D. *Present at the Creation: My Years in the State Department* (New York: Norton, 1969).

Alter, P. (ed.), *Spuren in die Zukunft: Deutscher Akademischer Austauschdienst 1925–2000* (Bonn: DAAD, 2000), 3 vols.

Auerbach, H. 'Die Gründung des Instituts für Zeitgeschichte', *Vierteljahrshefte für Zeitgeschichte*, 18 (1970), pp. 529–54.

Augstein, R., K. D. Bracher, and M. Broszat. *Historikerstreit: Die Dokumentation der Kontroverse um die Einzigartigkeit der nationalsozialistischen Judenvernichtung* (Munich: Piper, 1987).

Beattie, A. *Playing Politics with History: The Bundestag Inquiries into East Germany* (New York: Berghahn, 2008).

Berger, S., P. Lambert, and P. Schumann (eds), *Historikerdialoge: Geschichte, Mythos und Gedächtnis im deutsch-britischen kulturellen Austausch, 1750–2000* (Göttingen: Vandenhoeck & Ruprecht, 2003).

Bracher, K.-D. *Die Auflösung der Weimarer Republik: Eine Studie zum Machtverfall einer Demokratie* (Villingen: Ring-Verlag, 1971).

Clay, L. D. *Decision in Germany* (Garden City: Doubleday, 1950).

Conrad, C. and M. Kessel (eds), *Kultur und Geschichte: Neue Einblicke in eine alte Beziehung* (Stuttgart: Reclam, 1998).

Conrad, S. *The Quest for the Lost Nation: Writing History in Germany and Japan in the American Century* (Berkeley: University of California Press, 2010).

Conze, E., N. Frei, P. Hayes, and M. Zimmermann, *Das Amt und die Vergangenheit: Deutsche Diplomaten im Dritten Reich und in der Bundesrepublik* (Munich: Blessing, 2010).

Crew, D. 'Alltagsgeschichte: A New Social History from Below?', Central European History, 22 (1989), pp. 394–407.

Daum, A., H. Lehmann, and J. J. Sheehan (eds), The Second Generation: Émigrés from Nazi Germany as Historians (New York: Berghahn, 2016).

Davidson, E. The Trial of the Germans: An Account of the Twenty-Two Defendants Before the International Military Tribunal at Nuremberg (New York: Macmillan, 1966).

Dehio, L. Gleichgewicht oder Hegemonie (Krefeld: Scherpe, 1948).

Eckert, A. Der Kampf um die Akten: Die Westalliierten und die Rückgabe von deutschem Archivgut nach dem zweiten Weltkrieg (Stuttgart: Franz Steiner Verlag, 2004).

Eckert, A. 'The Transnational Beginnings of West German Zeitgeschichte in the 1950s', Central European History 40 (2007), pp. 63–87.

Eley, G. The 'Goldhagen Effect': History, Memory, Nazism – Facing the German Past (Ann Arbor: University of Michigan Press, 2000).

Eley, G. 'Labor History, Social History, "Alltagsgeschichte": Experience, Culture and the Politics of the Everyday – A New Direction for German Social History', Journal of Modern History, 61 (1989), pp. 297–343.

Eley, G. and D. Blackbourn. Peculiarities of German History: Bourgeois Society and Politics in Nineteenth Century Germany (Oxford: Oxford University Press, 1984).

Epstein, C. 'German Historians at the Back of the Pack: Hiring Patterns in Modern European History, 1945–2010', Central European History, 46 (2013), pp. 599–639.

Evans, R. In Hitler's Shadow: West German Historians and the Attempt to Escape from the Nazi Past (New York: Pantheon Books, 1989).

Faulenbach, B. Die Ideologie des deutschen Weges: Die deutsche Geschichte in der Historiographie zwischen Kaiserreich und Nationalsozialismus (Munich: Beck, 1980).

Feldman, G. D. Allianz and the German Insurance Business, 1933–1945 (New York: Cambridge University Press, 2001).

Gebhardt, B. Handbuch der deutschen Geschichte, Vol. IV (Stuttgart: Klett-Cotta, 1959).

Geyer, M. and C. Bright. 'World History in a Global Age', American Historical Review, 100 (1995), pp. 1034–60.

Goldhagen, D. J. Hitler's Willing Executioners: Ordinary Germans and the Holocaust (London: Little Brown, 1996).

Hagemann, K. and J. Quaetert. 'Geschichte und Geschlechter: Geschichtsschreibung und akademische Kultur in Westdeutschland und den USA im Vergleich', in K. Hagemann and J. Quaetert (eds), Geschichte und Geschlechter: Revisionen der neueren deutschen Geschichte (Frankfurt a. M.: Campus-Verlag, 2008), pp. 11–63.

Hamerow, T. S. Restoration, Revolution and Reaction: Economics and Politics in Germany, 1815–1871 (Princeton: Princeton University Press, 1958).

Hartshorne, E. Y. Academic Proconsul: Harvard Sociologist Edward Y. Hartshorne and the Reopening of German Universities: His Personal Account (Trier: Wissenschaftlicher Verlag Trier, 1998).

Heffter, H. 'Vom Primat der Außenpolitik', Historische Zeitschrift, 171 (1951), pp. 1–20.

Henke, K. D. Die amerikanische Besetzung Deutschlands (Munich: Oldenbourg, 1995).

Hoenicke-Moore, M. Know Your Enemy: The American Debate on Nazism 1933–1945 (Cambridge: Cambridge University Press, 2010).

Hoggan, D. L. Der erzwungene Krieg: Ursachen und Urheber des zweiten Weltkriegs (Tübingen: Grabert, 1961).

Hohls, R. and K. H. Jarausch. Versäumte Fragen: Deutsche Historiker im Schatten des Nationalsozialismus (Stuttgart: Deutsche Verlags-Anstalt, 2000).

Iggers, G., K. H. Jarausch, M. Middell, and M. Sabrow (eds), *Die DDR-Geschichtswissenschaft als Forschungsproblem* (Munich: Oldenbourg, 1998), Beiheft 27 of the *Historische Zeitschrift*.

James, H. *The Nazi Dictatorship and the Deutsche Bank* (Cambridge: Cambridge University Press, 2004).

Jarausch, K. H. *After Hitler: Recivilizing Germans, 1945–1995* (New York: Oxford University Press, 2006).

Jarausch, K. H. 'Contemporary History as Transatlantic Project: The German Problem, 1960–2010', *Historical Social Research*, Supplement 24 (2012).

Jarausch, K. H. 'Demokratie in der Globalisierung', *Francia*, 38 (2011), pp. 311–20.

Jarausch, K. H. 'Der nationale Tabubruch: Wissenschaft, Öffentlichkeit und Politik in der Fischer-Kontroverse', in M. Sabrow, R. Jessen, and K. Große Kracht (eds), *Zeitgeschichte als Streitgeschichte: Große Kontroversen seit 1945* (Munich: Beck, 2003), pp. 20–40.

Jarausch, K. H. (ed.), *Dictatorship as Experience: Towards a Socio-Cultural History of the GDR* (Oxford: Berghahn, 1999).

Jarausch, K. H. 'German Social History – American Style', *Journal of Social History*, 19 (1985), pp. 349–60.

Jarausch, K. H. *Out of Ashes: A New History of Europe in the 20th Century* (Princeton: Princeton University Press, 2015).

Jarausch, K. H. '"Wo man die stärksten Bindungen fühlt": Zur Remigration von Historikern nach 1945', in I. Löhr (ed.), *Kultur und Beruf in Europa* (Stuttgart: Steiner, 2012).

Jarausch, K. H. and M. Geyer. *Shattered Past: Reconstructing German Histories* (Princeton: Princeton University Press, 2003).

Jarausch, K. H. and K. Hardy. *Quantitative Methods for Historians: A Guide to Research, Data and Statistics* (Chapel Hill: University of North Carolina Press, 1991).

Jarausch, K. H. and T. Lindenberger (eds), *Conflicted Memories: Europeanizing Contemporary Histories* (New York: Berghahn, 2007).

Jarausch, K. H., H. Wenzel, and K. Goihl (eds), *Different Germans, Many Germanies* (New York: Berghahn, 2017).

Kirsch, J.-H. *Nationaler Mythos oder historische Trauer? Der Streit um ein zentrales 'Holocaust-Mahnmal' für die Berliner Republik* (Cologne: Böhlau, 2003).

Klessmann, C. *Zeitgeschichte in Deutschland nach dem Ende des Ost-West-Konflikts* (Essen: Klartext, 1998).

Kocka, J. 'German History before Hitler: The Debate about the German Sonderweg', *Journal of Contemporary History*, 23 (1988), pp. 3–16.

Kocka, J. *Sozialgeschichte: Begriff – Entwicklung – Probleme* (Göttingen: Vandenhoeck & Ruprecht, 1977).

Latzin, E. *Lernen von Amerika? Das US-Kulturaustauschprogramm und seine Absolventen in Bayern* (Stuttgart: Steiner, 2005).

Lehmann, H. and J. J. Sheehan (eds), *An Interrupted Past: German-Speaking Refugee Historians in the US after 1933* (Washington, DC: Cambridge University Press, 1991).

Lindenberger, T. and M. Sabrow (eds), *German Zeitgeschichte: Konturen eines Forschungsfeldes* (Göttingen: Wallstein Verlag, 2016).

Luedtke, A. (ed.), *Alltagsgeschichte: Zur Rekonstruktion historischer Erfahrungen und Lebensweisen* (Frankfurt: Campus-Verlag, 1989).

Maier, C. S. *The Unmasterable Past: History: Holocaust and German National Identity* (Cambridge, MA: Harvard University Press, 1988).

Meinecke, F. *Die deutsche Katastrophe: Betrachtungen und Erinnerungen* (Wiesbaden: Brockhaus, 1949).

Moses, A. D. *German Intellectuals and the Nazi Past* (Cambridge: Cambridge University Press, 2007).

Mosse, G. and W. Laqueur. 'Editorial Note', *Journal of Contemporary History*, 1 (1966), pp. iii–vi.

Novick, P. *The Holocaust in American Life* (Boston: Houghton Mifflin, 1999).

Osterhammel, J. *Globalization: A Short History* (Princeton: Princeton University Press, 2005).

Paxton, R. *Vichy France: Old Guard, New Order* (New York: Barrie & Jenkins, 1972).

Poiger, U. *Jazz, Rock and Rebels: Cold War Politics and American Culture in a Divided Germany* (Berkeley: University of California Press, 2000).

Remy, S. P. *The Heidelberg Myth: The Nazification and Denazification of a German University* (Cambridge: Harvard University Press, 2002).

Ritter, G. *Europa und die Deutsche Frage: Betrachtungen über die geschichtliche Eigenart des deutschen Staatsdenkens* (Munich: Münchner Verlag, 1948).

Ritter, G. A. (ed.), *Friedrich Meinecke: Akademischer Lehrer und emigrierte Schüler: Briefe und Aufzeichnungen 1910–1977* (Munich: Oldenbourg, 2006).

Ross, C. *The East German Dictatorship: Problems and Perspectives in the Interpretation of the GDR* (London: Arnold, 2002).

Rothfels, H. 'Zeitgeschichte als Aufgabe', *Vierteljahrshefte für Zeitgeschichte*, 1 (1953), pp. 1–8.

Rousso, H. *The Vichy Syndrome: History and Memory in France since 1944* (New York: Harvard University Press, 1991).

Sabrow, M. 'Writing Contemporary German History in the Present', in T. Lindenberger and M. Sabrow (eds), *German Zeitgeschichte: Konturen eines Forschungsfeldes* (Göttingen: Wallenstein Verlag, 2016), pp. 13–27.

Sabrow, T. and M. Sabrow (eds), *German Zeitgeschichte: Konturen eines Forschungsfeldes* (Göttingen: Wallenstein Verlag, 2016).

Satter, D. *It Was a Long Time Ago and it Never Happened Anyway: Russia and the Communist Past* (New Haven: Yale University Press, 2012).

Schildt, A. *Zwischen Abendland und Amerika: Studien zur westdeutschen Ideenlandschaft der 50er Jahre* (Munich: Oldenbourg, 1999).

Schorske, C. E. *German Social Democracy, 1905–1917: The Development of the Great Schism* (Cambridge: Harper & Row, 1955).

Schulin, E. *Traditionskritik und Rekonstruktionsversuch: Studien zur Entwicklung von Geschichtswissenschaft und historischem Denken* (Göttingen: Vandenhoeck & Ruprecht, 1979).

Schulze, W. *Deutsche Geschichtswissenschaft nach 1945* (Munich: Dt. Taschenbuch-Verlag, 1989).

Schwabe, K. and R. Reichardt (eds), *Gerhard Ritter: Ein politischer Historiker in seinen Briefen* (Boppard: Boldt, 1984).

Shandley, R. A. *Unwilling Germans? The Goldhagen Debate* (Minneapolis: University of Minnesota Press, 1998).

Stelzel, P. *Rethinking Modern German History: Critical Social History as a Transatlantic Enterprise*, dissertation (Chapel Hill, 2010).

Stern, F. *Five Germanys I Have Known* (New York: Farrar, Straus and Giroux, 2006).

Taylor, A. J. P. *The Origins of the Second World War* (New York: Hamilton, 1961).

Taylor, T. *The Anatomy of the Nuremberg Trials: A Personal Memoir* (New York: Little Brown, 1992).

Tent, J. *The Free University of Berlin: A Political History* (Bloomington: Indiana Univ. Press, 1988).

van Laak, D. 'Der Platz des Holocaust im deutschen Geschichtsbild', in K. H. Jarausch and M. Sabrow (eds), *Die historische Meistererzählung: Deutungslinien deutscher Nationalgeschichte nach 1945* (Göttingen: Vandenhoeck & Ruprecht, 2002), pp. 163–93.

Wagnleitner, R. *Coca-Colonization and the Cold War: The Cultural Mission of the US in Austria after the Second World War* (Chapel Hill: University of North Carolina Press, 1994).

Wehler, H.-U. (ed.), *Der Primat der Innenpolitik: Gesammelte Aufsätze zur preußisch-deutschen Sozialgeschichte im 19. und 20. Jahrhundert von Eckart Kehr* (Berlin: de Gruyter, 1965).

Wehler, H.-U. *Die Herausforderung der Kulturgeschichte* (Munich: Beck, 1998).

Wehler, H.-U. '*Eine lebhafte Kampfsituation:' Ein Gespräch mit Manfred Hettling und Cornelius Thorp* (Munich: Beck, 2006).

Welskopp, T. 'Identität *ex negativo*: Der "deutsche Sonderweg" als Metaerzählung in der bundesdeutschen Geschichtswissenschaft der siebziger und achtziger Jahre', in K. H. Jarausch and M. Sabrow (eds), *Die historische Meistererzählung: Deutungslinien deutscher Nationalgeschichte nach 1945* (Göttingen: Vandenhoeck & Ruprecht, 2002), pp. 109–39.

Wirsching, A. *Preis der Freiheit: Geschichte Europas in unserer Zeit* (Munich: Beck, 2012).

7

Towards a new diplomatic history of transatlantic relations: America, Europe, and the crises of the 1970s

Ariane Leendertz

In the twenty-first century, transatlantic relations no longer enjoy the prominence they had in both the foreign policies of the United States and of many Western European countries, as well as in the history of international relations during the second half of the twentieth century. Yet, transatlantic relations remain a focus of study by historians and political scientists, as America and the European Union still are, economically and politically (and, in the American case, militarily), two of the most powerful actors in international politics. Scholarship on the history of transatlantic relations tends to focus on political domains, particularly on foreign and security policy, and on economic and fiscal policy. Dominated by diplomatic history approaches, historical scholarship on the period after the 1970s has concentrated on government negotiations and conflicts between the United States and Europe as well as on decision-making processes, crisis management, bilateral and multilateral diplomacy, and international summits and agreements. Further, historians examine cultural exchange, public diplomacy,[1] and the influence of American popular culture in Western Europe.

In this chapter, neither the political history of transatlantic relations nor cultural exchange will stand at the centre. Instead, emphasis falls on the American view of the political *and* cultural relationship to Western Europe. My analysis proceeds on the level of discourse. Its hypothesis is that not only after the end of the Cold War, but already in the 1970s the position and the status of transatlantic relations changed decisively in the American political and public purview. My analysis documents the 'public political sphere', which is to say a realm of intersection and exchange between politics, academia, elite journalism, and the mass media. I explore the following questions. Why were transatlantic relations evaluated as good or bad? Was it considered desirable to improve these relations? What conceptual frameworks and social developments influenced the views and reflections of diplomatic actors and commentators in the United States? Which patterns of perception and judgement shaped their views and their assessments, their definitions of problems, and their options for action? By exploring perceptions, conceptual frameworks, and worldviews I wish to broaden the political history of transatlantic relations. This chapter therefore begins with some thoughts on the connection between cultural and political history, as far as transatlantic relations are concerned.

The cultural and political history of transatlantic relations

'The U.S. and the World', as it has been called in the past few years, provides a useful point of departure for this chapter – American History in a transatlantic and global context, that is.[2] Methodologically, this approach entails the widening of 'classical' diplomatic history to include cultural history. In the United States, this is called the 'cultural turn in international relations' or the 'New Diplomatic History'.[3] In Germany, this has been dubbed the 'new political history' and 'the cultural history of the political'.[4] I endorse Eckart Conze's view that cultural history has not created a new paradigm in the study of international history. Rather, cultural history opens to consideration dimensions of 'traditional' diplomatic history that had previously been given only marginal consideration.[5] Perspectives from cultural history, which often encompass intellectual history, underline the centrality of interpretations and webs of meaning, convictions, and perceptions, as 'imagined orders' in international relations, transmitted through communication, creating images of reality that inform thought and action, thereby gaining social and political relevance.[6] With respect to cultural and intellectual history, scholars embracing social and political history raise the thorny question of causality. What are the causal connections between worldviews, cultural dispositions, discourses, or mental maps, on the one hand, and 'concrete' foreign-policy decision-making and 'real' politics on the other?[7]

Cultural history is on the defensive when this question cannot be given a clear answer. The answer, however, lies not in cultural history but in the need to complicate the question of causality in relation to policy-making. Just as there is no simple causal relationship between ideas and political decisions, there is no simple causal relationship between discourse and politics. We should thus not try to explain 'concrete' political decisions through a model of cause and effect, rendering discourse the singular and absolute explanatory factor. If one limits oneself to a simplified cause and effect model, a diversity of factors involved in policy-making will get left out: ideas and ideology, information and knowledge; power interests and group interests, individual interests and preferences; the dynamics of process, organization, communication, and institutional structures; timing, situation, and accident – they all impact political action.[8]

How can we then best link discourse and political process in the analysis of America, Europe, and transatlantic relations? I will make this link empirically through an examination of contemporary debates and reflections, putting political deliberation at the core of my analysis. In this chapter, I investigate the structures of knowledge, intellectual dispositions, and perceptions which influenced the views and assessments of political actors in the transatlantic arena. I assume that the thinkable and the speakable constitute an essential precondition for the politically doable.[9] Convictions about what *is* 'reality' and what is considered true form the background for the determination of options for political action.[10] Ideas and discourses order and structure the perceptions of social phenomena and the definition of problems which must be addressed in policy-making.[11] The way a problem is described is actualized by suppositions, by knowledge positions, and by interests. Ideas and discourses are always present in political debates: they can determine political agendas, and they hold together various groups of actors. In addition, the mass media have a substantial impact on the ordering and interpretation of diplomatic developments and events, establishing for example specific patterns of argumentation. Scholars of media and of communications use the word 'framing' for this.[12]

On the conceptual level of key concepts, belief systems, and convictions, which structure the perception of problems and the conception of political action, political deliberation is not limited to the domain of the political system, but takes place to a great extent in public forums: public debates over transatlantic relations and the formation of opinion of policy-makers are tightly interwoven. Hence, the sphere of political deliberation can be defined alternatively as a 'public political sphere', in which social actors move and interact – namely, policy-makers and officials, experts and advisers, opinion leaders, commentators and journalists, as well as lobbyists and public interest groups. The mass media are thus to be understood as foreign-policy actors, as journalists do not only serve as experts, commentators, critics, and opinion-shapers in the public sphere but in the political sphere as well: the mass media were and are an irreplaceable resource for policy-makers,[13] and journalists can be seen as active creators of perception, interpretation, and meaning,[14] shaping political reflections on transatlantic relations.

This chapter will demonstrate that transatlantic-policy considerations in the 1970s were not conducted in a closed fashion, cut off from public debate. Further, they were connected to a set of other contemporary discussions and themes. American reflections on transatlantic relations had three important components, or determinants: American's self-perception and introspection; perceptions of Europe; and the broader context of world politics. First, social and cultural as well as political and economic developments internal to the United States, coupled with self-image and a sense of the United States' role in the world, did a great deal to colour American definitions and judgements of Europe. Second, European developments and American ideas of Europe shaped the way in which transatlantic relations were evaluated. Third, global developments and events played a role; that is the general condition of US foreign policy and contemporary understandings of global change and challenges.

Transatlantic relations in 1970s America[15]

Historians of transatlantic relations agree that the late 1960s led to dramatic change and that the 1970s witnessed a greater degree of conflict than had been the case before – even if the crises and conflicts were not at all new but rather were a constant of the US–European relationship.[16] Transatlantic conflicts arose, in the 1970s, over questions of currency and protective tariffs, over West Germany's *Ostpolitik*,[17] over the initiatives of Senator Mike Mansfield to reduce troop levels in Western Europe, over the Middle East and the Yom Kippur War,[18] over the first oil crisis and over Henry Kissinger's failed 'Year of Europe'.[19] By contrast, successful cooperation was exercised in the reaching of the Helsinki accords[20] and in the establishment of the G7. As Matthias Schulz and Thomas Schwartz have argued, conflict and cooperation waxed and waned in transatlantic relations. At the same time, they characterized the collisions of the 1970s as 'clearly more intense and bitter' than before.[21] Geir Lundestad followed a similar line of argument in pointing out that debates within NATO acquired a new quality in the 1970s. They were not simply disagreements on individual questions but divisions of opinion on fundamental matters: 'there had always been quarrels and debates among the NATO members; but these were more structural now than they had been earlier, in the sense that they touched basic relationships not only single issues.'[22] For Kenneth Weisbrode, the years of détente[23] were 'the worst climate in transatlantic relations since World War II'.[24]

Why were the conflicts of the 1970s more intense and more bitter, and why did major shifts of opinion occur in the United States in the transition from the late 1960s to the 1970s? An important reason can be found in the weakening sense of threat in the era of détente, which brought about some of the conflicts among the Western allies. The post-war anti-communist consensus, guided by the idea of containment, which had framed American foreign policy since the beginning of the Cold War and had been the backbone of the Western alliance, was fragmenting.[25] At the same time, the key actors in American foreign policy were changing, by the end of the 1960s: the State Department's European bureau, the American Atlanticists and the idea of 'Atlanticism'[26] were declining in political influence.[27] Power and influence in foreign policy-making shifted to the White House and the Pentagon, just as the National Security Council, too, was gaining in status.[28] Further, alongside the progression of the war in Vietnam since 1965, Europe no longer remained the exclusive focus of US world politics; and the traditionally Europhile East Coast establishment had, since the mid-1960s, been losing its dominant position.[29] By the early 1970s, economic questions had moved to the centre of transatlantic dispute, with President Nixon and Henry Kissinger speaking publicly about 'rivalry' and 'competition' between the United States and Europe.[30] That would have been unthinkable before the 1960s.

On the discursive level, American debates and deliberations about transatlantic relations in the 1970s revealed a heightened awareness of conflict and confusion, coupled with a tentative search for proper descriptions, and for new terms that could best describe the new conditions of the transatlantic relationship. Despite the close integration and manifold relations, despite common problems and shared values, there seemed to be more conflict, competition, and division of opinion between the United States and Europe.[31] Such was the puzzled judgement of J. Robert Schaetzel, American Ambassador to the European Community in Brussels. There were many explanations, and the situation seemed, in his view, full of paradoxes. One explanation for the confusion in transatlantic relations was that neither side knew what it wanted. There seemed to be a lack of vision and a lack of ideas: the course of European integration was unclear, as were the direction of American foreign policy and the future of the Atlantic Community beyond NATO. Stanley Hoffmann, one of the leading Atlanticist intellectuals and founding chairman of the Minda de Gunzburg Center for European Studies at Harvard University, wrote that Europe had become, in the 1970s, only a necessity and a possibility, but it was not a will and it was no longer much of an ideal.[32] Robert Schaetzel came to a similar conclusion, at the beginning of the decade, remarking that the old lustre of the grand idea of a partnership of equals was gone. The Europeans had no clear ideas on the shape of the European Community, which was contributing to the confusion on the American side.[33] Miriam Camps, a diplomat and expert on Europe, pondered whether the will existed to make the European Community much more than a customs union with an anachronistic agricultural policy. As the Europeans appeared themselves confused as to what they wished to build, they provided no guidelines according to which the United States might orient itself. In the United States, the formation of a 'European bloc' was feared, burdening relations, and Camps also saw grave self-doubts and uncertainty in the United States as to its role in the world.[34] She ascribed to these uncertainties on both sides to be the underlying source of much of the strain in the transatlantic relationship.[35]

The US policy towards Europe was entering a phase of reformulation or, as many observers felt, a phase of neglect. Both American and European Atlanticists warned that the United States and Europe were proceeding along different trajectories, which might imperil the stability of the West.[36] At the same time, the conviction that the relationship to Europe and the foundations of the transatlantic relationship should be rethought and redefined was gaining traction in American foreign-policy circles, in the early 1970s.[37] In a motif that was often repeated in the early 1970s, the post-war period was said to be over, and a new era was beginning. This claim was tightly connected to the perception of global transformation, such that the institutional and conceptual parameters of the post-war order were being undone.

As the examples of Henry Kissinger and Zbigniew Brzezinski illustrate, the Euro-Atlantic power constellations of the 1970s were being fit increasingly to a global pattern, to the bigger picture of world politics.[38] Transatlantic relations were being conceptualized as an integral part of the global situation characterized by new challenges and developments that had fundamental impacts on the Western world. Zbigniew Brzezinski, a political scientist and Jimmy Carter's National Security Adviser, saw the United States and Europe as passing into a new age, the so-called 'technetronic era'.[39] The democratic advanced-industrial societies were being confronted with increasingly 'complex' political and social questions, which they were incapable of answering on their own.[40] These new problems demanded new political attempts at cooperation, and Brzezinski believed that international politics and its institutions would have to adapt to the new reality of global integration. Brzezinski built on this analysis by initiating the Trilateral Commission in 1973, the International Energy Agency in 1974, and the establishment of the G7 in 1975.

In this new global order, America and Europe would have to stand together; so ran the argument then. 'The values and the way life – in a word, the civilization – of the West depend on the ability of America and West Europe to work closely together in weaving a new fabric of international affairs', Brzezinski wrote.[41] The danger of 'drifting apart' was frequently invoked.[42] If America and Europe would be unable to cooperate, the West would disintegrate and so too would the Cold War transatlantic alliance: 'the validity and wholeness of Western civilization are at stake', in the words of a 1970 report from the Atlantic Council, then one of the most influential Atlanticist networks.[43] Were this to happen, in the eyes of the future National Security Adviser, Brzezinski, there would be no 'community of the developed nations which can effectively address itself to the larger concerns confronting mankind'.[44] In light of new, common problems and increasing interdependence, especially in the sphere of economic integration, better coordination and new forms of collective management appeared to be necessary.[45] As Schaetzel, the Ambassador to the European Community, wrote about the so-called 'Nixon shock', that is the administration's unilateral decision to cancel the US dollar's convertibility to gold: Decision-makers now appeared to be almost 'overwhelmed by the complexities of the world, working with institutions inherited and designed to deal with simpler issues'. Desperate to find solutions, they tended to deal with related issues in isolation without reference to the side effects of decisions made unilaterally. This, according to Schaetzel, was both a conceptual and an institutional problem.[46]

Contemporary American discussions reflected large-scale social and global change, characterized in recent historical scholarship as 'after the boom' or 'the shock of the global'.[47] Looking inwards, American observers saw a society in rapid transition. America and the other Western industrial societies stood at the beginning of a new era that would be determined by 'interdependence', increasing 'complexity', and new kinds of problems.[48] The partners in the transatlantic relationship – the United States itself, the European Community, the individual European states and their societies – were changing as rapidly as was the global order in which their relations were embedded. Three themes emerge from the debates and discussions: interdependence, the 'crisis of confidence', and the already noted beginning of a 'new era'.

Implicit to the category of 'interdependence' that traversed political discourse in the 1970s was an altered worldview and definition of problems, as David Kuchenbach showed in analyzing debates over 'one world' or Daniel Sargent did when looking at Henry Kissinger's revised perception after the energy crisis of 1973/4.[49] In the eyes of contemporary observers, the world's political geography was changing. These changes were manifested in the evocations of economic, social, and ecological 'interdependence' (only later, in the mid-1980s, did people start talking of 'globalization' instead). That this overall impression of global change altered the condition of Europe and of the transatlantic relationship is apparent from the feeling of finding oneself on the threshold, such that the relationship to Europe at the 'end of the postwar era' had to be configured to a transformed global constellation.[50] Martin J. Hillenbrand, the American Ambassador to West Germany, in a speech to the Kassel Chamber of Commerce placed American–European relations in a global context, in 1974, in which much was indelibly interconnected: 'we live in an interdependent world in which all things seem to impact one another, in which issues of economics and politics are inter-woven to form the fabric of our relationship'.[51] Secretary of State Kissinger adopted the claims of the political scientists Joseph Nye and Robert Keohane by intoning inter-dependence and complexity (though both had ironically formulated their models in opposition to Kissingerian realism).[52] Kissinger declared the post-war period defini-tively over by the mid-1970s. A new era had begun: 'now we are entering a new era. Old international patterns are crumbling; old slogans are uninstructive; old solutions are unavailing. The world has become interdependent in economics, in communications, in human aspirations. No one nation, no one part of the world, can prosper or be secure in isolation.'[53] According to Kissinger in 1975, the 'simple' categories of the post-war period no longer matched the 'complex realities of the modern world'.[54]

'Complexity' and 'interdependence' had become central themes by 1974/5, much discussed in policy research and theories of contemporary international-relations scholarship. The political scientists Joseph Nye and Robert Keohane fashioned the theory of 'complex interdependence' in 1971. They presented their ideas as an urgently needed paradigm shift, as the erstwhile state-centred models were, in their view, incapable of explaining the phenomenon of what they called 'transnational relations': that is, relations across borders by non-state actors such as multilateral corporations or international organizations and movements, cross-border contacts, communication, trade, capital flows, travelling people, goods, and ideas.[55] Nye and Keohane saw these transnational relations as distinguished by multiple forms of dependence and inter-dependence. Further, they claimed that the number of actors in the field of international relations, and the number of transnational actors, was always increasing; as a consequence traditional forms of power politics were no longer adequate. Policy-makers had to learn a new way of looking at and imagining the world.[56] Only then could foreign policy take account of the changes. For Nye and Keohane, there was a strong connection between how the world was imagined and actual politics. The same goes for the political scientist David Calleo, who emphasized that the future American policy towards Europe and the reformulation of the Atlantic Community depended on new ways of seeing the world and, accordingly, of adjusting the United States' political stance towards Western Europe: Europe was not America's 'front porch', and the United States thus could not govern an Atlantic Community from Washington. 'The Europeans are our best friends in the world; they are also our equals', Calleo wrote. In addition, it was necessary to create new assumptions for foreign policy: 'there must be a shift in our imaginations – away from that two-dimensional myth of blocs and challenges to a vision that represents that plural squirming world which is reality'.[57] The Cold War binary way of thinking, therefore, had to be replaced by new theories and concepts that emphasized interdependence and global change.

The theme of interdependence also recurred in the articles of the *New York Times*'s James Reston, then one of the best-known journalists in America. To properly address the challenges of a 'post-Vietnam world', Reston argued for joint solutions to common problems.[58] For the popular journalist, writing from Paris in 1972, the new world order was characterized by a different West European attitude towards the United States. As Reston diplomatically put it, Western Europe's attitude had become 'more independent'. He connected this to the advance of European integration. On the other hand, the perception and image of the United States had changed in Europe: 'Vietnam has clearly challenged the American assumption of both moral and military superiority, and convinced even our friends in Europe that maybe we don't have the superior answer to the problem of the world order, and that our "muddling through" is not much better than Europe's way in the nineteenth century.' In Western Europe as in Japan, the United States was no longer conceived as a model of innovation, management, and marketing; on matters of social welfare the United States had ever smaller powers of attraction. 'As for the American ideal of unity and equality at home', Reston wrote, 'and generosity and pity abroad, the magic of the American dream has lost much of its allure in Europe'.[59]

In a similar vein, *Time* magazine published a cover story on 'Europe: America's New Rival' in March 1973. The article affirmed that 'today the average informed American views Europe as a wealthy, technologically advanced, comfortable and somewhat expensive society that has somehow learned to get the most out of life without sacrificing its values'.[60] Only two months after the Paris Peace accords with North Vietnam many Americans could fill in the blanks. Western Europe was different from the United States, and after the peace treaty, America could return the mundane issues of transatlantic politics: 'with Vietnam out of the way at last, a measured American recessional resumes with negotiations on trade and troop reductions'. Against this background, the old US–European 'Atlantic Community' then seemed to be 'rapidly evolving into a spirited international rivalry'. The rivalry extended beyond economics: 'the new sense of rivalry is real, not only in trade, but in less tangible matters, including the nature of progress and the good life'.[61] The European model of civilization, discredited in the Second World War, was gaining in attractiveness on the American dream.

The descriptions of *Time* and of James Reston exemplify the efforts of American journalists, especially the foreign correspondents and those writing for *Time*, to take Europe's pulse and to provide the American public with reports on the mood beyond the great political and economic matters. What is striking about Reston's description is that it was less about European perceptions of America than it was a projection of *domestic* cultural criticism onto Europe's perceptions of the United States. 'Crisis of confidence' was the theme that surfaced in Reston's musings, a common trope of the years between 1968 and 1979, which, in the 1970s, left its traces in the analysis of European–American relations.[62]

Today 'crisis of confidence' is a theme most readily associated with Jimmy Carter's septet to the nation on July 15, 1979, the so-called 'malaise speech', which was marked by the impression of social crisis. The energy crisis, about which Carter had been trying to speak, was not the country's actual problem; it was only a symptom of many other problems. The real problem, Carter emphasized, was deeper, deeper than the long lines at the gas stations and the rationing of gasoline, deeper than inflation and recession. According to Carter, the country found itself in a 'crisis of confidence', a crisis of belief in its own future, of faith in its own capacities, of self-confidence in the nation itself.[63] Carter had not been the first to speak in public about a 'crisis of confidence'. This had been the title of a book by the historian and adviser to JFK, Arthur Schlesinger, Jr., which was published in 1969 and was already in its second edition in 1969. As stated on its dust jacket:

for the first time in their history Americans have begun to wonder whether the problems they face might be too much for them. Until recently we had been sustained by a conviction of physical and moral strength which seemed to render us invulnerable to any serious threat. Now, beset by discord, fanaticism and violence, we are no longer so sure. With cities and universities torn by revolt, with faith in military power and moral purpose depleted in a meaningless war, with social change apparently out of control, confidence in our destiny is shaken.[64]

Diagnoses of crisis such as Schlesinger's were motivated by racial unrest in many American cities, by mass protests with many deaths, by the assassination of Martin Luther King and Robert Kennedy, by riots surrounding the Democratic National Convention in Chicago in 1968, by rebelling students, by the anti-war movement, the environmental movement and the counter-culture, by rising criminality and drug consumption, by the war in Vietnam. These were followed by serious economic crises and by Watergate, which shook people's faith in their political institutions.[65]

The 'crisis of confidence' and the overall crisis discourse also coloured *political* analyses of transatlantic relations. In 1971, the diplomat Martin Hillenbrand wrote a memo for the Secretary of State with the alarming title, 'Tensions in U.S. Relations with Europe'. Hillenbrand identified what he called 'a problem of growing concern', and this was a European loss of confidence in the United States. Hillenbrand's pretext was President Nixon's decision to take the dollar off the gold standard. For Hillenbrand, this decision marked a turning-point in US economic policy: 'from twenty-five years of international economic cooperation to a new pattern of confrontation to achieve our own objectives at the expense of the Europeans'. This gave the crisis of confidence a new quality: 'while we have had crises of confidence before, they have not been of the same severity and depth'.[66]

Hillenbrand was likely referring here to data from USIA, which regularly conducted opinion polls for the State Department on attitudes towards America and on the image of the United States. The USIA could confirm in 1973 (and in 1976) that confidence in the United States had diminished, that a majority believed the United States to be 'on the way down'.[67] Only a few days before the 1976 presidential election supporters of Jimmy Carter referenced further USIA reports in the *New York Times*, which put the results on its front page: 'Poll in West Europe Finds U.S. Prestige Lowest in 22 Years'.[68] European attitudes towards the United States had become a weapon in the presidential election. The polling data bolstered Carter's accusation that under Gerald Ford's leadership the United States was losing respect. The USIA qualified the low numbers by pointing to American polls, in which the state of affairs in the United States was judged even more severely than in Europe. In the 1970s, American public opinion agencies were trying to measure the 'crisis of confidence' in the United States.[69] 'Foreign views of America's future are not nearly so harsh as those of Americans themselves', the USIA reported in 1973. 'The weight of evidence suggests that this harsher American view, rather than [being] more accurate than foreign opinion, is possibly indicative of an undue loss in national self-esteem'.[70] By comparison with the American self-image America's image in Europe was not so bad, in the USIA's evaluation, and the situation not as bad as Hillenbrand had implied.

To come back to the often cited theme of a 'new era', it is worth pointing out the frequency with which the notion of a turning point in transatlantic relations appeared in the debates of the 1970s – for example in the observations of J. Robert Schaetzel,[71] of Stanley Hoffmann,[72] or Martin J. Hillenbrand, who had been director of the European bureau at the State Department before becoming ambassador to West Germany. Hillenbrand also regarded the post-war period as over, with an uncertain future ahead: 'sometime in the late 1960s the so-called post-war era ended. We are clearly in an era of transition'.[73] Kenneth Rush, the acting Secretary of State, in 1974 came to a similar conclusion: 'Western Europe has waxed wealthy and has been moving, not without difficulty, toward economic and perhaps ultimately political unity. The United States welcomes this and sees this transitional time as a critical juncture.'[74]

The proposition that this was an era of transition and of transformation could also be found in the period's social theory, most prominently in the arguments about the advent of a post-industrial society. These debates had taken place among intellectuals and sociologists already from the mid-1960s, finding a wide resonance even before the publication of Daniel Bell's famous book, *The Coming of Post-Industrial Society*, in 1973. In 1970 the Atlantic Council published a study devoted to the question of how the relationship between Europe and the United States would develop in the next ten years. The authors worried about whether Europe would follow the United States into the post-industrial era or whether Europe and the United States would grow apart.[75] The debates then current in foreign-policy circles about a world in transition did not just concern the world outside of the United States. They included the role of the United States in this new world, the United States being a society in the midst of internal transition. This was made clear, for instance, by Winston Lord, director of the State Department's Office of Policy Planning: 'at a time when the world is in flux and a new American role emerging, we are subjected as well to profound changes at home. A nation which first explored its own frontiers, and then stretched its presence around the world, now requires a new horizon.' This new horizon was not to be found outside the United States but within. The country had lost one president to assassination, another to Vietnam, and a third to scandal, Lord recited. America had 'agonized through our longest and most inconclusive war'. America's once uncontested strengths were under threat and the once almighty dollar was getting 'battered'. The country had endured social unrest, political murder, racial and generational conflict, a cultural revolution, and Watergate. In Lord's opinion, 'our next frontier is to find peace within ourselves. Let us begin by restoring our self-confidence'.[76] Should this not come to pass, there would be paralysis and the danger of being overcome by change.[77]

Conclusion

During the 1970s, American debates about the relationship between the United States and Europe were shaped by uncertainty and a search for appropriate terms and descriptions. These reflections were closely connected to debates over American identity and the self-image of being an imperiled superpower. The United States had lost some of its standing in Western Europe. The relationship with Europe was strained by economic competition between the United States and the European Community, by protectionist measures on both sides of the Atlantic, and this was perceived as a danger to Cold War transatlantic unity. Simultaneously, America's role in the world seemed to be changing after the Vietnam War, and in political circles there was a widely held view that many of the core ideas and assumptions, taken to be self-evident in post-war foreign policy, had to be revised. The perception of increasing global 'interdependence' fostered the search for new solutions to common problems and new forms of cooperation. This found its clearest expression in the foreign-policy conceptions of the Nixon and Ford administrations as well as in the Carter era. From the viewpoint of transatlantic actors – and this applied equally to politicians, diplomats, political scientists, and journalists – much was in flux. Popular social theory, such as that of the post-industrial society, strengthened the sense among those involved in foreign affairs that they stood at a turning, facing the beginning of a new era. Policy-makers, experts, and public intellectuals saw themselves in a period of transition, in which established patterns of thought were perceived to be outdated. This made it difficult to define new parameters for the relationship to Europe. These impressions and uncertainties must be taken seriously if one is trying to explain the high degree of sensitivity to transatlantic conflicts and tensions in these years. Outside concerns were interwoven with the crises of domestic politics and internal affairs, leading to a pessimistic view of transatlantic relations. Studying discourses and perceptions that underlie and frame the stances and decisions ultimately taken by foreign policy-makers thus not only helps to deepen our understanding of the history of transatlantic relations, but it could also serve to enhance our comprehension of contemporary diplomacy between America and Europe.

Notes

1 Public diplomacy refers to political efforts to improve relationships between countries that are not directed at other diplomats or governments, but at the public. Student exchange is one example of this.

2 T. Bender, *Rethinking American History in a Global Age* (Berkeley: University of California Press, 2002); K. K. Patel, 'Jenseits der Nation: Amerikanische Geschichte in der Erweiterung', in M. Berg and P. Gassert (eds), *Deutschland und die USA in der Internationalen Geschichte des 20. Jahrhunderts* (Stuttgart: Steiner, 2004), pp. 40–57.

3 See T. W. Zeiler, 'The Diplomatic History Bandwagon: A State of the Field', *Journal of American History*, 95:4 (2009), pp. 1053–73; M. J. Hogan, 'The "Next Big Thing": The Future of Diplomatic History in a Global Age', *Diplomatic History*, 28:1 (2004), pp. 1–21; A. Iriye, 'Culture and International History', in M. J. Hogan and T. G. Paterson (eds.), *Explaining the History of American Foreign Relations* (Cambridge: Cambridge University Press, 2004), pp. 241–56; J. Gienow-Hecht and F. Schumacher (eds), *Culture and International History* (New York: Berghahn, 2003). 'New Diplomatic History' is an informal scholarly network devoted to broadening the study of diplomacy through new approaches from cultural studies, sociology, ethnology, and other disciplines. See http://newdiplomatichistory.org.

4 B. Stollberg-Rilinger (ed.), *Was heißt Kulturgeschichte des Politischen?* (Berlin: Duncker und Humblot, 2005); U. Frevert and H. G. Haupt (eds), *Neue Politikgeschichte. Perspektiven einer historischen Politikforschung* (Frankfurt/Main: Campus, 2005);

H.-C. Kraus and T. Nicklas (eds), *Geschichte der Politik. Alte und neue Wege* (Munich: Oldenbourg, 2007); E. Conze, 'Moderne Politikgeschichte: Aporien einer Kontroverse', in G. Müller (ed.), *Deutschland und der Westen: Internationale Beziehungen im 20. Jahrhundert* (Stuttgart: Steiner, 1998), pp. 19–30.

5 E. Conze, 'States, International Systems, and Intercultural Transfer: A Commentary', in Gienow-Hecht and Schumacher, *Culture and International History*, pp. 198–205.

6 E. Conze, 'Jenseits von Männern und Mächten: Geschichte der internationalen Politik als Systemgeschichte', in Kraus and Nicklas, *Geschichte der Politik*, pp. 41–64.

7 See D. Reynolds, 'International History, the Cultural Turn and the Diplomatic Twitch', *Cultural and Social History*, 3:1 (2006), pp. 75–91; V. Depkat, 'Cultural Approaches to International Relations: A Challenge?', in Gienow-Hecht and Schumacher, *Culture and International History*, pp. 175–97.

8 See P. Jackson and P. Bourdieu, 'The "Cultural Turn" and the Practice of International History', *Review of International Studies*, 34 (2008), pp. 155–81; A. Siniver, *Nixon, Kissinger, and U.S. Foreign Policy Making: The Machinery of Crisis* (Cambridge: Cambridge University Press, 2011).

9 See W. Steinmetz, *Das Sagbare und das Machbare. Zum Wandel politischer Handlungsspielräume: England 1780–1867* (Stuttgart: Klett-Cotta, 1993).

10 J. Goldstein and R. O. Keohane (eds), *Ideas and Foreign Policy: Beliefs, Institutions, and Political Change* (Ithaca: Cornell University Press, 1993); A. Leendertz and W. Meteling (eds), *Die neue Wirklichkeit. Semantische Neuvermessungen und Politik seit den 1970er Jahren* (Frankfurt/Main: Campus, 2016).

11 See P. Weingart, *Die Stunde der Wahrheit? Zum Verhältnis der Wissenschaft zu Politik, Medien und Wirtschaft in der Wissensgesellschaft* (Weilerswist: Verbrück Wissenschaft, 2005).

12 See especially R. M. Entman, 'Declarations of Independence: The Growth of Media Power after the Cold War', in B. L. Nacos, R. Y. Shapiro, and Pierangelo Isernia (eds), *Decisionmaking in a Glass House: Mass Media, Public Opinion, and American and European Foreign Policy in the 21st Century* (Lanham: Rowman and Littlefield, 2000), pp. 11–26; R. M. Entman, *Projections of Power: Framing News, Public Opinion, and U.S. Foreign Policy* (Chicago: University of Chicago Press, 2004).

13 See in particular D. A. Graber, *Mass Media and American Politics*, 6th edn (Washington, DC: CQ Press, 2002).

14 D. Geppert, *Pressekriege: Öffentlichkeit und Diplomatie in den deutsch-britischen Beziehungen 1896–1912* (Munich: Oldenbourg, 2007), p. 435.

15 The following sections are based on A. Leendertz, 'Interdependenz, Krisenbewusstsein und der Beginn eines neuen Zeitalters: Die USA und die Neuverortung der transatlantischen Beziehungen in den 1970er Jahren', in F. Bösch and P. Hoeres (eds), *Außenpolitik im Medienzeitalter: Vom späten 19. Jahrhundert bis zur Gegenwart* (Göttingen: Wallstein, 2013), pp. 232–50.

16 R. Markowitz, 'Im Spannungsfeld von Amerikanisierung, Europäisierung und Westernisierung: Die Zäsur der 1960er und 1970er Jahre für die transatlantische Europadebatte', in C. Metzger and H. Kaelble (eds), *Deutschland - Frankreich - Nordamerika: Transfers, Imaginationen, Beziehungen* (Stuttgart: Steiner, 2006), pp. 98–123; G. Lundestad, *The United States and Western Europe since 1945: From 'Empire' by Invitation to Transatlantic Drift* (Oxford: Oxford University Press, 2003); M. Del Pero and F. Romero (eds), *Le crisi transatlantiche: Continuità e trasformazioni* (Rome: Ed. di Storia e Letteratura, 2007).

17 *Ostpolitik* refers to the foreign policy of the German government under Chancellor Willy Brandt to improve relations with Eastern Germany, Poland, and the Soviet Union in the early 1970s.

18 On the Jewish holiday of Yom Kippur on 6 October 1973, Egyptian and Syrian military attacked Israel to retaliate for land annexations dating back to 1967. The war ended with a ceasefire by the end of the month.

19 M. Schulz and T. A. Schwartz (eds), *The Strained Alliance: U.S.-European Relations from Nixon to Carter* (Cambridge: Cambridge University Press, 2010).

20 The Helsinki accords of August 1975 were a major diplomatic agreement between the superpowers and thirty-three other nations during the Cold War, when both sides declared their willingness to promote cooperation in various policy fields and pledged to recognize human rights and fundamental freedoms. The Helsinki Final Act is commonly seen as encouraging human rights movements in Eastern Europe, ultimately contributing to the collapse of the Soviet Union.

21 Schulz and Schwartz, *The Strained Alliance*, p. 355.

22 Lundestad, *The United States and Western Europe*, 169.

23 Détente describes a period of the Cold War when tensions between the United States and the Soviet Union were eased through increased communication, cooperation, and agreements. There is different periodization regarding its beginning, either starting with the end of the Cuban missile crisis of 1962, or with the foreign policy of Richard Nixon and Henry Kissinger after they came into office in 1969. The period of détente ended in 1979 when the USSR invaded Afghanistan.

24 K. Weisbrode, *The Atlantic Century: Four Generations of Extraordinary Diplomats Who Forged America's Vital Alliance with Europe* (Cambridge, MA: Da Capo Press, 2009), p. 220.

25 M. Del Pero, '"Europeanizing" U.S. Foreign Policy: Henry Kissinger and the Domestic Challenge to Détente', in M. Vaudagna (ed.), *The Place of Europe in American History: Twentieth Century Perspectives* (Torino: Otto, 2007), pp. 187–212.

26 Atlanticism refers to an orientation in foreign policy that privileges relations between the United States and Europe within the broader foreign policy frameworks of both sides, emphasizing that Europe and the United States share a host of common interests and values, and that they are historically and culturally connected in a way that makes them ideal partners. However, this orientation lost much of its traction since the end of the Cold War. With reference to Atlanticism, also see Giles Scott-Smith's remarks on the 'transatlantic era' in this volume.

27 Weisbrode, *The Atlantic Century*. This was also due to a generational shift, as shown by R. Kreis, 'Bündnis ohne Nachwuchs? Die "Nachfolgegeneration" und die deutsch-amerikanischen Beziehungen in den 1980er Jahren', *Archiv für Sozialgeschichte*, 52 (2012), pp. 607–31.

28 Siniver, *Nixon, Kissinger and U.S. Foreign Policy Making*.

29 See P. Roberts, '"All the Right People": The Historiography of the American Foreign Policy Establishment', *Journal of American Studies*, 26:3 (1992), pp. 409–34.

30 See, for example, R. M. Nixon, 'Second Annual Report to the Congress on United States Foreign Policy: Feb. 25, 1971', in *Public Papers of the Presidents of the United States: Richard M. Nixon, 1971* (Washington, DC, 1972), pp. 219–345; H. Kissinger, 'The Year of Europe', *The Department of State Bulletin*, 14 May (1973), pp. 593–8.

31 See J. R. Schaetzel, 'U.S. Policy Toward Western Europe – In Transition: Off the record speech, Royal College of Defense Studies, London, Nov. 1, 1971', Princeton University, Seeley G. Mudd Library, George Ball Papers, Box 85, Fol. 8.

32 S. Hoffmann, 'Fragments Floating in the Here and Now', *Daedalus*, 108:1 (1979), pp. 1–26, p. 3.

33 Schaetzel, 'U.S. Policy Toward Western Europe', p. 5; similarly W. R. Burgess and J. R. Huntley, *Europe and America: The Next Ten Years* (New York: Walker, 1970), p. 6.

34 M. Camps, 'Sources of Strain in Transatlantic Relations', *International Affairs*, 48 (1972), pp. 573–4.

35 *Ibid.*, p. 562; similarly: R. Vernon, 'Rogue Elephant in the Forest: An Appraisal of Transatlantic Relations', *Foreign Affairs*, 51:3 (1973), pp. 573–87.

36 Burgess and Huntley, *Europe and America*; K. Kaiser and H.-P. Schwarz (eds), *Amerika und Westeuropa: Gegenwarts- und Zukunftsproblem* (Stuttgart: Belser, 1977).

37 Especially Camps, 'Sources of Strain'; Z. Brzezinski, 'America and Europe', *Foreign Affairs*, 49 (1970), pp. 11–30.

38 See Weisbrode, *The Atlantic Century*, p. 277.

39 Z. Brzezinski, *Between Two Ages: America's Role in the Technetronic Era* (New York: Viking Press, 1970).

40 Brzezinski, 'America and Europe', p. 13.

41 *Ibid.*, p. 17.

42 J. R. Schaetzel, *The Unhinged Alliance: America and the European Community* (New York: Harper & Row, 1975), pp. 3–4.

43 Burgess and Huntley, *Europe and America*, p. 62.

44 Brzezinski, 'America and Europe', p. 29.

45 Camps, 'Sources of Strain', p. 572.

46 Schaetzel, 'U.S. Policy Toward Western Europe', p. 7.

47 A. Doering-Manteuffel and L. Raphael, *Nach dem Boom: Perspektiven auf die Zeitgeschichte seit 1970*, 3rd edn (Göttingen: Vandenhoeck und Ruprecht, 2012); N. Ferguson, C. S. Maier, E. Manela and D. J. Sargent (eds), *The Shock of the Global: The 1970s in Perspective* (Cambridge, MA: Belknap Press of Harvard University Press, 2010).

48 A. Leenderts, 'Das Komplexitätssyndrom: Gesellschaftliche Komplexität als intellektuelle und politische Herausforderung in den 1970er Jahren', MPIfG Discussion Paper 15/7 (2015). Online, available at www.mpifg.de/pu/mpifg_dp/dp15-7.pdf (accessed 10 October 2016).

49 D. Kuchenbuch, '"Eine Welt": Globales Interdependenzbewußtsein und die Moralisierung des Alltags in den 1970er und 1980er Jahren', *Geschichte und Gesellschaft*, 38 (2012), pp. 158–84; D. J. Sargent, 'The United States and Globalization in the 1970s', in Ferguson *et al.*, *The Shock of the Global*, pp. 49–64.

50 Charles Maier's appeal, in this volume, to embed transatlantic relations and Atlantic History into the broader framework of global history thus seems to reflect exactly the observational shifts experienced by foreign policy actors in the mid-1970s.

51 M. J. Hillenbrand, 'U.S.-German-European Community Economic Relations: The Need for Common Approaches to Common Problems', *Department of State Bulletin*, 20 May (1974), pp. 548–54, p. 548.

52 See B. Kohler-Koch, 'Interdependenz', in V. Rittberger (ed.), *Theorien der Internationalen Beziehungen: Bestandaufnahme und Forschungsperspektiven* (Opladen: Westdeutscher Verlag, 1990), pp. 110–29.

53 H. Kissinger, 'A New National Partnership', *Department of State Bulletin*, 17 February (1975), p. 197.

54 H. Kissinger, 'American Unity and the National Interest', *Department of State Bulletin*, 15 September (1975), p. 390.

55 J. S. Nye and R. O. Keohane (eds), *Transnational Relations and World Politics* (Cambridge: Cambridge University Press, 1971).

56 R. O. Keohane and J. S. Nye, *Power and Interdependence: World Politics in Transition* (Boston: Little, Brown & Co, 1977).

57 D. Calleo, *The Atlantic Fantasy: The U.S., NATO, and Europe* (Baltimore: Johns Hopkins University Press, 1970), pp. ix–x.

58 J. Reston, 'Mr. Whiskers', *New York Times*, 8 September 1971.

59 J. Reston, 'Europe in the Spring', *New York Times*, 2 April 1972.

60 N. N., 'How America Looks at Europe', *Time Magazine*, 12 March 1973.

61 N. N., 'Here Comes the "European Idea"', *Time Magazine*, 12 March 1973.

62 For an interpretation of the 1970s as a decade of multiple crises P. Jenkins, *Decade of Nightmares: The End of the Sixties and the Making of Eighties America* (New York and Oxford: Oxford University Press, 2006).

63 J. Carter, 'Energy and National Goals: Address to the Nation, July 15, 1979', in *Public Papers of the Presidents of the United States: Jimmy Carter, 1979*, Vol. 2 (Washington, DC, 1980), pp. 1235–41.

64 A. M. Schlesinger, Jr., *The Crisis of Confidence: Ideas, Power and Violence in America* (Boston: Houghton Mifflin, 1969).

65 See M. Isserman and M. Kazin, *America Divided: The Civil War of the 1960s*, 3rd edn (New York and Oxford: Oxford University Press, 2008); B. Schulman, *The Seventies: The Great Shift in American Culture, Society, and Politics* (New York: Da Capo Press, 2002).

66 M. J. Hillenbrand, 'Tensions in US Relations with Europe: Memorandum for the Secretary of State, Nov. 15, 1971', NARA, RG 59, Box 2362: Subject Numeric Files, 1970–1973: Political and Defense.

67 N. N., 'The Image of America's Future in Foreign Public Opinion', U.S.I.A. Research Report, July, 1973. NARA, RG 306, Entry P 160, Box 34.; N. N., 'Some Indications of Trends and Current Opinions About the U.S. and NATO in Western Europe', 2 November 1976. NARA, RG 306, Entry P 160, Box 37.

68 *New York Times*, 20 October 1976, referring to the polls in 'The Standing of the U.S. and of NATO in West European Public Opinion', 22 September 1976. NARA, RG 306, Entry P 160, Box 37.

69 See E. Carll Ladd, Jr., 'The Polls: The Question of Confidence', *Public Opinion Quarterly*, 40:4 (1976), pp. 544–52; W. Watts and L. A. Free, *State of the Nation III* (Lexington: Lexington Books, 1978).

70 N. N., 'The Image of America's Future in Foreign Public Opinion'.

71 Schaetzel, 'U.S. Policy', pp. 2–3.

72 S. Hoffmann, 'Uneven Allies: An Overview', in D. S. Landes (ed.), *Western Europe: The Trials of Partnership* (Lexington: Lexington Books, 1977), p. 69.

73 Quoted in Weisbrode, *The Atlantic Century*, p. 268.

74 K. Rush, 'European-American Relations: A Case for Cooperative Endeavor', *Department of State Bulletin*, 11 March (1974), p. 238.

75 Burgess and Huntley, *Europe and America*.

76 W. Lord, 'America's Purposes in an Ambiguous Age', *Department of State Bulletin*, 4 November (1974), pp. 621–2.
77 See *ibid.*, p. 617.

References

Bender, T. *Rethinking American History in a Global Age* (Berkeley: University of California Press, 2002).

Brzezinski, Z. 'America and Europe', *Foreign Affairs*, 49 (1970), pp. 11–30.

Brzezinski, Z. *Between Two Ages: America's Role in the Technetronic Era* (New York: Viking Press, 1970).

Burgess, W. R. and J. R. Huntley. *Europe and America: The Next Ten Years* (New York: Walker, 1970).

Calleo, D. *The Atlantic Fantasy: The U.S., NATO, and Europe* (Baltimore: Johns Hopkins University Press, 1970).

Camps, M. 'Sources of Strain in Transatlantic Relations', *International Affairs*, 48 (1972), pp. 559–78.

Carll Ladd, Jr., E. 'The Polls: The Question of Confidence', *Public Opinion Quarterly*, 40:4 (1976), pp. 544–52.

Carter, J. 'Energy and National Goals: Address to the Nation, July 15, 1979', in *Public Papers of the Presidents of the United States: Jimmy Carter, 1979*, Vol. 2 (Washington, DC, 1980), pp. 1235–41.

Conze, E. 'Jenseits von Männern und Mächten: Geschichte der internationalen Politik als Systemgeschichte', in H.-C. Kraus and T. Nicklas (eds), *Geschichte der Politik: Alte und neue Wege* (Munich: Oldenbourg, 2007), pp. 41–64.

Conze, E. 'Moderne Politikgeschichte: Aporien einer Kontroverse', in G. Müller (ed.), *Deutschland und der Westen: Internationale Beziehungen im 20. Jahrhundert* (Stuttgart: Steiner, 1998), pp. 19–30.

Conze, E. 'States, International Systems, and Intercultural Transfer: A Commentary', in J. Gienow-Hecht and F. Schumacher (eds), *Culture and International History* (New York: Berghahn, 2003), pp. 198–205.

Del Pero, M. '"Europeanizing" U.S. Foreign Policy: Henry Kissinger and the Domestic Challenge to Détente', in M. Vaudagna (ed.), *The Place of Europe in American History: Twentieth Century Perspectives* (Torino: Otto, 2007), pp. 187–212.

Del Pero, M. and F. Romero (eds), *Le crisi transatlantiche: Continuità e trasformazioni* (Rome: Ed. di Storia e Letteratura, 2007).

Depkat, V. 'Cultural Approaches to International Relations: A Challenge?', in J. Gienow-Hecht and F. Schumacher (eds), *Culture and International History* (New York: Berghahn, 2003), pp. 175–97.

Doering-Manteuffel, A. and L. Raphael. *Nach dem Boom: Perspektiven auf die Zeitgeschichte seit 1970*, 3rd edn (Göttingen: Vandenhoeck & Ruprecht, 2012).

Entman, R. M. 'Declarations of Independence: The Growth of Media Power after the Cold War', in B. L. Nacos, R. Y. Shapiro, and P. Isernia (eds), *Decisionmaking in a Glass House: Mass Media, Public Opinion, and American and European Foreign Policy in the 21st Century* (Lanham: Rowman & Littlefield, 2000), pp. 11–26.

Entman, R. M. *Projections of Power: Framing News, Public Opinion, and U.S. Foreign Policy* (Chicago: University of Chicago Press, 2004).

Ferguson, N., C. S. Maier, E. Manela and D. J. Sargent (eds), *The Shock of the Global: The 1970s in Perspective* (Cambridge, MA: Belknap Press of Harvard University Press, 2010).

Frevert, U. and H. G. Haupt (eds), *Neue Politikgeschichte: Perspektiven einer historischen Politikforschung* (Frankfurt/Main: Campus, 2005).

Geppert, D. *Pressekriege: Öffentlichkeit und Diplomatie in den deutsch-britischen Beziehungen 1896–1912* (Munich: Oldenbourg, 2007).

Gienow-Hecht, J. and F. Schumacher (eds), *Culture and International History* (New York: Berghahn, 2003).

Goldstein, J. and R. O. Keohane (eds), *Ideas and Foreign Policy: Beliefs, Institutions, and Political Change* (Ithaca: Cornell University Press, 1993).

Graber, D. A. *Mass Media and American Politics*, 6th edn (Washington, DC: CQ Press, 2002).

Hillenbrand, M. J. 'Tensions in US Relations with Europe: Memorandum for the Secretary of State, Nov. 15, 1971', NARA, RG 59, Box 2362: Subject Numeric Files, 1970–1973: Political and Defense.

Hillenbrand, M. J. 'U.S.-German-European Community Economic Relations: The Need for Common Approaches to Common Problems', *Department of State Bulletin*, 20 May (1974), pp. 548–54.

Hoffmann, S. 'Fragments Floating in the Here and Now', *Daedalus*, 108:1 (1979), pp. 1–26.

Hoffmann, S. 'Uneven Allies: An Overview', in D. S. Landes (ed.), *Western Europe: The Trials of Partnership* (Lexington: Lexington Books, 1977), pp. 55–110.

Hogan, M. J. 'The "Next Big Thing": The Future of Diplomatic History in a Global Age', *Diplomatic History*, 28:1 (2004), pp. 1–21.

Iriye, A. 'Culture and International History', in M. J. Hogan and T. G. Paterson (eds), *Explaining the History of American Foreign Relations* (Cambridge: Cambridge University Press, 2004), pp. 241–56.

Isserman, M. and M. Kazin. *America Divided: The Civil War of the 1960s*, 3rd edn (Oxford and New York: Oxford University Press, 2008).

Jackson, P. and P. Bourdieu. 'The "Cultural Turn" and the Practice of International History', *Review of International Studies*, 34 (2008), pp. 155–81.

Jenkins, P. *Decade of Nightmares: The End of the Sixties and the Making of Eighties America* (New York and Oxford: Oxford University Press, 2006).

Kaiser, K. and H.-P. Schwarz (eds), *Amerika und Westeuropa: Gegenwarts- und Zukunftsproblem* (Stuttgart: Belser, 1977).

Keohane, R. O. and J. S. Nye. *Power and Interdependence: World Politics in Transition* (Boston: Little, Brown & Co, 1977).

Kissinger, H. 'American Unity and the National Interest', *Department of State Bulletin*, 15 September (1975), pp. 389–96.

Kissinger, H. 'A New National Partnership', *Department of State Bulletin*, 17 February (1975), pp. 197–207.

Kissinger, H. 'The Year of Europe', *Department of State Bulletin*, 14 May (1973), pp. 593–8.

Kohler-Koch, B. 'Interdependenz', in V. Rittberger (ed.), *Theorien der Internationalen Beziehungen: Bestandsaufnahme und Forschungsperspektiven* (Opladen: Westdeutscher Verlag, 1990), pp. 110–29.

Kraus, H.-C. and T. Nicklas (eds), *Geschichte der Politik: Alte und neue Wege* (Munich: Oldenbourg, 2007).

Kreis, R. 'Bündnis ohne Nachwuchs? Die "Nachfolgegeneration" und die deutsch-amerikanischen Beziehungen in den 1980er Jahren', *Archiv für Sozialgeschichte*, 52 (2012), pp. 607–31.

Kuchenbuch, D. "'Eine Welt": Globales Interdependenzbewußtsein und die Moralisierung des Alltags in den 1970er und 1980er Jahren', *Geschichte und Gesellschaft*, 38 (2012), pp. 158–84.

Leendertz, A. 'Interdependenz, Krisenbewusstsein und der Beginn eines neuen Zeitalters: Die USA und die Neuverortung der transatlantischen Beziehungen in den 1970er Jahren', in F. Bösch and P. Hoeres (eds), *Außenpolitik im Medienzeitalter: Vom späten 19. Jahrhundert bis zur Gegenwart* (Göttingen: Wallstein, 2013), pp. 232–50.

Leendertz, A. 'Das Komplexitätssyndrom: Gesellschaftliche Komplexität als intellektuelle und politische Herausforderung in den 1970er Jahren', MPIfG Discussion Paper 15/7 (2015). Online, available at (accessed 10 October 2016).

Leendertz, A. and W. Meteling (eds), *Die neue Wirklichkeit: Semantische Neuvermessungen und Politik seit den 1970er Jahren* (Frankfurt/Main: Campus, 2016).

Lord, W. 'America's Purposes in an Ambiguous Age', *Department of State Bulletin*, 4 November (1974), pp. 617–22.

Lundestad, G. *The United States and Western Europe since 1945: From 'Empire' by Invitation to Transatlantic Drift* (Oxford: Oxford University Press, 2003).

Markowitz, R. 'Im Spannungsfeld von Amerikanisierung, Europäisierung und Westernisierung: Die Zäsur der 1960er und 1970er Jahre für die transatlantische Europadebatte', in C. Metzger and H. Kaelble (eds), *Deutschland - Frankreich - Nordamerika: Transfers, Imaginationen, Beziehungen* (Stuttgart: Steiner, 2006), pp. 98–123.

N. N. 'How America Looks at Europe', *Time Magazine*, 12 March 1973.

N. N. 'Here Comes the "European Idea" ', *Time Magazine*, 12 March 1973.

N. N. 'The Image of America's Future in Foreign Public Opinion', U.S.I.A. Research Report, July, 1973. NARA, RG 306, Entry P 160, Box 34.

N. N. 'Some Indications of Trends and Current Opinions About the U.S. and NATO in Western Europe', 2 November 1976. NARA, RG 306, Entry P 160, Box 37.

N. N. 'The Standing of the U.S. and of NATO in West European Public Opinion', 22 September 1976. NARA, RG 306, Entry P 160, Box 37.

Nixon, R. M. 'Second Annual Report to the Congress on United States Foreign Policy: Feb. 25, 1971', in *Public Papers of the Presidents of the United States: Richard M. Nixon, 1971* (Washington, DC, 1972), pp. 219–345.

Nye, J. S. and R. O. Keohane (eds), *Transnational Relations and World Politics* (Cambridge: Cambridge University Press, 1971).

Patel, K. K. 'Jenseits der Nation. Amerikanische Geschichte in der Erweiterung', in M. Berg and P. Gassert (eds), *Deutschland und die USA in der Internationalen Geschichte des 20. Jahrhunderts* (Stuttgart: Steiner, 2004), pp. 40–57.

Reston, J. 'Europe in the Spring', *New York Times*, 2 April 1972.

Reston, J. 'Mr. Whiskers', *New York Times*, 8 September 1971.

Reynolds, D. 'International History, the Cultural Turn and the Diplomatic Twitch', *Cultural and Social History*, 3:1 (2006), pp. 75–91.

Roberts, P. "'All the Right People": The Historiography of the American Foreign Policy Establishment', *Journal of American Studies*, 26:3 (1992), pp. 409–34.

Rush, K. 'European-American Relations: A Case for Cooperative Endeavor', *Department of State Bulletin*, 11 March (1974), pp. 237–41.

Sargent, D. J. 'The United States and Globalization in the 1970s', in N. Ferguson *et al.* (eds), *The Shock of the Global: The 1970s in Perspective* (Cambridge, MA: Belknap Press of Harvard University Press, 2010), pp. 49–64.

Schaetzel, J. R. *The Unhinged Alliance: America and the European Community* (New York: Harper & Row, 1975).

Schaetzel, J. R. 'U.S. Policy Toward Western Europe – In Transition: Off the record speech, Royal College of Defense Studies, London, Nov. 1, 1971', Princeton University, Seeley G. Mudd Library, George Ball Papers, Box 85, Fol. 8.

Schlesinger, Jr., A. M. *The Crisis of Confidence: Ideas, Power and Violence in America* (Boston: Houghton Mifflin, 1969).

Schulman, B. *The Seventies: The Great Shift in American Culture, Society, and Politics* (New York: Da Capo Press, 2002).

Schulz, M. and T. A. Schwartz (eds), *The Strained Alliance: U.S.-European Relations from Nixon to Carter* (Cambridge: Cambridge University Press, 2010).

Siniver, A. *Nixon, Kissinger, and U.S. Foreign Policy Making: The Machinery of Crisis* (Cambridge: Cambridge University Press, 2011).

Steinmetz, W. *Das Sagbare und das Machbare: Zum Wandel politischer Handlungsspielräume: England 1780–1867* (Stuttgart: Klett-Cotta, 1993).

Stollberg-Rilinger, B. (ed.), *Was heißt Kulturgeschichte des Politischen?* (Berlin: Duncker und Humblot, 2005).

Vernon, R. 'Rogue Elephant in the Forest: An Appraisal of Transatlantic Relations', *Foreign Affairs*, 51:3 (1973), pp. 573–87.

Watts, W. and L. A. Free. *State of the Nation III* (Lexington: Lexington Books, 1978).

Weingart, P. *Die Stunde der Wahrheit? Zum Verhältnis der Wissenschaft zu Politik, Medien und Wirtschaft in der Wissensgesellschaft* (Weilerswist: Verbrück Wissenschaft, 2005).

Weisbrode, K. *The Atlantic Century: Four Generations of Extraordinary Diplomats Who Forged America's Vital Alliance with Europe* (Cambridge, MA: Da Capo Press, 2009).

Zeiler, T. W. 'The Diplomatic History Bandwagon: A State of the Field', *Journal of American History*, 95:4 (2009), pp. 1053–73.

8

Transatlantic Catholicism and the making of the 'Christian West'

Giuliana Chamedes

The post-war ideological construct of the Atlantic order rested on two distinct visions for the post-war world. These visions were characterized by radically different genealogies and long-term aims; indeed, their only point of convergence was in a minimalist consensus on the imperative of greater transatlantic cooperation. The first vision – born and bred by liberal-democratic American and British intellectuals – called upon the United States to strengthen its political and economic ties with Europe so as to protect the shared democratic institutions and practices that purportedly united the Atlantic World. According to this view, the United States had much to teach European countries, most of which had strayed far from democracy in the interwar years and needed to be brought back into the fold. The second vision – advanced by the Holy See, a handful of European Christian Democratic leaders, and certain key American Catholic opinion-makers – did not have democracy as its endgame. Rather, it proposed to build a peaceful post-war order through the reconstitution of the 'Christian West', which was defined as an imagined community built on a shared commitment to Christian principles. As envisioned by these thinkers, the Christian West – which united Western Europe, Eastern Europe, and the United States in common cause – stood poised against the Soviet Union, which was presented as the greatest extant challenge to Christianity and religiosity in the post-war world. The chapter will focus in particular on a small group of American Catholic opinion-makers who sought to Christianize the concept of the Atlantic in the mid-1940s.

Catholic Atlanticism after the Great War

Genealogies of the concept of the 'Atlantic' in the twentieth century have tended to focus on the role of Anglo-American secular democratic thinkers. It was these thinkers, the standard story goes, that led to the popularization of the phrases Atlantic order, Atlantic Community, and their cognates in the early post-war period. But proponents of the Atlantic were not only liberal-democratic defenders of a post-war order dominated by Great Britain and the United States. Rather, the prominence of Atlantic talk in the post-war years was also due to the adoption of the phrase by religious, anti-liberal, anti-communist conservatives in the mid-1940s. These figures sought out a new language that enabled them to speak to transatlantic audiences about the twin evils of secularism and materialism, which they considered embodied by liberal and communist political movements. These figures were, by and large, Catholics. In order to understand how and why they made the Atlantic their own in the mid-1940s, we must turn our attention, albeit briefly, to the evolution of mainstream Catholic political thought in the years between the First World War and the Second World War.

American and European Catholics began strongly positing the need for greater transatlantic ties in the years immediately following the First World War. Scholars have just begun to demonstrate the transatlantic turn of Roman Catholicism after the First World War. Though the subject is certainly too vast to address in its fullness here, a few factors deserve special mention. First, the growing visibility and internationalization of the Holy See, which by the early post-war years had vastly expanded its diplomatic corps and its bases in North, Central, and South America. Second, the expansion of Catholic anti-communist groups and ideologies, particularly following the founding in the early 1930s of the Vatican's transnational Secretariat on Atheism, which produced printed propaganda and travelling exhibitions highlighting the inherently transatlantic ambitions of the Soviet Union. Third, the increased migration of European Catholics to North America, particularly as a result of political unrest in Italy, Germany, and Austria. And fourth, the growing economic power of the United States, along with the increased dependency of the Holy See on donations from American Catholics.[1]

During the years immediately following the Great War, the Pope, higher clergy, and a core group of American Catholic opinion-makers began to harp on a series of shared themes. According to these figures, the Great War represented the culmination of decades of violence (real and imagined) against the Catholic Church and the place of Catholicism in European history. The 'civilized world', as Pope Benedict XV put it, 'overwhelmed by universal madness', had had a close brush with 'suicide' as a result of its straying from the religious path.[2] The response to this state of affairs was a return to Christ and to the Catholic Church. For thinkers such as the American Catholic convert Ross Hoffman, to whom we shall return, Catholicism was exonerated from all responsibility in the breakdown of European civilization because it had been sent into exile by Europe's political leaders. For Pope Benedict XV, the Church's 'absolute impartiality' during the Great War placed it in a unique position to offer a resolution to the 'crisis of civilization' that had overtaken the European continent.

What was the solution to the post-First World War crisis of civilization, according to these Catholic theorists? The road out, according to the Pope and like-minded Catholic thinkers, was to cultivate a third-way solution that avoided the 'twin errors' of socialism and liberalism. This third-way approach eschewed the dangers of hyper-collectivism and hyper-individualism, taking as its source of inspiration the political-religious order of the Middle Ages. In the interwar years, the imperative for a third-way Christian solution was signalled through appeal to the phrase 'Western Christendom'.

In a bid to restore the centrality of religion to everyday life, these thinkers called for a return to a tradition defined as 'all those doctrines, principles courtesies, and noble refinements of life which have been honored in the Christian past'. Without this return to Christian tradition, 'man and society must inevitably be disillusioned'.[3]

The flavour of appeals to Western Christendom was slightly different in the United States as compared to the European continent. In the United States, these appeals were presented as compatible with the imperative to return to, and study the foundations of, 'Western civilization'. After the Great War, the study of Western civilization had enjoyed a heyday in the United States, something of which scholars are increasingly taking note. Columbia University had introduced the first Western civilization course, and many other universities had quickly followed suit.[4] Interestingly, in American Catholic circles, the call for the return to the tradition of Western Christendom elided the messiness of what was meant by 'West', running roughshod over the important distinction between a Greco-Roman West and a Christian one. Thus, the growing interest in Western civilization in the immediate aftermath of the Great War was cast as potentially compatible with Christian revivalism.[5] As we shall see, this smoothing over of potentially rival conceptions of the West would become quite relevant in the Catholic recasting of the Atlantic in the mid-1940s.

The call for a refounding of 'Western Christendom' only intensified in Catholic circles in the 1930s and early 1940s. For if the Great War had proved Armageddon averted, spectres of global dissolution appeared on the horizon once again following the 1929 Wall Street Crash and the Great Depression and effloresce of worker activism that followed. Increasingly, Catholics on both sides of the Atlantic began to read developments as disparate as the resurgence of anti-religious legislation in Mexico and the declaration of the Spanish Republic in 1931 as ominous signs that the world was bent on destroying organized religion in general, and Roman Catholicism in particular. More pointedly, they read these events as the work of what they called 'Bolshevik atheism', a movement whose ideological origins supposedly could be traced to the French Revolution. Yoked to a long tradition of counter-revolutionary thought, Catholic theorists argued that the French Revolution had gone terribly wrong in its attempt to remove religion from the public sphere and its glorification of popular sovereignty. In the process, the Revolution had displaced more convincing justificatory frameworks that understood state authority and human aims in society through appeal to the super-natural. On this reading, the French Revolution was the great-grandfather of the communists, according to whom history could be explained, and states erected, through appeal to this-worldly rather than other-worldly factors. In the interwar years, Catholics discussed the need to defend their own tradition against this alternate and purportedly Eastern import, as the imperative of saving 'Western Christendom' from its destroyers. Therefore, in the interwar years, a distinct Catholic anti-communist ideology developed, and this negative ideology was the flipside of the positive vision calling for the re-Christianization of public and private life.

It is worth emphasizing that Catholic theorists in the interwar years were speaking of 'the West' and 'Western Christendom'; they were not yet mobilizing the language of Atlanticism. At this point in time, the term remained solidly in the preserve of

Anglo-American liberal-democrats. Following his 1917 call for US intervention in the Great War, the American publicist Walter Lippmann was the leading figure associated with the phrase the Atlantic, and the Atlantic Community. And despite Lippmann's growing suspicions of popular sovereignty and the irrationality of 'the masses', the American writer remained committed to a chastened vision of democracy as the ideal political form. Throughout the interwar years, democracy remained, by contrast, distinctly unappealing to Catholics close to the Pope in the 1920s and 1930s; instead, they were more comfortable with authoritarian, anti-democratic, political experiments, such as Dollfuss's Austria, and Mussolini's Italy, in so far as these experiments openly refuted the legacy of secularism of the French Revolution.

It would not be until 1944–5 that Catholics – and, in particular, border-crossing American Catholics – took up the language of 'the Atlantic' and made it their own. In a contentious and surprising move, these American Catholics worked in the final years of the Second World War to redefine the term Atlantic as synonymous and co-extensive with Western Christendom and the Christian West. As they did so, they unhinged the Atlantic from two of its principal interwar associations: first, as a binding Anglo-American commitment to the Atlantic Ocean as a shared space of diplomatic-economic activity; and second, as a solidly liberal-democratic project. As a response to older understandings of the Atlantic, these thinkers called for the inclusion of markedly non-democratic countries, such as Spain, into the Atlantic order. They also made a strong case for the participation in the Atlantic project of countries that had no geographic connection whatsoever to the Atlantic Ocean: countries like Poland and Italy. In the process, they appealed to the fathers of Atlantic talk and tried to seize them as their own. It was thanks in no small part to the efforts of these thinkers that non-democratic, non-Atlantic powers could not only claim membership in the Atlantic order after the Second World War but become among its staunchest supporters.

In what follows, I will focus on three key sites for the reconfiguration of Atlanticism by American Catholics in the final years of the Second World War: the Edmund Burke Society of Fordham University, founded in May of 1945; the annual meeting of the American Historical Association and the United States Catholic Historical Society in 1945; and the Polish Institute of Arts and Sciences in America, founded in New York in 1942. These sites were by no means the only sites in which American and European Catholics reinvented the Atlantic and baptized it as a specifically Catholic project. Nonetheless, all three sites represented important platforms for the diffusion of this new idea. All were populated by Catholic border-crossers with deep ties to the European continent. And all were the breeding grounds for a new variety of conservatism in American politics that came into its own in the 1950s; a species of conservatism that championed the Atlantic as coextensive with Western Christendom, and that presented the revival of religious beliefs and practices as the best response to the catastrophes of the twentieth century writ large, and Soviet communism in particular. In many respects, this new conservatism flew in the face of an older tradition of American conservatism. Rather than wedded to laissez-faire capitalism and the self-regulatory powers of the invisible hand, the new conservatism of the post-war years called for an interventionist economic order that protected workers and families.

Furthermore, it proposed the existence of an objective moral order, grounded in natural law, which it was one's duty to realize in political and social life. In keeping with interwar Catholic thought, liberalism and communism were cast as the leading political enemies, with communism enjoying pride of place. In addition to Edmund Burke, the heroes of the new Catholic conservatism were figures like Alexis de Tocqueville, Georges Bernanos, and José Ortega y Gasset.[6]

Catholicizing Walter Lippmann

The post-war Christianization of the Atlantic involved, among other things, an attempt to wrest the concept itself out of liberal-democratic hands. In the late 1930s, the wheel was set in motion by Ross Hoffman, a fiesty American Catholic convert who taught history at Fordham University, and would go on to found the Burke Society in 1945. In 1937, Hoffman had begun the process of recuperating the liberal makers of Atlantic talk for Catholic ends. In a strongly opinionated review of Walter Lippmann's latest work, *The Good Society*, Hoffman had in fact noted that the father of the phrase Atlantic Community was finally beginning to see the light.[7] The American publicist had until recently been hailed as a hero for the liberal left-wing. However, 'today', Hoffman noted, with evident glee, 'Mr. Lippmann's name is jeered and derided by the Left; his writings are syndicated in the conservative press; and he is well on his way to becoming a twentieth-century Burke'. The reason for this transformation had one simple explanation: Lippmann had 'grown wise with age'. Why? As Hoffman saw it, Lippmann had come into his own in three particularly important respects. First, Lippmann had gained 'a heightened awareness that the crisis of modern civilization is of the spirit'. Indeed, Lippmann had begun to contemplate 'the acids of modernity and the much graver spiritual condition produced by modern man's apostasy from ancestral religion'. Not only had Lippmann correctly diagnosed the crisis of civilization as a spiritual one due to the rejection of religion, he had also – on Hoffman's reading, that is – begun to demonstrate 'a larger respect for traditional wisdom and experience', characterized in particular by his veneration for 'the spirituality and mystical grandeur of man' and 'the unique treasures of Christendom'. In other words, Lippmann had begun to celebrate the importance and the positive contributions of the Christian tradition to history. Third, and most pointedly, Lippmann had finally gained cognizance of the 'gigantic heresy' about which Catholics and the papacy had been warning for quite some time: the heresy of what the Popes called 'statolatry' and 'hyper-nationalism': the worship of the state, as a surrogate and disturbing substitute for the worship of God.[8]

The central thrust of Hoffman's review of *The Great Society* was undoubtedly positive. However, Hoffman also had some predictable criticisms for the once-darling of the liberal Left. For Hoffman, Lippmann had taken his critique of the all-powerful state a bit too far. This was doubtless because Lippmann remained committed to a fundamental error: the belief in liberalism, and as such an excessively minimalistic understanding of the state's role in society. The second problem that Hoffman found with Lippmann was in his assimilation of Bolshevism and fascism. For Hoffman, Bolshevism and fascism were not 'twin aspects of one dread evil', as Lippmann maintained. Rather, 'the regime of Italian Fascism is rather a strong and bitter medicine for the cure of an ill society'.[9] In his diary of 1936, following a visit to Italy, Hoffman had gone a step further, praising Mussolini for erecting an effective barrier against 'the pestilential heresy of Communism', and for creating 'a spiritual environment favorable to the Christian religious tradition'.[10]

Despite Lippmann's wrong-sighted liberalism and his mistaken assimilation of fascism and communism, Hoffman concluded his review on a positive note. Lippmann, he noted, was to be applauded for one crucial thing. In *The Good Society*, on Hoffman's reading, Lippmann had conclusively demonstrated that a society can be 'good' and 'free' only if it 'restores its allegiance to truths enshrined in the religious tradition of Christendom'.[11] Surely, this reading was an exercise in selective truth – for though it might be the case that Lippmann grew increasingly interested in the Christian heritage of the West, shunning, whenever possible, his own identification as Jewish, Lippmann was certainly not setting sail on the same ship as Hoffman.[12] For as Hoffman busied himself in the project of restoring Western Christendom, lambasting liberalism and communism, Lippmann remained, as ever, a chastened liberal thinker.

Thus notwithstanding, this was neither the first nor the last time that Lippmann's name would serve the rather particularistic ends of American Catholics in the 1930s and 1940s. Indeed, in the final years of the Second World War, American Catholic thinkers would repeatedly quote selectively from Lippmann in order to buttress their own views. In particular, Catholic historians would repeatedly use Lippmann's name in their rewriting of the history of the Atlantic. In 1945, Lippmann was in fact the key figure to whom American Catholic historians referred as they addressed the American historical profession, in the effort to recode the study of the Atlantic as the study of a shared, transatlantic, Christian heritage.

In 1945, an American Catholic historian by the name of Carlton Hayes drew heavily on Lippmann's writings in his December address to the American Historical Society in Washington, DC. Hayes had recently been named president of the American Historical Society, in a contentious election that pitted liberals against conservatives. Just before, Hayes had served as US Ambassador to Spain under Roosevelt, and the controversy swirling about him had much to do with his perceived sympathies to the Franco regime. In his keynote lecture at the American Historical Society, Hayes drew on his recent experience in Spain to launch a clarion call to American historians. He announced that American historians needed to cast aside petty provincialisms. Rather, they needed to begin to write as members of 'a great historic culture, the Western civilization, which, taking its rise around the Mediterranean, has long since embraced the Atlantic, creating what Mr. Walter Lippmann has appropriately designated the "Atlantic Community"'.[13] What Lippmann had called the Atlantic Community, Hayes explained, should be understood as one and the same as Western civilization. And that was not the end of it. In the same address, Hayes quoted Hoffman as well, so as to argue that the Atlantic Community and Western civilization had their shared origin in European Christendom. Quoting Hoffman verbatim, Hayes affirmed that 'every state of the North and South American continents originated from Western European

Christendom'. Indeed, it was Western Christendom that made 'the Atlantic Ocean the inland sea of Western civilization' and 'an historical and geographical extension of the Mediterranean'.[14]

In summary, in Hayes's view, the Atlantic should be understood as 'the inland sea' of Western Christendom, and the United States should proudly claim its role as the protector and defender of this rich tradition. As was the case with Hoffman, Hayes's quoting of Lippmann in his American Historical Society speech betrayed no sympathy with Lippmann's political views. In fact, Hayes was a sharp critic of modern American liberalism if there ever was one. In his sweeping 1941 history of late-nineteenth-century Europe, titled *A Generation of Materialism, 1871–1900*, Hayes had argued that American liberalism had cast aside Christian teachings and become increasingly secular and materialistic. In the process, it had put too much faith in democracy and nationalism, making itself thus vulnerable to political manipulation. In place of hyper-nationalism and the cult of democracy, Hayes advocated a return to Catholic principles and politics.

Similar points were raised by Hoffman, in his 1945 speech before the United States Catholic Historical Association. Hoffman delivered the keynote at the conference, which was held in New York City in mid-December of 1945. Hoffman's talk was appropriately titled, 'The American Republic and Western Christendom'. In it, Hoffman focused on the possibility of being 'a passionate American patriot no less than a devoted Catholic'. Pulling from a series of historical examples, Hoffman sought to demonstrate that Catholics had historically 'believed that just as it was the mission of the Church to incorporate all mankind in one divinely appointed communion, so it was the destiny of the American Republic to fulfill in the political order those conditions requisite to the completion of that divine mission'.[15] In other words, Hoffman's speech was perfectly in line with Hayes, in its call to the United States to recognize its membership in a Christian tradition, and the compatibility of its own national mission with a distinctly religious one.[16] In the closing sections of his speech, Hoffman quoted an extensive section from Lippmann's 1943 work, *U.S. Foreign Policy*. Hoffman's purpose in doing so was to demonstrate that historically the community of Western Christendom was organized 'around the Atlantic basin'.[17] For Hoffman, the United States must take stock of this 'historic fact' and commit to protecting and promoting Western Christendom as an idea and as a space of operation. Thus, Hoffman had once again redefined Lippmann's liberal-democratic thought in Catholic terms.

One final example will, I hope, demonstrate the pervasiveness of Lippmann in Catholic circles in the mid-1940s. In 1945, Paul Levack, a Catholic historian teaching at Fordham University, was giving a graduate lecture course entitled, 'The Atlantic Community'. At the time, it was perhaps the first of its kind. The course aims were described as follows: 'It provides a grand framework for studying the colonization and development of three continents by the nations of Western European Christendom, and for the development of the foreign policy of the United States.'[18] In other words, seizing on the phrase coined by Walter Lippmann, Levack sought to show that the Atlantic Community was coextensive with the history of Western European Christendom and its defence by US foreign policy. In a talk delivered in

January of 1945 before the Polish Institute of Arts and Sciences in America, Levack elaborated on some of these points. The talk was entitled, 'The Atlantic Community as a Historical Concept'. Rather thin on arguments, the talk nonetheless aimed to demonstrate that historically the Atlantic Community included many non-democratic states as well. Thus, Levack approvingly cited the Portuguese dictator Salazar, who referenced the necessity of an Atlantic Community emerging after the war in 1943, alongside, of course, Ross Hoffman himself. Finally, Levack picked up on the well-known sections of Walter Lippmann's *United States Foreign Policy*. Though he celebrated Lippmann's foresight on many questions, Levack did close by emphasizing that Lippmann was overly focused on the German peril. What of the Russian, Levack asked? 'The future must be considered in light of the resurrection of Russian power and the possibility of its extension', Levack noted, suggesting that the containment and/or elimination of the communist threat should be the core aim of the reconstituted 'Atlantic Community'.[19] In sum, Lippmann was, in a sense, a tool put to rather unlikely ends by Catholic conservatives like Hoffman, Hayes, and Levack, who roundly criticized his commitment to liberalism but nonetheless found his Atlanticism praiseworthy.

Putting the past to new purposes: Burke, Tocqueville, Vitoria, and the Christian Atlantic

But the Christianization of the Atlantic did not only take place via the appropriation of figures like Lippmann. In fact, during the mid-1940s, there were several other thinkers who were rescued from history and elevated to hero-status so as to buttress the theory and practice of the Christian Atlantic. The figure who loomed largest among them was the eighteenth-century English writer, Edmund Burke. Just as Hoffman, Hayes, and Levack were busy lambasting liberals and communists at historical conventions in 1945, they were also helping create a new site for the flowering of Catholic conservative thought after the Second World War: the Edmund Burke Society, founded at Fordham University in May of 1945.

Fordham University – the pre-eminent Jesuit university of New York – was a congenial home for the ambitious project of resurrecting Burke as the father of counter-revolutionary thought. Not only had the university 'faithfully championed and transmitted the principles and traditions of Christendom', as the founders of the Burke Society dutifully noted.[20] Fordham – along with Georgetown University – had from the interwar years crafted itself as the bastion of an aggressive, interventionist Catholicism; one that had relevance to modern society and was prepared to demonstrate it. Fordham had won repeated acclaim from the papacy in the interwar years for its activism. In 1936, the university had been visited by then-papal Secretary of State and future Pope Pius XII, Eugenio Pacelli, whom it honoured with an honorary degree. In addition, Fordham was conveniently located in the heart of New York City, the city which had become one of the premier hubs of American Catholic activism and European émigré activity in the interwar years.

In the inaugural conference of the Burke Society, the Society's purpose was defined in expansive terms. As its founders specified, the purpose of the Society was 'to promote the study and analysis of modern political society, from a historical and philosophical viewpoint, and in the light of the principles and traditions that have ever been essential characteristics of the international society of Christendom'. By bringing together historians, political scientists, and assorted other social scientists, the Burke Society proposed to promote not only the study of the 'international society of Christendom', but also to speak on its behalf. In the process, the Burke Society would raise awareness of the historical contributions of 'Christendom' to politics and political thought. The project of the Burke Society was ambitious indeed. Stated in the broadest terms, it was to reverse 'national and world disorder' through a return to Christian principles. As one of the founding members of the Society noted, the Burke society's recuperation of Christian traditions was 'indispensable if minds are to grapple effectively with the political, social, economic, juridical, and educational problems that will confront governments and citizens for many years after the present crisis of war'.[21]

To be sure, the Burke Society was not named after Edmund Burke by accident. Burke was an attractive figure for Hoffman and his cohort for several reasons. First, his status as one of the earliest and most articulate critics of the French Revolution gave him an important position within the history of European conservatism. Second, Burke was a border-crosser who had lived in Europe and the United States and spoken to both audiences – thus laying the practical foundations for transatlantic conservatism. Finally, Burke was an inspiring example for American Catholic activists because he had found the wherewithal to formulate a sophisticated analysis of European affairs at a time of great political and social turmoil; a time that seemed analogous, in many respects, to the world in 1945. Indeed, Burke's opposition to the French Revolution was readily extended by mid-century American Catholics to cover what they considered the two most dangerous children of the French Revolution: liberalism and communism. Thus, for post-war Catholic border-crossers, Burke's writings were eminently topical and useful, in that they helped Catholics foreground their own role in the moral and material reconstruction of European and American political and social life after the Second World War.

The Burke Society sponsored an outpouring of texts and activities in the 1940s that sought to bolster the Christianization of the Atlantic as a conceptual space and as a space of operation. Within a few years, Ross Hoffman and Paul Levack issued an important new edition of Burke's writings, titled *Burke's Politics: Selected Writings and Speeches on Reform, Revolution, and War*. In the rather incendiary preface to the volume, Hoffman and Levack made a strong case for the relevance of Burke's thought to the contemporary Atlantic. In particular, they emphasized Burke's commitment to Christian traditions and his relevance in a modern-day age of revolution. In subsequent writings on Burke, Hoffman in particular laid a great deal of stress on the transatlantic relevance of this figure, terming Burke a 'New York agent', and publishing Burke's personal correspondence during his time in New York City, where he had served as a representative of the British crown.[22]

The Burke Society began its ambitious project of orienting the post-war order by attempting to provide a Christian veneer to the concept of the Atlantic in its first annual symposium of 1945. It did so through appeal to another emerging star for the new Catholic conservatives: Alexis de Tocqueville, the nineteenth-century French politician and thinker. Ross Hoffman gave the introductory speech at the conference, as well as the concluding reflections 'on religion in democracy' in Tocqueville. In both speeches, Hoffman returned repeatedly to the theme of the Atlantic. 'The Atlantic Ocean', he noted, 'had no doubt widened – in a political sense – since Jackson had defeated the British at New Orleans, but a single political civilization span[s] it'. That single political civilization was synonymous with 'Christendom', a term which, Hoffman noted with evident delight, Tocqueville employed on several occasions in his best-known work, *Democracy in America*. As Hoffman emphasized, Tocqueville's recommendations were relevant not only in Europe; they also 'have an obvious relevance on this side of the Atlantic today'. In particular, it was noted that Tocqueville saw religious faith as a central component of a functioning political system. Without religion, political systems became despotic and dysfunctional; 'when the religion of a people is destroyed', in Tocqueville's words, 'doubt gets hold of the highest portions of the intellect and half paralyzes all the rest of its powers … Such a condition cannot but enervate the soul, relax the springs of the will, and prepare a people for servitude'. For Hoffman, this, 'of the many precepts of political wisdom set forth in Tocqueville's work', was 'the most important and least appreciated'.[23]

In the late 1940s and 1950s, the Burke Society continued to defend the idea of a reborn Christian Atlantic by making a point of bringing non-democratic and non-Atlantic powers into the fold of the Atlantic Community. In 1946, for instance, the founders of the Society celebrated Carlton Hayes's mission to Spain through a series of articles. In the 1940s, Hayes had begun to come under fire in certain circles on account of his rigid anti-communism and what was read as his apologetic defences of Franco's side during the Spanish Civil War. Additionally, Hayes was faulted for having done little to help Jewish refugees during his time as U.S. Ambassador to Spain, between 1942 and 1945. In 1945, Hayes's publication of his memoirs as Ambassador to Spain – titled *Wartime Mission in Spain* – did little to halt the criticisms. To the contrary, as book reviewers noted on the pages of *Foreign Affairs* and the *Journal of Modern History*, Hayes's memoirs had fanned the fires of controversy, suggesting to critics that Hayes indeed 'was not sufficiently critical of Franco and his régime'.[24] According to these reviewers, Hayes had used his memoirs to 'continue the conflict between Catholic Franco and communist Russia', clearly betraying his own allegiance to Catholicism, 'with all the ardor of a convert'.[25] Indeed, part of the point of Hayes's book was to make a case for non-intervention in Spain's internal affairs, and to emphasize that the United States had much to gain from establishing greater economic and cultural ties with the Spanish people. Furthermore, Hayes did not spare a few sharp words for 'decadent democracies' and sectors of the British and American governments.

In 1946, the members of the Edmund Burke Society rose to Hayes's defence. They wrote that Hayes had performed perhaps the most important and delicate diplomatic mission of the war: the mission of keeping Spain neutral. 'Upon the success of [Hayes's] enterprise depended not only the fate of Africa, but of the Mediterranean and the Near and Middle East.'[26] No superlatives were spared in the celebration of Hayes's actions and Hayes-the-man by his colleagues and friends at the Burke Society. Indeed, Hayes was 'a great historian', a 'first-rate political thinker', and an 'exemplary Catholic'; indeed 'it would be hard to imagine anyone better equipped to comprehend the realities of contemporary Spain'. It was likely for these reasons that Roosevelt had entrusted Hayes with the delicate diplomatic mission, in what was 'one of [Roosevelt's] shrewdest actions'.[27] Finally, Hayes deserved to be celebrated because he had laid the foundations for a diplomatic and cultural partnership between the United States and Spain – one grounded in a shared, Christian, Atlanticist, tradition.

Interesting, in the mid-1940s, the Society worked to promote the idea of Spain as a member of the Atlantic Community in other ways as well. It did so, for instance, by publicizing Ross Hoffman's trip to Spain, in an effort to revive another border-crossing ideologue of times past: Francisco de Vitoria.[28] Vitoria, the Renaissance Spanish Catholic philosopher, had played a key role in the rebirth of Thomism in his own time. In the immediate aftermath of the Second World War, Vitoria piqued the interest of conservative Catholic thinkers for several reasons. First, Hoffman perceived Vitoria as a border-crosser who had helped lay the foundations for the Christianization of the post-war Atlantic order. In two of his most famous lectures – 'De Indis Noviter Inventis' and 'De Jure Bellis Hispanorum in Barbaros' – Vitoria had famously explored whether the Spanish empire was justified in its violence against the native peoples of North America. In his investigation of the topic, Vitoria had concluded that what he called Amerindian resistance to conversion was a violation of *jus gentium* and thus cause for war. Indeed, Vitoria asserted, Christian practices should not be considered limited in scope to the Christian world; rather, they should be viewed as universal rules endorsed by *jus gentium*.[29] The take-away for Hoffman from Vitoria's famous lectures was as follows: Christian universalism – and Christian legal teachings – could and should apply broadly, to Christians and non-Christians alike. There was no reason to limit Christian universalism to Christian-majority territories or to the old continent; North America could and should be part of its scope as well, as should be countries that contained significant non-Christian populations. In other words, the Atlantic could and should be Christianized. In so far as Hoffman was putting forward these theses in the immediate aftermath of the massacre of European Jewry, some of the implications of his positions were eerie indeed.

Vitoria was attractive to mid-century American Catholics for a second reason: centuries prior, Vitoria had launched a heartened defence and updating of natural-law theory, presenting this as an answer to the conundrum of how one might create a universally binding system of law. As Hoffman and other Catholics noted, the newly formed United Nations had much to learn from the Catholic natural-law tradition, which derived law from God's will and saw it as an objective rule given from on high. As the lawyers associated with the UN busily sought to create a new system of universal principles and legal practices, these Catholics suggested, they would do well to heed one of the fathers of a specifically *Christian* variety of legal universalism. Indeed, from as early as 1940, Hoffman had explained that the League of Nations had faltered due to its commitment to liberalism and its aversion to religion as a social and cultural source of unity.[30] In 1945, he worried that the United Nations was wrongly conceived; it had erred by positing itself as 'an alliance formed for mutual defense by nations that have no common law, no common religion, or culture, or historical tradition'. In other words, it committed the grave mistake of including the Soviet Union within its ranks. Rather, what was needed was the creation of 'a genuine international community' grounded in the 'permanent political reality [of] Western civilization', which arose in the context of 'the international European political community of Christendom'.[31] Hoffman's call for a robust, Christian, understanding of international obligation, grounded in natural-law theories, was far from a cry in the dark. To the contrary, in 1945, the Vatican, in consortium with representatives of the American hierarchy, had just provided the funds necessary for the creation of a Catholic United Nations office, which would be based in New York City and staffed by laypeople.[32] The purpose of the office would be to advance a specifically Catholic vision of the post-war order at the new international body, among other things through the promotion of natural-law thinking, and the pressuring of individual UN representatives on legal questions of interest to the Catholic Church. Thus, Vitoria had a lesson for the United Nations as well, and it was this: Christian natural-law theories were applicable in transatlantic, universal, terms.

In sum, between 1944 and 1945, Catholic conservatives in the United States undertook an ambitious project of historical recuperation. Figures like Edmund Burke, Alexis de Tocqueville, and Francisco de Vitoria were recuperated as spokespersons for a new Christian, Atlantic, order. From Burke, Catholic conservatives took the message that the theory and practice of counter-revolution was noble and necessary, and one that could unite individuals both in Europe and the United States. From Tocqueville, Catholic conservatives cherry-picked the Frenchman's writings to find endorsements of Christianity and of 'the single political civilization' that spanned the Atlantic. Finally, from Vitoria, Catholic conservatives concluded that it was warranted and advisable for Catholics to impose their legal-moral order on non-Catholics and non-Christians. Indeed, things would be amiss should Catholics fail to live up to their task to do so.

How Poland and Italy joined the 'Atlantic'

American Catholics of the 1940s thus sought to Christianize the practice and conceptual history of the Atlantic in various ways. First, they reclaimed the liberal-democratic makers of the concept as their own, creatively reinterpreting their writings so as to emphasize agreement over disagreement. Second, they restored a series of key thinkers – including Edmund Burke, Alexis de Tocqueville, and Francisco de Vitoria – who were cumulatively read as the fathers of Christian Atlanticism. Third, they posited the need to include non-democratic countries – such as Franco's Spain – into the fold, on cultural-historic grounds. In these immediate post-war years, American Catholics took their thinking one step further: they argued that powers that were not on the shores of the Atlantic Ocean at all deserved full membership within the Atlantic Community. The two key countries at stake here were Italy (a former axis power) and Poland. I will focus on the latter in what follows.

On January 22, 1945, the Polish Institute of Arts and Sciences in America organized what they called a public 'discussion meeting' in New York on 'the problem of the Atlantic Community'. The timing was impeccable. The invited speakers included Ross Hoffman, Paul Levack, and Richard Nikolaus Eijiro von Coudenhove-Kalergi, the conservative Austrian aristocrat who would become a pioneer of European integration. The lectures were followed by a discussion, in which Oscar Halecki, the Polish historian and Catholic activist, and Erik Maria Ritter von Kuehnelt-Leddihn, the prominent Austrian conservative, were featured participants. Halecki was one of the key organizers of the event, which had as its undertone the 'scandal' of Yalta, in which Poland had been promised to the Soviet Union. Erik Maria Ritter von Kuehnelt-Leddihn did much to orient the conversation in this direction, as he had personally just received an award from the Vatican for a rather unsophisticated anti-communist novel that sought to raise awareness of the communist menace for Catholics through the genre of the adventure novel.

At the 1945 discussion meeting on 'the problem of the Atlantic Community', Ross Hoffman gave the opening address. In his introductory remarks, he got right to the heart of the paradox of the Atlantic Community, as advanced in Catholic circles: namely, that many of the members of this community were not on the Atlantic Ocean at all. 'On first thought it may appear a little odd that a meeting to discuss the Atlantic Community should take place at the Polish Institute', Hoffman noted. However, Hoffman went on to argue, Poland had geographic, cultural-historical, and geopolitical reasons to claim membership in the Atlantic Community. First, 'it is arguable indeed that she belongs to [the Atlantic Community], for Poland is a Baltic country and the Baltic is an Atlantic bay'. Second, Poland should be included in the Atlantic Community on geostrategic grounds, in so far as 'the solidarity of the West depends on its ability to set limits to the advance of Soviet imperialism in Europe'. Finally, and most importantly, Poland deserved membership in the Atlantic Community because of its proud Christian heritage. Indeed, in Hoffman's words,

> If this Atlantic Community is the modern form of Western Christendom – a society of nations who are the progeny of a world once formed and impregnated by classical traditions and Catholic Christianity – then surely Poland is a great and honored member.

If the Atlantic was a modern-day synonym for Western Christendom then a Christian power like Poland was a necessary member of the club. According to Hoffman, individuals in 1945 had attained the 'sharpened awareness [that] the Atlantic Community [is] not an ideology, not a mere strategic conception, not a post-war plan, not a "block" of "Powers," but a political and historical reality'.[33] In other words, he was not the only one making the claim that the Atlantic and Western Christendom should be considered the same thing.

After the Second World War, Catholic border-crossers grew increasingly interested in reimagining the political geography of West Christendom as an Atlantic space of operation. As envisioned by these thinkers, the 'Christian West' stood poised against the twin dangers of secularism and materialism. The most dangerous incarnation of these tendencies was the Soviet Union. In their theorizing, these Catholic writers also highlighted the 'heresy' of hyper-individualism, associated with liberal democracy. Over and above the cult of the nation, the individual, and the collective, Catholics called for a reinvigorated, values-grounded, international society that took its cues from Catholic teachings. In doing so, post-war Catholic hermeneutics provided a comprehensive interpretation of the horrors of the Second World War, and a relatively clear prescription for the future. Ironically, the call for the re-founding of Christian civilization – which carried with it the imperative of converting non-Christians to the one true religion, and presenting the Catholic Church as the leading victim of communism – came on the heels of the largest massacre of European Jewry known to history.

Notes

1 On these topics, see J. Pollard, *Money and the Rise of the Modern Papacy: Financing the Vatican, 1850–1950* (Cambridge: Cambridge University Press, 2005); P. D'Agostino, *Rome in America: Transnational Catholic Ideology from the Risorgimento to Fascism* (Chapel Hill: University of North Carolina Press, 2004); J. Connelly, *From Enemy to Brother: The Revolution in Catholic Teaching on the Jews, 1933–1965* (Cambridge, MA: Harvard University Press, 2012); U. Greenberg, *The Weimar Century: German Émigrés and the Ideological Foundations of the Cold War* (Princeton: Princeton University Press, 2014); and G. Chamedes, 'The Vatican, Nazi-Fascism, and the Making of Transnational Anticommunism in the 1930s', *Journal of Contemporary History*, 51:2 (2016), pp. 261–90.
2 Pope Benedict XV, 'Note to the Heads of Belligerent Peoples' (1 August 1917).
3 J. Husslein, S.J., 'Preface', in R. Hoffman (ed.), *Tradition and Progress and Other Historical Essays in Culture, Religion, and Politics* (Milwaukee: The Bruce Publishing Company, 1938), p. ix.
4 For a helpful overview, see M. Kimmage, 'The Rise and Fall of the West: An American Story', *Telos*, 168 (Fall 2014), pp. 22–44.
5 In *Tradition and Progress*, Hoffman for instance argued that it is a mistake to refer to the Church as a heritage of the Middle Ages. Rather, 'It was the Hellenic-Roman culture which existed in the days of Christ. It was this culture which the Church Christianized, and so handed down in the West as a heritage to the Middle Ages'. The tradition was also referred to in the same text as 'the Christianized classic tradition'. Husslein, 'Preface', pp. x, xiii.
6 On the explosion of this variety of conservatism after the Second World War, see P. Allitt, *Catholic Intellectuals and Conservative Politics in America, 1950–1985* (Ithaca: Cornell University Press, 1993); M. Kimmage, *The Conservative Turn: Lionel Trilling, Whittaker Chambers, and the Lessons of Anti-Communism* (Cambridge, MA: Harvard University Press, 2009).

7 R. Hoffman, 'Walter Lippmann Grows Wise with Age: From his Prefaces to his Book on the Good Society', *America* (20 November 1937), pp. 150–1.

8 In his approving summary of Lippmann, Hoffman noted that according to Lippmann the world had 'lost its way' because it had 'withdrawn its faith not only from God but from man', insofar as it 'has succumbed to a "gigantic heresy"'; which is the mad doctrine that the social order can be planned and administered by an omni-competent political power'. *Ibid.*, pp. 150–1.

9 *Ibid.*, pp. 150–1.

10 R. Hoffman, *Rome Diary*, 7 August 1936. As quoted in Allitt, *Catholic Intellectuals*, p. 222.

11 Hoffman, 'Walter Lippmann', p. 151.

12 In the late 1920s, Lippmann had favourably reviewed the writings of the founder of the Italian Popular Party, Luigi Sturzo, celebrating the anti-statism of Thomas Aquinas and Catholic corporatist thought. See W. Lippmann, 'Autocracy vs. Catholicism', *Commonweal* (13 April 1927), p. 627. In 1941, Lippmann had delivered a speech at the American Catholic Philosophical Association in which he chided 'secular man' for his 'ideal of secular progress, which is totally alienated from and profoundly opposed to the real character of a human person'. In the same year, Lippmann also gave a speech before the Phi Beta Kappa society entitled 'Education vs. Western Civilization' in which he condemned modern educators for 'abandoning the classical religious culture of the West' in their teaching. Even though Lippmann was Jewish, he would never speak before Jewish groups. He even refused to accept an award from the Jewish Academy of Arts and Sciences. In a letter to his wife of the late 1930s, Lippmann wrote about how at home he felt in 'the classical and Christian heritage'. When the *Commonweal* editor asked Lippmann to assist Jewish refugees during the war, Lippmann said no; however, he did not hesitate to help out when approached by a committee that was seeking to restore an old convent once used by Thomas Aquinas for teaching purposes. All of this had led some commentators to conclude that Lippmann was more comfortable with Christianity than he was with Judaism. See, e.g., B. Riccio, *Walter Lippmann: Odyssey of a Liberal* (New Brunswick, NJ: Transaction Press, 1994).

13 C. J. Hayes, 'The American Frontier – Frontier of What?' *American Historical Review* (1946), pp. 199–216.

14 R. Hoffman, 'Europe and the Atlantic Community', *Thought*, 25 (March, 1945), as quoted in Hayes, 'The American Frontier', pp. 199–216.

15 R. Hoffman, 'American Republic and Christendom', *Historical Records and Studies*, XXXV (1946), pp. 3–17, here p. 7.

16 *Ibid.*, p. 10.

17 *Ibid.*, p. 13.

18 R. Hoffman, 'Activities of Sections: Section of Historical and Political Sciences: Lectures and Discussion Meetings', *Bulletin of the Polish Institute of Arts and Sciences in America*, III (1944), pp. 599–601.

19 *Ibid.*, p. 603.

20 W. J. Schlaerth, 'Preface', in *Alexis de Tocqueville's Democracy in America: A Symposium* (New York: Fordham University Press, 1945).

21 *Ibid.*

22 R. Hoffman, *Edmund Burke, New York Agent, with His Letters to the New York Assembly and Intimate Correspondence with Charles O'Hara, 1761–1776* (Philadelphia: American Philosophical Society, 1956).

23　Schlaerth, 'Preface', p. 41.
24　R. G. Woolbert, 'Wartime Mission in Spain, 1942–5', *Foreign Affairs* (April 1946).
25　L. M. Sears, 'Review: *Wartime Mission in Spain 1942–1945* by Carlton J. H. Hayes', *The Journal of Modern History*, 18:4 (December 1946), p. 363.
26　R. Hoffman, 'Editorial: The Hayes Mission to Spain', *Thought*, 23 (March 1946), p. 5.
27　*Ibid.*, p. 7.
28　For a discussion of Ross Hoffman's trip to Spain to deliver talks on Francisco de Vitoria, see *Thought* (March 1946), p. 394; and R. Hoffman, 'Vitoria and American Political Thinking', *Thought*, 21 (September 1946), pp. 394–400. Hoffman's lectures were published the following year in an eighteen-page pamphlet under the title, *American Political Thinking and the Vitorian Tradition* (Madrid: Institute Francisco de Vitoria del Consejo Superior de Investigaciones Cientificas, 1947).
29　A. Anghie, 'Francisco De Vitoria and the Colonial Origins of International Law', *Social & Legal Studies*, 5:3 (1996), pp. 321–36.
30　See R. Hoffman, 'Christendom and the Organization of Peace', *The Catholic World*, 151 (September 1940), pp. 651–9; R. Hoffman, *The Great Republic* (New York: Sheed & Ward, 1942), chapter 6; and R. Hoffman, 'Peacemaking after Ideological Wars', *Thought*, 20 (September 1945), pp. 404–26, esp. p. 419.
31　Hoffman, 'American Republic and Christendom', p. 11.
32　On this, see J. S. Rossi, *Uncharted Territory: The American Catholic Church at the United Nations, 1946–1972* (Washington, DC: Catholic University Press, 2006).
33　Hoffman, 'Activities of Sections', pp. 599–600.

References

Allitt, P. *Catholic Intellectuals and Conservative Politics in America, 1950–1985* (Ithaca: Cornell University Press, 1993).

Anghie, A. 'Francisco De Vitoria and the Colonial Origins of International Law', *Social & Legal Studies*, 5:3 (1996), pp. 321–36.

Pope Benedict XV, 'Note to the Heads of Belligerent Peoples' (1 August 1917).

Chamedes, G. 'The Vatican, Nazi-Fascism, and the Making of Transnational Anticommunism in the 1930s', *Journal of Contemporary History*, 51:2 (2016), pp. 261–90.

Connelly, J. *From Enemy to Brother: The Revolution in Catholic Teaching on the Jews, 1933–1965* (Cambridge, MA: Harvard University Press, 2012).

D'Agostino, P. *Rome in America: Transnational Catholic Ideology from the Risorgimento to Fascism* (Chapel Hill: University of North Carolina Press, 2004).

Greenberg, U. *The Weimar Century: German Émigrés and the Ideological Foundations of the Cold War* (Princeton: Princeton University Press, 2014).

Hayes, C. J. 'The American Frontier – Frontier of What?', *American Historical Review* (1946), pp. 199–216.

Hoffman, R. 'Activities of Sections: Section of Historical and Political Sciences: Lectures and Discussion Meetings', *Bulletin of the Polish Institute of Arts and Sciences in America*, III (1944), pp. 599–601.

Hoffman, R. *American Political Thinking and the Vitorian Tradition* (Madrid: Institute Francisco de Vitoria del Consejo Superior de Investigaciones Cientificas, 1947).

Hoffman, R. 'American Republic and Christendom', *Historical Records and Studies*, XXXV (1946), pp. 3–17.

Hoffman, R. 'Christendom and the Organization of Peace', *The Catholic World*, 151 (September 1940), pp. 651–9.

Hoffman, R. 'Editorial: The Hayes Mission to Spain', *Thought*, 23 (March 1946), pp. 5–12.

Hoffman, R. *Edmund Burke, New York Agent, with His Letters to the New York Assembly and Intimate Correspondence with Charles O'Hara, 1761–1776* (Philadelphia: American Philosophical Society, 1956).

Hoffman, R. 'Europe and the Atlantic Community', *Thought*, 25 (March 1945), pp. 21–36.

Hoffman, R. *The Great Republic* (New York: Sheed & Ward, 1942).

Hoffman, R. 'Peacemaking after Ideological Wars', *Thought*, 20 (September 1945), pp. 404–26.

Hoffman, R. 'Vitoria and American Political Thinking', *Thought*, 21 (September 1946), pp. 394–400.

Hoffman, R. 'Walter Lippmann Grows Wise with Age: From his Prefaces to his Book on the Good Society', *America* (20 November 1937), pp. 150–1.

Husslein, S. J. 'Preface', in R. Hoffman (ed.), *Tradition and Progress and Other Historical Essays in Culture, Religion, and Politics* (Milwaukee: The Bruce Publishing Company, 1938), pp. ix–xiii.

Kimmage, M. 'The Rise and Fall of the West: An American Story', *Telos*, 168 (Fall 2014), pp. 22–44.

Kimmage, M. *The Conservative Turn: Lionel Trilling, Whittaker Chambers, and the Lessons of Anti-Communism* (Cambridge, MA: Harvard University Press, 2009).

Lippmann, W. 'Autocracy vs. Catholicism', *Commonweal* (13 April 1927).

Pollard, J. *Money and the Rise of the Modern Papacy: Financing the Vatican, 1850–1950* (Cambridge: Cambridge University Press, 2005).

Riccio, B. *Walter Lippmann: Odyssey of a Liberal* (New Brunswick: Transaction Press, 1994).

Rossi, J. S. *Uncharted Territory: The American Catholic Church at the United Nations, 1946–1972* (Washington, DC: Catholic University Press, 2006).

Schlaerth, W. J. 'Preface', in *Alexis de Tocqueville's Democracy in America: A Symposium* (New York: Fordham University Press, 1945), p. 7.

Sears, L. M. 'Review: *Wartime Mission in Spain 1942–1945* by Carlton J. H. Hayes', *The Journal of Modern History*, 18:4 (December 1946), p. 363.

Woolbert, R. G. 'Wartime Mission in Spain, 1942–5', *Foreign Affairs* (April 1946), p. 558.

9

From denationalizing history to decanonizing teaching history: A programme for the teaching of history in the post-national era

Thomas Adam

Teaching history at American colleges and universities currently undergoes significant changes and transformations. Fundamental questions are raised about how we teach history and what we teach as history. There is the pressure of university administrations and boards of regents to develop online courses which students can take at their own pace. The large survey courses in American and World History are relocated from lecture halls into the virtual world of the internet where students are guided through the material with interactive tools and online lectures. The internationalization and transnationalization of teaching history is another keyword for the reconstruction of history in the pursuit of endowing history education with new relevance in an increasingly globalized world. If history is to be relevant to students' life in the twenty-first century, it needs to relate to their experience and problems. And challenges from migration to terrorism are global in nature and cannot be explained by referencing a national framework.

There are many ways to achieve a state of history teaching that connects the current global experiences of students with past events and provides explanations for the challenges of our time. The most prominent way to reconfigure our historical knowledge and its presentation is offered by the approach of Transnational History. Transnational History emerged since the early 1990s as a counter-model to the paradigm of national history. It is focused on the circulation of ideas, concepts, and practices across various cultures and societies. Rather than seeing history as a function of nation states and only in its national variants, Transnational History considers history as a universal and global project. Transnational History is based upon the fundamental belief that humans live in an interconnected world. Instead of researching and writing the history of a particular phenomenon such as eugenics within the confines of a given nation state, Transnational History encourages historians to follow a particular phenomenon wherever it leads us. This approach not only unearths the hidden connections and exchanges that occurred below the level of nation states in the past, but it also prevents historians from making misleading assumptions about the uniqueness of certain nations and developments within these nations.[1]

The approach of Transnational History overlaps to a certain degree with the approach of global history. Both Transnational and Global History are focused on phenomena rather than on the history of isolated nations and both approaches stress connections and exchanges of material and immaterial products that create spaces of their own. The most significant difference rests, according to Pierre-Yves Saunier, with the time frame. While Global History focuses on the history of humankind since the late fifteenth century and Christopher Columbus's journey to the Americas, Transnational History focuses on the period since the American and French revolutions that created the modern nation state. Global historians concern themselves more with early modern history while transnational historians have located their studies more in the nineteenth century. The most significant difference between Global and Transnational History rests with their relationship to national history. Global History can, because of its longer time span and its starting point around 1500, co-exist with national history. Transnational History, by contrast, competes with national history for exactly the same time period.[2]

The approach of Transnational History has also given rise to the concept of Transatlantic History as it will be used in this chapter. Since defining Transatlantic History as a subfield of Transnational History has not been accepted by all scholars, it is necessary to explore the different concepts of Transatlantic History that have emerged within the last five decades. There are at least four distinct schools of Transatlantic History which have little in common beyond their name. The first part of this chapter is, therefore, dedicated to a brief historiographical review of four different concepts while the second part of this chapter addresses the challenges of teaching Transatlantic and Transnational History and of introducing students to the study of Intercultural Transfers.

The national history paradigm

Since the birth of history as an academic discipline at the beginning of the nineteenth century, professors and students came to accept the notion that nation states seemingly formed the natural skin to the body of history. It appeared that the nation needed history as much as history needed the nation. 'Nationalism as it first developed in the nineteenth century', Thomas Baker reminds us, 'both shaped and was shaped by the field of historical study as it was then coming to be constituted in the West'.[3] History has been part of the 'national project' from its inception and provided legitimacy to the nation states created during the nineteenth century. And while not

all histories of the day were national in scope or outlook, histories of nations – that is, histories that sought to document and thereby conjure a culturally or politically powerful nascent 'national' consciousness from a welter of memories, myths, traditions, and established 'facts' – were among the most characteristic works of mid-nineteenth-century historiography. Men such as Jules Michelet (1798–1874) in France, Thomas Babington Macaulay (1800–59) in Great Britain, and George Bancroft (1800–91) in the United States, whose multi-volume 'people's' histories explicitly promoted the moral purpose of nation building, emerged as some of their generation's best known and most influential historians. Since these men often simultaneously held positions of public trust as politicians, diplomats, or popular lecturers *and* spoke directly to an expansive new middle-class readership rather than to an audience of professionally trained historians alone, they shaped public opinion much more directly than did either their precursors or descendants.[4]

Historians, thus, told the story of how nations were born, with which unique characteristics they had been endowed, and which territories they could claim rightfully their own. As a result, a mutually beneficial relationship emerged between the historical profession and the nation states they helped to legitimize.[5] This is not to suggest that the historical profession should be reduced to a tool of politicians and nationalists in their pursuit of making nation states. Historians simply absorbed and reflected the culture in which they grew up, in which they were trained, and which they perceived as the logical framework for their research and writing. This condition of historical writing applies to the production of all works of history and all interpretations from national history to Atlantic and transnational history. Historians, as we should remember, are always the product of their culture and environment.

This is not to say that the production of national history was without alternative. 'There existed', as Stefan Berger asserts, 'many traditions of historical writing' in the nineteenth century. It 'was by no means a foregone conclusion that the national perspective would come to dominate' the writing of history 'in the second half of the nineteenth century'.[6] Regional and local history had a great appeal for historians. The Göttingen scholars Johann Christian Gatterer, August Ludwig Schlözer, and Ludwig Timotheus Spittler, who have been credited with creating the first 'intellectual community which defined methodological ground rules for the writing of history distinct from other forms of writing' and thereby established history as an academic discipline, 'wrote predominantly regional, social and economic history rather than national history'.[7] And there were even conceptual alternatives to national history as for instance the Marxist approach towards history. In Karl Marx's theories about social organization and historical development, nations and nation states played only a marginal role. His insistence that the structural forces of capitalism transcend national borders provided, already in the nineteenth century, an alternative – although a strongly deterministic one – to the nationalist histories in which the virtues and exceptional values of single nations were extolled. Marxist theory had, however, little impact on the writing and teaching of history before the Second World War since selective admissions policies to universities, state control in the case of public universities, and the influence of donors in the case of private universities prevented the integration of alternative views and interpretations inspired by Marxism.[8] It appears to be an irony of history that Marxism, channelled into orthodox Stalinism and orthodox Maoism, took a nationalist turn at the exact moment at which universities across the Western world were opened to students from a diverse socio-economic and political-ideological background. In the post-Second-World-War era, conservative, liberal, and Marxist historians largely agreed that history was best served by being presented as national history.

Atlantic and Transatlantic Histories

In the context of the Cold War, history obtained new significance. In the same way as the emergence of nationalism and nation states had shaped the historical profession in the nineteenth century, the climate of the Cold War with its entrenched East–West confrontation and the formation of the two antagonistic military alliances, NATO[9] and Warsaw Pact,[10] were not without consequences for doing history. Interpretations of historical events and the development of historical concepts never occur in a vacuum. Historians in Eastern Europe as well as Western Europe willingly provided historical justification for the rearrangement of national borders as in the case of post-war Poland and Germany and embarked on the search for the historical foundation for Western European and Eastern European integration. The most productive outcome of these historical ruminations was the thesis of the Atlantic Revolution and the concept of Atlantic History developed by Jacques Godechot and Robert R. Palmer.[11] 'In its first, original phase', Bernard Bailyn wrote,

> Atlantic history in the broadest sense is the story of the creation of a vast new marchland of European civilization, an ill-defined, irregular outer borderland, thrust into the world of indigenous peoples in the Western Hemisphere and in the outer reaches of the British archipelago. Life in this contested marchland was, literally, barbarous: that is, in its initial stages it was, in large areas, a scene of conflict with alien people, alien in language and mores, hostile in purpose, savage and uncultivated. Europeans, native Americans, and displaced Africans, all – each from their own point of view – saw it that way. For all, others were intent on destroying the civility – European, native American, African, that had once existed.[12]

This rather far-reaching and inclusive approach provided the intellectual stimulus for path-breaking books such as Alfred Crosby's *The Columbian Exchange*[13] and Bernard Bailyn's *The Peopling of British North America*.[14] Both books made important contributions towards the understanding of imperial and colonial conquest, migration voluntary and forced, trade and biological exchanges.

And yet, Atlantic History had its critics from the very beginning. Palmer and Godechot were accused 'then and later, of being apologists for NATO and the new-fangled idea of an Atlantic community'.[15] There can be no doubt that the 1950s were conducive to concepts that espoused a closer relationship between Western Europe and North America. Historians do not operate outside of society and their interpretations are always influenced by the culture in which the historian operates. There are, however, more serious scholarly problems associated with the concept of Atlantic History. For many historians, the Atlantic World has, as Philip D. Morgan and Jack P. Greene have pointed out, 'little coherence and no real unity'.[16] Historians are quick to assert that there was an English Atlantic, a Spanish Atlantic, etc., but they remain reluctant to see an integrated Atlantic World in which people from different parts of Europe and the Americas interacted and formed an Atlantic culture. While research about the shares European populations claimed within the Atlantic World has moved from the British to include the Spanish, the French, the Dutch, and more recently also African people,[17] the contributions of other significant groups such as the Germans and Russians, to name just two examples, are still not explored. What are the shares of the Germans and the Russians within the Atlantic World as explorers, merchants, and settlers? The German case provides an intriguing opportunity to reconsider concepts of Atlantic History since Germany is the only European country to have provided migrants for all regions and parts of North and South America without ever having possessed colonies on either continent.[18] Yet, Germans developed also colonizing visions and even provided strategies for their relationship with Native American populations in North America which markedly differed from the British approach. German settlers in the Mohawk Valley, as Philip Otterness shows, created friendly relations with the Mohawks, sent their children to live with them, and obtained rights to land through negotiation rather than conquest.[19] This pattern was not confined to this cluster of German settlements but was repeatedly applied in other regions from Pennsylvania to Texas.[20]

The focus on the British, Spanish, Portuguese, and Dutch shares of the Atlantic World points to another problem of Atlantic History. It all too often seems to be colonial history in disguise, which too long privileged the role of Europeans in the formation of the Atlantic World. The self-imposed timeframe according to which Atlantic History begins with the great exploration of the Spanish following Christopher Columbus's first voyage in 1492 and ends somewhere between 1774 and 1825 seems to support the suspicion that Atlantic History is not more than colonial history.[21] The emergence of nation states in Europe and North America did not, as many historians have wrongly assumed, result in an interruption of cultural contacts and exchanges between people of different languages, cultures, and traditions within the Atlantic World. The Atlantic remained, as Daniel T. Rodgers established, 'a connective lifeline – a seaway for the movement of people, goods, ideas, and aspirations'[22] even after the formation of nation states. In fact, people moved closer together within the Atlantic World because of the improvements of travel with the introduction of steam ships that revolutionized transatlantic transportation. While migrants sailing across the Atlantic in the eighteenth century needed about thirty-six days to make the journey, steam ships travelled from Europe to North America in just thirteen days by the end of the nineteenth century. And the cost for a ticket on board one of the new steam ship liners decreased significantly from the 1860s to the turn of the century.[23] Travel became within a few decades faster, more affordable, and safer. These changes allowed people of different social background to cross the Atlantic in both directions and thereby intensified intercultural transfers of ideas for social and cultural institutions from museums and libraries to housing companies and social welfare institutions between various communities within the Atlantic World that contributed to the creation of urban infrastructures and cityscapes on both sides of the Atlantic.[24]

The spatial and temporal limitations imposed by the approach of Atlantic History appear as too artificial for a complex and multifaceted region such as the Atlantic World. The term Atlantic History has been mistaken to suggest that there was one unified Atlantic World, culture, or civilization. Such a suggestion is, of course, grossly misleading. Instead, multiple centres emerged within the Atlantic World and multiple cultures and societies were formed, destroyed, and recreated within the Atlantic

World. The most serious objection against Atlantic History rests with its sole definition by space. Atlantic History is defined by the geography of the Atlantic and its
surrounding continents. This approach is rather simplistic and privileges the Atlantic
over other regions such as the Pacific or the Mediterranean. More than four decades
of research have not produced a single innovative theory or theoretical concept for the
interpretation of Atlantic History.

The North Atlantic world in the post-Second-World-War era was not the exclusive
resort for Atlantic historians; scholars who studied international relations and diplomacy explored the relationship between the United States and its Western European
allies within the context of the Transatlantic World. While Atlantic historians limited
themselves to the era before 1825, scholars of foreign relations saw the First World War
as their starting point. The cultural and economic Americanization of Western Europe,
in which ideas, practices, and patterns of behaviours that were developed in the United
States were adopted in other countries, and anti-American resistance to the American
presence in Western Europe have received much attention from European scholars.[25]
Most scholarship, however, focused on the dominating role of the United States in
post-Second-World-War Western Europe and its relations with its Western European
allies.[26] In these writings the notion of an increasingly integrated Transatlantic World
emerged from the 1950s onwards. This Transatlantic World was clearly dominated by
the United States as the hegemonic power of the West. Its relationship with Western
European countries has been variably described as an 'empire by invitation', an 'empire
by consensus', and more recently as the 'irresistible empire'.[27]

The end of the Cold War led to a considerable reorientation within the field of foreign relations studies and to a reinvention of scholars of foreign relations as transatlantic
scholars. Jessica Gienow-Hecht spoke of a 'virtual palace revolution' which occurred
in the early 1990s and led scholars of foreign relations to consider 'analytical concepts
such as gender, literary criticism, travel, environmentalism, race, and culture'.[28] Culture
in particular emerged as a new powerful concept in international relations and caused
scholars such as Akira Iriye and Gienow-Hecht to rebrand older concepts of diplomacy and international relations as cultural diplomacy and intercultural relations.[29]
While nations and governments remain important agents in this field of study, transatlantic scholars recognized the roles non-governmental actors play in transatlantic
relations. 'Historians of international relations … had', as Akira Iriye reminds us, 'vir-
tually ignored' the activities of non-governmental organizations.[30] Yet, the activities of
non-governmental associations such as Greenpeace reminded scholars that there were
powers outside the realm of traditional state authority. Gienow-Hecht observed:

> Aware of the crucial role played by non-governmental actors such as mission-
> aries, teachers, and other cultural envoys in international relations, scholars have
> recognized that these actors constitute ambassadors and diplomats in their own
> right. Diplomacy thus refers not only to state-to-state relations conducted by
> officials on the payroll of their governments but, increasingly, to other forms of
> overt or covert negotiation by individuals acting – often unwittingly – in the name
> or the interest of the state.[31]

While Atlantic History received its organizational centre with the 'International Seminar on the History of the Atlantic World', established by Bernard Bailyn in 1995 at Harvard University,[32] transatlantic scholars created their Transatlantic Studies Association (TSA) in 2002, which was initially based at Dundee University and which publishes *The Journal of Transatlantic Studies*.[33] The concept of Transatlantic History espoused by this organization and its journal proves to be even more restrictive than the concept of Atlantic History. The editors of *The Journal of Transatlantic Studies* define the scope of their field as being limited to the period from 1945 to the present time. It also limits the geographic region to the North Atlantic and Northwestern Europe and is – when it comes to space and time frame – even more exclusive than the concept of Atlantic History.

A third and often overlooked approach to Atlantic and Transatlantic Studies has been the result of the rebranding of ethnic studies. In 1998 scholars from around the Atlantic founded the Society for Multi-Ethnic Studies: Europe and the Americas (MESA). Going beyond traditional academic divisions, this organization seeks to bridge literary and historical approaches towards the study of people who have lived in lands that surround the Atlantic. It created in 2004 with the journal *Atlantic Studies* an interdisciplinary journal that sought so far unsuccessfully to integrate various approaches to the study of the Atlantic World.[34]

Since Atlantic History comes, according to its proponents, to an end at around 1825 and Transatlantic History begins, according to its proponents, with the drawing of the United States into the First World War, the time in between – the nineteenth century – had become a black box in between both trans-oceanic approaches. This temporal gap and the arrival of Transnational History in the 1990s caused historians to reconsider concepts of Atlantic and Transatlantic History and the place of the nation state in nineteenth-century history.[35] The result was a new concept of Transatlantic History which was not defined solely by space (the Atlantic) but more importantly by the approach of Intercultural Transfer Studies. This approach emerged in the context of researching the mutual influences of French and German history from the eighteenth to the nineteenth centuries. The focus on intercultural transfers provided a useful instrument for historical inquiry into the transatlantic connections and exchanges that had been written out of history by national historians on both sides of the Atlantic.[36]

Processes of the transfer of material and immaterial goods between different cultures had already attracted the attention of historians interested in processes of Americanization. However, historians have all too hastily employed a terminology of copying, influencing, and modelling to label these processes. Many historians still embrace concepts of diffusion – of which the notion of Americanization is the most prominent – to conceptualize such transfers. Yet, neither of the terms of copying or modelling nor the idea of diffusion grasps the complexity of the processes of intercultural transfer. They mistake transfers as a one-way road. They wrongly strip the receiving culture of all agency. And they wrongly infer that the product transferred to the receiving culture is identical to the product provided by the giving culture. Such concepts simply cannot explain the conundrum of the modern world: that the world becomes more similar and more dissimilar at the same time.[37]

If we study intercultural transfers closely and attentively, we will see that phenomena transferred from one culture to another experienced significant mutations and transformations that occurred in the process of transfer and which were determined by the actions of the agents of transfer as well as the needs and expectations of the receiving culture. Intercultural transfers occurred because of a need to fill a perceived gap in the receiving culture. Transfers were often accompanied by a discourse in which the giving culture was described as being superior. However, the giving culture had no, or a very limited, role in the process of transfer beyond presenting a phenomenon for selection.[38]

The phenomenon selected for transfer was made to fit into the receiving society by members of that society. The fitting into the receiving society was often done in ways that the origins of the transferred phenomenon were almost obscured and members of the receiving culture began to believe over time that this phenomenon had always been part of their culture and history. Terminology and naming often obscured relatedness between objects in two different cultures. The study of intercultural transfers could, therefore, be compared to an archaeological excavation since the task of the scholar is to unearth connections and influences which have been buried deep under many layers of modification and interpretation.

Because of the transformations and mutations ideas and objects undergo in the process of intercultural transfer some scholars have doubted that such transfers actually occurred. For Gabriele Lingelbach, who studied the introduction of the 'German university model' into American higher education, public claims of American reformers such as Herbert Baxter Adams to having brought the superior model of German graduate education to American universities appear simply as a public relations trick rather than a successful implementation of a perceived German model.[39] The systems of education seemed to be too far apart, the understanding of German ways of instruction among American observers too superfluous, and the result of the publicly claimed transfer too different from graduate education at German universities. As Daniel T. Rodgers reminds us, however, no idea 'came through the transnational networks of debate and connection unaltered' and 'every imported idea and scheme was, by necessity, multiply transformed'.[40]

This new approach of Transatlantic History is based upon a concept of transnational history which emphasizes the interconnected nature of human experiences and cultures. In this radical reinterpretation of history, nation states are seen as superimposed upon cultures and societies over which they exercised only very limited control. Communities in distant regions and on opposite sides of an ocean were connected through travel and migration, which produced an ongoing and multi-directional transfer of ideas, concepts, and models for the organization of communities and civil society. Intercultural transfer contributed to the creation of urban infrastructures and cityscapes that included museums and opera houses, subways and streetcars as well as apartment buildings and city parks. All these institutions of modern cities resulted from intercultural transfers within the Atlantic World. These transfers were not the result of government activities but rather the outcome of the activities of non-governmental associations and individual citizens. If one explores these intercultural transfers and the integration of the transferred ideas and concepts, it becomes clear that nation states were not necessary to write the history of nineteenth-century cultures and societies within the Atlantic World.

The transfer of concepts for urban infrastructures occurred outside of the control of state governments, was initiated by members of the receiving societies, and involved multiple processes of modification and transformation of the idea transferred between the giving and the receiving end. In this interpretation of history, all cultures within the Atlantic World emerged as hybrid cultures that incorporated ideas and concepts from other cultures within the Atlantic World. This concept, thus, does not suggest that there was just one Atlantic culture or one Atlantic civilization. It rather proposes an understanding of the Atlantic World as a space created through human activities and the connections humans made in the process of populating and creating the Atlantic World.[41]

This approach of Transatlantic History still privileges the Atlantic World over other geographic regions, but in contrast to the concept of Atlantic History, it contains an innovative methodological and theoretical component which makes it possible to gain from the study of Atlantic societies and cultures insights that also might apply to other regions of the world. The Atlantic, thus, is no longer a preferred subject of investigation but just one example to gain fundamental insights into the nature of intercultural transfer. In the process, the concept of Intercultural Transfer has been advanced and expanded. The investigation of the transfer of holiday traditions such as Christmas from German-speaking Central Europe to the United States or the transfer of the game of football from Britain to various South American countries affords us opportunities to test the concept of intercultural transfer and to modify it based upon our findings. It has become clear from case studies that intercultural transfer succeeds only if initiated and controlled by the receiving society. Agents of intercultural transfer who almost always come from the receiving culture were in charge of selecting, modifying, transferring, and integrating ideas from one culture to another. From the beginning the receiving culture is in charge of the transfer.[42]

Travel and migration were conducive to intercultural transfer across the Atlantic, but in some cases such as the writings of Karl May, a German author who produced with his *Winnetou* novels iconic representations of American native people, travel was not part of the process. May received his ideas about American culture and landscapes from reading novels and travel reports written by authors who actually had been to North America. Yet, it was May who developed the image of America that stuck in the minds of many Europeans who have a concrete image of America in their minds long before (if ever) they encounter American society and landscapes.[43] While direct contact might not be a precondition for intercultural transfer, the contact of cultures was. And when cultures come into contact, something always results from this contact. It does not always lead to transfers; it can also result in the rejection of a certain cultural practice or idea. But this rejection occurred only because of the previous contact and is, thus, shaped by the contact. In other words, the rejection occurred only because of the contact.

Teaching Transatlantic History

This approach of Transatlantic History found its institutional home with the programme in Transatlantic History at the University of Texas at Arlington (UTA). The doctoral students of this programme established in 2000 the Transatlantic History Student Organization (THSO), which organized the annual graduate student workshop in Transatlantic History and which publishes, since 2011, the online journal *TRAVERSEA*.[44] The doctoral programme at UTA has been the only doctoral programme in the United States specifically dedicated – some would say limited – to the teaching and research of Transatlantic History. It was envisioned that this programme would break with national history in both structure and content. Steven Reinhardt, one of the programme's founders, suggested that this post-national concept of history is 'defined primarily by its conceptual approach, which focuses on the interconnectedness of human experience over the centuries in the Atlantic Basin'. It is, further, 'problem oriented and dedicated to analyzing the dynamic process of encounter and interchange among the peoples on all sides of the Atlantic Ocean'.[45] From these social and cultural interchanges hybrid identities and cultures emerged that formed the core characteristic of transatlantic communities.[46]

The PhD programme has been characterized by a very unique organization of course work. Instead of traditional courses, which would introduce the student to particular topics and problems within one national history, the courses designed for this programme were to provide a view across cultures and societies following a particular theme or topic. Students started with two introductory courses into Atlantic History and Transatlantic History. These courses were intended to provide an overview of the theoretical and methodological approaches towards these fields of history as well as an overview of the major works in the field. The first course was, following the more traditional and established approach of Atlantic History, focused on the times from 1492 to around 1800. The second course introduced students, following newer transnational approaches to history, to the long nineteenth century. This sequence of courses appeared to be necessary since the arrival of the nation state at the beginning of the nineteenth century was a turning point for history in the Atlantic World. Since proponents of Atlantic History have not developed a theoretical framework for their research and have deliberately defined their field to the time before the nation state, traditional accounts of Atlantic History cannot provide guidance for the interpretation of nineteenth-century history. While 1800 or 1825 is certainly not the end to Atlantic History, it is a turning point with regards to the theoretical and methodological approaches to history. Transatlantic History approaches for the nineteenth century have to deal with the concepts of nation and nation state. In this context, Transnational History and Intercultural Transfer Studies provide tools and frameworks that are essential to understand transatlantic cultures and societies in the nineteenth century.

Building upon these two introductory courses, students were expected to engage the four major themes of Transatlantic History – exploration and cartography, migration and settlement, revolutions and transformation, and identities and encounters – in four colloquia which were to provide a general introduction to the literature on these topics. Two research seminars provided students with the opportunity to research a particular topic of Transatlantic History in detail. All these classes were expected to be taught as topical classes rather than classes in American or European or African history. The fundamental principle of this programme was to break with the established national-history narratives in teaching and researching by forcing professors and students to go beyond national frameworks and to follow topics across regions, countries, and oceans. For both professors and students this innovative structure presented a serious challenge. When the programme was created in 1998, most professors were not prepared for leaving national history behind. Historians have been trained in national histories rather than comparative or transnational studies. Incoming students too had become used to choosing classes that were organized as courses in the history of a particular nation state and not according to topics and themes. For both sides, such a break, which represents nothing short of a decanonization – the gradual deconstruction of an established history canon – proves to be a long, complicated, and open-ended learning process.[47]

The general goal of the PhD programme at UTA was to present topics such as migration in their transatlantic setting and complexity. Leaving the notion of immigration history behind, courses in transatlantic migration required the professor to be proficient in the history of at least two national histories and the general theoretical debates on migration that is not part of just one national discourse.[48] It also includes what is frequently left out: the passage across the Atlantic and the discussion of migrants' identities. Migrants leaving German-speaking areas in Central and Eastern Europe for North and South America during the eighteenth and nineteenth centuries were often identified by the authorities created by colonial powers and the new states that took their place as Germans based on the language they spoke. Yet, these migrants probably would not have called themselves Germans when they left Prussia, Saxony, Bavaria, or the Volga region in Russia.[49] As Philip Otterness has shown in his masterful book about the German migration from the Palatinate in 1709/10, first to London and from there to British North America, identities created for the migrants by English authorities were sometimes quickly embraced by these migrants if they saw an advantage in accepting these identities. The very same migrants soon felt the pressure to adopt yet another identity: that of the receiving colony. This represents an interesting conundrum in that German-speaking migrants from Central Europe became Germans in the process of migration and, yet, they were also on their way to becoming Americans. Neither identity was fixed at the time. It offered migrants an opportunity to shape both identities.[50]

While students might already be acquainted with topics such as migration, colonization, and cartography, the study and teaching of intercultural transfers poses the greatest challenge to students. The transfer of ideas and concepts is not always visible since the ideas transferred have been modified in the process. The integration of these ideas and concepts into the receiving society led to the appropriation of the idea by the local population. Over decades and centuries, the idea transferred was integrated into the receiving culture so deeply that its members no longer remember that it once had been an alien idea and even suggest that this idea could only be a true part of their own culture. One such example would of course be the bagel.[51] Few Americans can identify the (Eastern European) origin of the bagel and instead assume that it has been part of American culture from its invention. Such transfers are often invisible to the untrained eye. Other cases such as the transfer of football from England to Germany are more visible and yet they are not necessarily easier to comprehend.

From fall 2011 to fall 2012, I organized a sequence of three courses with a group of twelve MA and PhD students to study the global transfer of football from its English home to places as far as Turkey, Argentina, the French Caribbean, and Mexico.[52] Each student was expected to pick one country matched with his or her language skills since this research project depended on studying secondary publications produced in the countries selected for this project. Students were asked to investigate the circumstances of transfer, the actors involved, the integration of the game into the receiving culture, and the changes that occurred in the process. All students made a series of presentations, first, of their research proposal and, second, of their research paper in which the concrete example was used to expand our understanding of how intercultural transfer works. It also revealed processes of identity construction since football quickly became integrated into national cultures and national identities. It further led students to explore the construction of founding myths about the arrival of football in a particular country and the creation of national football cultures. Working on these projects was a learning experience for all – students and professor – involved.

Football is a unique example when it comes to intercultural transfer. In spite of its deep integration into national cultures, its English origin is still rather visible and more or less known. The need to play against other teams from other cities and even other countries prevented the introduction of too many modifications to this object of transfer. The need for rules and regulations which provide a basis for competition as well as the formation of an international body – the Federation Internationale de Football (FIFA) – in 1904 assured a transnational football culture. In other cases such as holiday customs (Christmas) or the organization of art museums the origins of the underlying concepts are not so obvious.[53]

To make intercultural transfers visible in these cases, students need to acquire a solid understanding of at least two different cultures and they need to develop an eye for those elements of a particular culture that might be connected to elements of another culture. Since these elements are not always similar on their surface, students need to develop a sense for related historical phenomena, which have often been labelled in very distinct ways to create the image of separateness and uniqueness. A different terminology, as for instance in the case of philanthropy (in the United States) versus patronage (in Germany), does not point to different phenomena.[54] It rather reflects different intellectual traditions which led to different terminological systems. Differences in naming do not always represent differences in essence. The study of Intercultural Transfers, thus, involves studying phenomena beyond language (terminology) and context.

National histories and narratives still hold significant interpretative power over people in modern societies. Students grow up with the idea that American history is fundamentally different – even exceptional – from that of other countries.[55] High school and undergraduate education often unwittingly reinforce positions of American exceptionalism and superiority by limiting their scope needlessly to the American story instead of locating developments in American society and culture within its global setting. One of the greatest tasks is, therefore, to challenge established stereotypes presented by textbooks, teachers, and the media. The lack of textbooks with a transnational and transatlantic focus does not make things easier. Maria Grever recently argued with an eye on high school education and textbooks:

> A particularly difficult problem historians now face is how to write a readable (non-nationalist) history that can do justice to the plurality of voices. The urge to resuscitate national plot lines and relationships with the past that cannot really come to terms with our 'post-national' era tends to petrify historical consciousness, discouraging and obstructing dissenting perspectives.[56]

This problem becomes obvious on three different levels: (1) we need textbooks that are truly comparative in nature and which highlight the interconnectedness of the human experience. Most historical phenomena from institutions such as kindergartens to movements such as eugenics were global rather than national in scope and their story can only be told meaningfully from a global rather than a national perspective. Laws about forced sterilization introduced in states across the United States influenced the creation of similar laws across Europe in the 1920s and 1930s. And the American experience with forced sterilizations had an impact on eugenic practices in Nazi Germany during the 1930s. Any attempt to tell the story of eugenics in Nazi Germany separated from the story of eugenics in the United State distorts the historical record and would lead to serious misinterpretations.[57] (2) We need textbooks that offer a truly transnational terminology which is capable of providing terms for analyzing similar phenomena in different cultural settings across the Atlantic World. All too often do we encounter 'national' terminologies that refer to phenomena, which appear or are presented as specific to a particular culture. Differences in naming phenomena do not necessarily reflect structural differences. This becomes clear in the attempts by Sven Beckert to jumpstart research about the American bourgeoisie.[58] For many decades, American historians contended that there was no American bourgeoisie or that the American upper class could not be compared to the European bourgeoisie.[59] Terms such as 'middle class', 'upper class', 'bourgeoisie', 'Bürgertum', and 'leisure class' point to the confusion of concepts, descriptions, and interpretations. We need to find a transnational term that is suitable to be used as a descriptive term and concept for the American and the European context. Thorstein Veblen's concept of the leisure class, which refers to a social class defined by a public and excessive consumption of resources, seems to be the most suitable of the terms available.[60] (3) We need a new transnational history of the United States that takes the contributions of all migrant groups into account. The United States did not become a multicultural society through the addition of 'immigrants' and 'minorities', which were expected over time to assimilate to the dominant Anglo-Saxon culture; America was a multiethnic society from its founding. The American story cannot just be traced back to Jamestown, but needs to include the multiple founding of settlements by Spanish, Dutch, German, Russian and French people and provide an image of the United States as a state that included various language groups with distinct centres and particular shares in the shaping of American society from its inception. Such a contributionist paradigm should centre, as John Higham has insisted, on 'the relations between national identity and group identities'.[61] It should include discussions of integration, repression, and resistance. And it should answer the question raised by Kathleen Conzen about the contributions of migrants, in her case of German migrants, to American culture and society. We need to be able to answer her questions: 'What difference has it made to America that these people were here, and that they constructed for themselves the kinds of lives and ethnic cultures that they did?'[62]

Transnational and Transatlantic History has not been welcomed with open arms everywhere. Some see in Transnational History a danger for national history and the structures which are in place for history instruction. Abolishing national history would eradicate – that is the fear – positions and limit history instruction to an extended version of American history. The PhD programme at UTA had its critics inside and outside the history department and the university from its inception. Critics pointed out that the programme trained historians for a job market that is simply not there. And while many historians have embraced transnational approaches and the term 'transnational' is frequently used to spice up conference papers and book titles, a real job market for transnational and transatlantic historians has yet to emerge. There are no positions in Transnational History. H-NET has not even a category in its job database for 'transnational' or 'transatlantic' history positions. And even the leading proponents of Transnational History such as Thomas Bender and Ian Tyrrell continue to write books about the history of one nation (the United States), reinforcing the point that one is first a national historian and only second a transnational historian.[63] Writing a dissertation in Transnational and Transatlantic History appears to be career suicide. As Thomas N. Baker has recently observed:

> For all of post-modern scholars' efforts to deconstruct the myths and presuppositions that sustain nationalist modes of thinking, for instance, the shape and programs of many of today's academic departments continue to reflect the nationalist assumptions that the founders of the historical discipline took from their forebears. Graduate study programs (in many of the humanities and social sciences as well as in history departments themselves) more regularly offer 'national' fields of concentration than they do ones that are international or thematically comparative in scope.[64]

In order to break this mould, a complete and radical reorganization of history instruction in the United States is needed. The organization of history instruction along national lines is neither natural nor necessary. In an increasingly globalized world in which identities are more and more determined by transnational spaces created in the virtual world of the internet and online media such as Facebook, national history will quickly lose its relevance. If history as an academic discipline is to survive, it needs to connect to the new reality of its students and provide stories that have relevance in the modern world. Discussions about eugenics, the definition of family and marriage, migration and citizenship resonate with students who seek guidance for forming their opinion. The most successful classes I have taught involved group projects and group discussions about eugenics and end-of-life decisions (assisted suicide laws), which have gained significant ground in the United States over the last few years. History has the potential to provide a real and virtual space for discussions about central aspects of our lives in the twenty-first century by focusing on topics rather than the cramming of facts.

Notes

1 P. Saunier, *Transnational History* (New York: Palgrave Macmillan, 2013); T. Adam, *Intercultural Transfers and the Making of the Modern World: 1800–2000* (New York: Palgrave Macmillan, 2012); A. Iriye, *Global and Transnational History: The Past, Present, and Future* (New York: Palgrave Macmillan, 2013); I. Tyrrell, *Transnational Nation: United States History in Global Perspective since 1789* (New York: Palgrave Macmillan, 2007); T. Bender, *A Nation Among Nations: America's Place in World History* (New York: Hill & Wang, 2006).
2 Saunier, *Transnational History*, pp. 1–12; S. Conrad, *What is Global History?* (Princeton and Oxford: Princeton University Press, 2016); D. Olstein, *Thinking History Globally* (New York: Palgrave Macmillan, 2015).
3 T. Baker, 'National History in the Age of Michelet, Macaulay, and Bancroft', in L. Kramer and S. Maza (eds), *A Companion to Western Historical Thought* (Malden, MA, Oxford, and Carlton: Blackwell Publishing, 2006), p. 185.
4 *Ibid.*, pp. 185–6.
5 J. Breuilly, 'Historians and the Nation', in Peter Burke (ed.), *History and Historians in the Twentieth Century* (New York: Oxford University Press, 2002), pp. 55–87; S. Berger, 'The German Tradition of Historiography: 1800–1995', in Mary Fulbrook (ed.), *German History since 1800* (London: Arnold, 1997), pp. 477–92; E. Breisach, *Historiography: Ancient, Medieval & Modern* (Chicago and London: University of Chicago Press, 1999), pp. 228–67.
6 Berger, 'The German Tradition of Historiography: 1800–1995', p. 478.
7 *Ibid.*, p. 477; Baker, 'National History in the Age of Michelet, Macaulay, and Bancroft', p. 185.
8 G. Iggers, *Historiography in the Twentieth Century: From Scientific Objectivity to the Postmodern Challenge* (Hannover and London: Wesleyan University Press, 1997), pp. 78–94; Breisach, *Historiography*, pp. 291–302; R. Hofstadter and W. Metzger, *The Development of Academic Freedom in the United States* (New York: Columbia University Press, 1955), pp. 413–67.
9 The North Atlantic Treaty Organization (NATO) was founded in 1949 as a military defence alliance of Western powers including the United States, Belgium, Canada, Denmark, France, Iceland, Italy, Luxembourg, the Netherlands, Norway, Portugal, and the United Kingdom. Its goal was to protect Western European countries from Soviet aggression and initially a resurgence of German aggression.

10 The Warsaw Pact was founded in 1955 as a military defence alliance of Eastern European countries including the Soviet Union, Albania, Bulgaria, Czechoslovakia, East Germany, Hungary, Poland, and Romania. It was created after the admission of West Germany into NATO in 1955 and conceived of as a defence alliance against American aggression.

11 B. Bailyn, *Atlantic History: Concept and Contours* (Cambridge, MA and London: Harvard University Press, 2005), pp. 24–30; R. R. Palmer, *The Age of the Democratic Revolution: A Political History of Europe and America, 1760–1800* (Princeton: Princeton University Press, 1959–64); J. Godechot, *France and the Atlantic Revolution of the Eighteenth Century, 1770–1799* (New York: Free Press, 1965).

12 Bailyn, *Atlantic History*, pp. 62–3.

13 A. Crosby, *The Columbia Exchange: Biological and Cultural Consequences of 1492* (Westport: Greenwood Press, 1972).

14 B. Bailyn, *The Peopling of British North America: An Introduction* (New York: Alfred A. Knopf, 1986).

15 Bailyn, *Atlantic History*, p. 28.

16 P. Morgan and J. Green, 'Introduction: The Present State of Atlantic History', in J. P. Green and P. D. Morgan (eds), *Atlantic History: A Critical Appraisal* (Oxford and New York: Oxford University Press, 2009), p. 5.

17 P. Gilroy, *The Black Atlantic: Modernity and Double Consciousness* (Cambridge, MA: Harvard University Press, 1993).

18 See the articles about German migration and settlement in North and South America in T. Adam (ed.), *Germany and the Americas: Culture, Politics, and History*, 3 vols (Santa Barbara, Denver, and Oxford: ABC CLIO, 2005).

19 P. Otterness, *Becoming German: The 1709 Palatine Migration to New York* (Ithaca and London: Cornell University Press, 2004), pp. 113–54.

20 C. G. Calloway, 'Historical Encounters across Five Centuries', in C. G. Calloway, G. Gemünden, and S. Zantop (eds), *Germans and Indians: Fantasies, Encounters, Projections* (Lincoln and London: University of Nebraska Press, 2002), pp. 47–63.

21 Morgan and Green, 'Introduction', pp. 6, 9, 21.

22 D. Rodgers, *Atlantic Crossings: Social Politics in a Progressive Age* (Cambridge, MA and London: The Belknap Press of Harvard University Press, 1998), p. 1.

23 M. Rennella, *The Boston Cosmopolitans: International Travel and American Arts and Letters* (New York: Palgrave Macmillan, 2008), pp. 17–21.

24 Rodgers, *Atlantic Crossings*; T. Adam, *Buying Respectability: Philanthropy and Urban Society in Transnational Perspective, 1840s to 1930s* (Bloomington and Indianapolis: Indiana University Press, 2009).

25 R. Kroes, *If You've Seen One, You've Seen the Mall: Europeans and American Mass Culture* (Urbana: University of Illinois Press, 1996); J. Gienow-Hecht, *Transmission Impossible: American Journalism as Cultural Diplomacy in Postwar Germany, 1945–1955* (Baton Rouge: Louisiana State University Press, 1999); R. Willett, *The Americanization of Germany, 1945–1949* (New York: Routledge, 1989); V. Berghahn, *The Americanization of West German Industry* (Leamington Spa: Berg, 1986); D. Diner, *America in the Eyes of the Germans: An Essay on Anti-Americanism* (Princeton: Markus Wiener Publishers 1996); J. Servan-Schreiber, *The American Challenge* (New York: Atheneum, 1968).

26 R. L. Moore and M. Vaudagna (eds), *The American Century in Europe* (Ithaca: Cornell University Press, 2004); D. Junker, P. Gassert, W. Mausbach, and D. Morris (eds), *The*

United States and Germany in the Era of the Cold War, 2 vols (New York: Cambridge University Press, 2004); M. Jonas, *The United States and Germany: A Diplomatic History* (Ithaca: Cornell University Press, 1984).

27 V. de Grazia, *Irresistible Empire: America's Advance through Twentieth-Century Europe* (Cambridge, MA and London: The Belknap Press of Harvard University Press, 2005); G. Lundestadt, "'Empire by Invitation" in the American Century', *Diplomatic History*, 23 (1999), pp. 189–217; G. Lundestadt, *'Empire' by Integration: The United States and European Integration, 1945–1997* (Oxford: Oxford University Press, 1998).

28 J. Gienow-Hecht, *Sound Diplomacy: Music and Emotions in Transatlantic Relations, 1850–1920* (Chicago and London: University of Chicago Press, 2009), p. 3.

29 Iriye, *Global and Transnational History*, p. 8; J. Gienow-Hecht and F. Schumacher (eds), *Culture and International History* (New York: Berghahn Books, 2003).

30 Iriye, *Global and Transnational History*, p. 14.

31 Gienow-Hecht, *Sound Diplomacy*, p. 4.

32 www.fas.harvard.edu/~atlantic/ (accessed 9 April 2018).

33 www.transatlanticstudies.com/ (accessed 9 April 2018).

34 See for instance D. Gabaccia, 'A Long Atlantic in a Wider World', *Atlantic Studies*, 1:1 (2004), pp. 1–27.

35 Rodgers, *Atlantic Crossings*; Adam, *Buying Respectability*; S. Reinhardt and D. Reinhartz (eds), *Transatlantic History* (College Station: Texas A & M University Press, 2006); T. Adam and R. Gross (eds), *Traveling between Worlds: German-American Encounters* (College Station: Texas A & M University Press, 2006); T. Adam and U. Luebken (eds), *Beyond the Nation: United States History in Transnational Perspective* (Bulletin of the German Historical Institute Supplement Number 5) (Washington, DC: German Historical Institute, 2008).

36 M. Espagne and M. Werner, 'Deutsch-französischer Kulturtransfer als Forschungsgegenstand: Eine Problemskizze', in *Transferts: Les Relations Interculturelles dans L'Espace Franco-Allemand (XVIIIe et XIXe siècles). Textes réunis et présentés par Michel Espagne et Michael Werner* (Paris: Editions Recherches sur les Civilisations, 1988), pp. 11–34; G. Lingelbach, 'Intercultural Transfer and Comparative History: The Benefits and Limits of Two Approaches', *Traversea*, 1 (2011), pp. 1–14; J. Paulmann, 'Internationaler Vergleich und interkultureller Transfer: Zwei Forschungsansätze zur europäischen Geschichte des 18. bis 20. Jahrhunderts', *Historische Zeitschrift*, 267 (1998), pp. 649–85; M. Werner and B. Zimmermann, 'Beyond Comparison: Histoire Croisée and the Challenge of Reflexivity', *History and Theory*, 45 (February 2006), pp. 30–50.

37 T. Adam, 'New Ways to Write the History of Western Europe and the United States: The Concept of Intercultural Transfer', *History Compass*, 11:10 (2013), pp. 880–92; Adam, *Intercultural Transfers*, pp. 1–7.

38 Adam, 'New Ways to Write the History of Western Europe and the United States'; Adam, *Intercultural Transfers*, pp. 1–7.

39 G. Lingelbach, 'Cultural Borrowing or Autonomous Development: American and German Universities in the Late Nineteenth Century', in Adam and Gross, *Traveling between Worlds*, pp. 100–23.

40 Rodgers, *Atlantic Crossings*, p. 31.

41 Adam, *Intercultural Transfers*.

42 Adam, 'New Ways to Write the History of Western Europe and the United States'; T. Adam, 'The Intercultural Transfer of Football: The Contexts of Germany and Argentina', *Sport in Society*, 20:10 (2017), pp. 1371–89.

43 P. Goral, *Cold War Rivalry and the Perception of the American West* (New York: Palgrave Macmillan, 2014); see also H. Glenn Penny, *Kindred By Choice: Germans and American Indians since 1800* (Chapel Hill: University of North Carolina Press, 2015).

44 https://journals.tdl.org/traversea/index.php/traversea/index (accessed 9 April 2018).

45 Reinhardt and Reinhartz, *Transatlantic History*, p. ix.

46 D. Buisseret, 'Introduction', in D. Buisseret and S. Reinhardt (eds), *Creolization in the Americas* (College Station: Texas A & M University Press, 2000), p. 5.

47 M. Grever, 'Plurality, Narrative and the Historical Canon', in M. Grever and S. Stuurman (eds), *Beyond the Canon: History for the Twenty-First Century* (Basingstoke and New York: Palgrave Macmillan, 2007), pp. 31–47.

48 D. Hoerder, *Cultures in Contact: World Migrations in the Second Millennium* (Durham, NC: Duke University Press, 2002); D. Hoerder, 'Migrations and Belongings', in E. Rosenberg (ed.), *A World Connecting, 1870-1945* (Cambridge, MA and London: The Belknap Press of Harvard University Press, 2012), pp. 435–589.

49 D. Hoerder, 'The German-Language Diasporas: A Survey, Critique, and Interpretation', *Diaspora*, 11:1 (2002), pp. 7–44.

50 Otterness, *Becoming German*, pp. 37–112.

51 M. Balinska, *The Bagel: The Surprising History of a Modest Bread* (New Haven and London: Yale University Press, 2008).

52 This project was inspired by R. Wollons (ed.), *Kindergartens and Cultures: The Global Diffusion of an Idea* (New Haven and London: Yale University Press, 2000).

53 J. Perry, *Christmas in Germany: A Cultural History* (Chapel Hill: University of North Carolina Press, 2010); P. Restad, *Christmas in America: A History* (New York and Oxford: Oxford University Press, 1995); Adam, *Buying Respectability*, pp. 13–31; A. Wallach, 'The Birth of the American Art Museum', in S. Beckert and J. Rosenbaum (eds), *The American Bourgeoisie: Distinction and Identity in the Nineteenth Century* (New York: Palgrave Macmillan, 2010), pp. 247–56.

54 T. Adam (ed.), *Philanthropy, Patronage, and Civil Society: Experiences from Germany, Great Britain, and North America* (Bloomington: Indiana University Press, 2004); T. Adam, S. Lässig, and G. Lingelbach (eds), *Stifter, Spender und Mäzene: USA und Deutschland im historischen Vergleich* (Stuttgart: Franz Steiner Verlag, 2009).

55 D. T. Rogers, 'Exceptionalism', in A. Molho and G. Wood (eds), *Imagined Histories: American Historians Interpret the Past* (Princeton: Princeton University Press, 1998), pp. 21–40.

56 Grever, 'Plurality, Narrative and the Historical Canon', p. 32.

57 Adam, *Intercultural Transfers*, pp. 60–76.

58 S. Beckert and J. B. Rosenbaum (eds), *The American Bourgeoisie: Distinction and Identity in the Nineteenth Century* (New York: Palgrave Macmillan, 2010); S. Beckert, *The Monied Metropolis: New York City and the Consolidation of the American Bourgeoisie, 1850-1896* (Cambridge, MA: Cambridge University Press, 2001).

59 J. Kocka and A. Mitchell (eds), *Bourgeois Society in Nineteenth-Century Europe* (Oxford and Providence: Berg, 1993).

60 T. Veblen, *The Theory of the Leisure Class: An Economic Study of Institutions* (New York: Modern Library, 1934), pp. 68–101.

61 Cited after K. Neils Conzen, 'Phantom Landscapes of Colonization: Germans in the Making of a Pluralist America', in F. Trommler and E. Shore (eds), *The German-American Encounter: Conflict and Cooperation between Two Cultures, 1800-2000* (New York and Oxford: Berghahn Books, 2001), p. 10.

62 *Ibid.*, p. 10.
63 Bender, *A Nation Among Nations*; Tyrrell, *Transnational Nation*.
64 Baker, 'National History in the Age of Michelet, Macaulay, and Bancroft', p. 201.

References

Adam, T. *Buying Respectability: Philanthropy and Urban Society in Transnational Perspective, 1840s to 1930s* (Bloomington and Indianapolis: Indiana University Press, 2009).

Adam, T. (ed.), *Germany and the Americas: Culture, Politics, and History*, 3 vols. (Santa Barbara, Denver, and Oxford: ABC CLIO, 2005).

Adam, T. 'The Intercultural Transfer of Football: The Contexts of Germany and Argentina', *Sport in Society*, 20:10 (2017), pp. 1371–89.

Adam, T. *Intercultural Transfers and the Making of the Modern World: 1800–2000* (New York: Palgrave Macmillan, 2012).

Adam, T. 'New Ways to Write the History of Western Europe and the United States: The Concept of Intercultural Transfer', *History Compass*, 11:10 (2013), pp. 880–92.

Adam, T. (ed.), *Philanthropy, Patronage, and Civil Society: Experiences from Germany, Great Britain, and North America* (Bloomington: Indiana University Press, 2004).

Adam, T. and R. Gross (eds), *Traveling between Worlds: German-American Encounters* (College Station: Texas A & M University Press, 2006).

Adam, T. and U. Luebken (eds), *Beyond the Nation: United States History in Transnational Perspective* (Bulletin of the German Historical Institute Supplement Number 5) (Washington, DC: German Historical Institute, 2008).

Adam, T., S. Lässig, and G. Lingelbach (eds), *Stifter, Spender und Mäzene: USA und Deutschland im historischen Vergleich* (Stuttgart: Franz Steiner Verlag, 2009).

Bailyn, B. *Atlantic History: Concept and Contours* (Cambridge, MA and London: Harvard University Press, 2005).

Bailyn, B. *The Peopling of British North America: An Introduction* (New York: Alfred A. Knopf, 1986).

Baker, T. 'National History in the Age of Michelet, Macaulay, and Bancroft', in Lloyd Kramer and Sarah Maza (eds), *A Companion to Western Historical Thought* (Malden, MA, Oxford, and Carlton: Blackwell Publishing, 2006).

Balinska, M. *The Bagel: The Surprising History of a Modest Bread* (New Haven and London: Yale University Press, 2008).

Beckert, S. *The Monied Metropolis: New York City and the Consolidation of the American Bourgeoisie, 1850–1896* (Cambridge, MA: Cambridge University Press, 2001).

Beckert, S. and J. B. Rosenbaum (eds), *The American Bourgeoisie: Distinction and Identity in the Nineteenth Century* (New York: Palgrave Macmillan, 2010).

Bender, T. *A Nation Among Nations: America's Place in World History* (New York: Hill & Wang, 2006).

Berger, S. 'The German Tradition of Historiography: 1800–1995', in Mary Fulbrook (ed.), *German History since 1800* (London: Arnold, 1997), pp. 477–92.

Berghahn, V. *The Americanization of West German Industry* (Leamington Spa: Berg, 1986).

Breisach, E. *Historiography: Ancient, Medieval & Modern* (Chicago and London: University of Chicago Press, 1999).

Breuilly, J. 'Historians and the Nation', in Peter Burke (ed.), *History and Historians in the Twentieth Century* (New York: Oxford University Press, 2002), pp. 55–87.

Buisseret, D. 'Introduction', in D. Buisseret and S. Reinhardt (eds), *Creolization in the Americas* (College Station: Texas A & M University Press, 2000), pp. 3–17.

Calloway, C. G. 'Historical Encounters across Five Centuries', in Colin G. Calloway, Gerd Gemünden, and Susanne Zantop (eds), *Germans and Indians: Fantasies, Encounters, Projections* (Lincoln and London: University of Nebraska Press, 2002), pp. 47–63.

Conrad, S. *What is Global History?* (Princeton and Oxford: Princeton University Press, 2016).

Crosby, A. *The Columbia Exchange: Biological and Cultural Consequences of 1492* (Westport: Greenwood Press, 1972).

Diner, D. *America in the Eyes of the Germans: An Essay on Anti-Americanism* (Princeton: Markus Wiener Publishers, 1996).

Espagne, M. and M. Werner. 'Deutsch-französischer Kulturtransfer als Forschungsgegenstand: Eine Problemskizze', in *Transferts: Les Relations Interculturelles dans L'Espace Franco-Allemand (XVIIIe et XIXe Siècle). Textes réunis et présentés par Michel Espagne et Michael Werner* (Paris: Editions Recherce sur les Civilisations, 1988), pp. 11–34.

Gabaccia, D. 'A Long Atlantic in a Wider World', *Atlantic Studies*, 1:1 (2004), pp. 1–27.

Gienow-Hecht, J. *Sound Diplomacy: Music and Emotions in Transatlantic Relations, 1850–1920* (Chicago and London: University of Chicago Press, 2009).

Gienow-Hecht, J. *Transmission Impossible: American Journalism as Cultural Diplomacy in Postwar Germany, 1945–1955* (Baton Rouge: Louisiana State University Press, 1999).

Gienow-Hecht, J. and F. Schumacher (eds), *Culture and International History* (New York: Berghahn Books, 2003).

Gilroy, P. *The Black Atlantic: Modernity and Double Consciousness* (Cambridge, MA: Harvard University Press, 1993).

Glenn Penny, H. *Kindred By Choice: Germans and American Indians since 1800* (Chapel Hill: University of North Carolina Press, 2015).

Godechot, J. *France and the Atlantic Revolution of the Eighteenth Century, 1770–1799* (New York: Free Press, 1965).

Goral, P. *Cold War Rivalry and the Perception of the American West* (New York: Palgrave Macmillan, 2014).

de Grazia, V. *Irresistible Empire: America's Advance through Twentieth-Century Europe* (Cambridge, MA and London: The Belknap Press of Harvard University Press, 2005).

Grever, M. 'Plurality, Narrative and the Historical Canon', in M. Grever and S. Stuurman (eds), *Beyond the Canon: History for the Twenty-First Century* (Basingstoke and New York: Palgrave Macmillan, 2007), pp. 31–47.

Hoerder, D. *Cultures in Contact: World Migrations in the Second Millennium* (Durham, NC: Duke University Press, 2002).

Hoerder, D. 'The German-Language Diasporas: A Survey, Critique, and Interpretation', *Diaspora*, 11:1 (2002), pp. 7–44.

Hoerder, D. 'Migrations and Belongings', in E. Rosenberg (ed.), *A World Connecting, 1870–1945* (Cambridge, MA and London: The Belknap Press of Harvard University Press, 2012), pp. 435–589.

Hofstadter, R. and W. Metzger. *The Development of Academic Freedom in the United States* (New York: Columbia University Press, 1955).

Iggers, G. *Historiography in the Twentieth Century: From Scientific Objectivity to the Postmodern Challenge* (Hannover and London: Wesleyan University Press, 1997).

Iriye, A. *Global and Transnational History: The Past, Present, and Future* (New York: Palgrave Macmillan, 2013).

Jonas, M. *The United States and Germany: A Diplomatic History* (Ithaca: Cornell University Press, 1984).

Junker, D., P. Gassert, W. Mausbach, and D. Morris (eds), *The United States and Germany in the Era of the Cold War*, 2 vols (New York: Cambridge University Press, 2004).

Kocka, J. and A. Mitchell (eds), *Bourgeois Society in Nineteenth-Century Europe* (Oxford and Providence: Berg, 1993).

Kroes, R. *If You've Seen One, You've Seen the Mall: Europeans and American Mass Culture* (Urbana: University of Illinois Press, 1996).

Lingelbach, G. 'Cultural Borrowing or Autonomous Development: American and German Universities in the Late Nineteenth Century', in T. Adam and R. Gross (eds), *Traveling between Worlds: German-American Encounters* (College Station: Texas A & M University Press, 2006), pp. 100–23.

Lingelbach, G. 'Intercultural Transfer and Comparative History: The Benefits and Limits of Two Approaches', *Traversea*, 1 (2011), pp. 1–14.

Lundestadt, G. '"Empire by Invitation" in the American Century', *Diplomatic History*, 23 (1999), pp. 189–217.

Lundestadt, G. *'Empire' by Integration: The United States and European Integration, 1945–1997* (Oxford: Oxford University Press, 1998).

Moore, R. L. and M. Vaudagna (eds), *The American Century in Europe* (Ithaca: Cornell University Press, 2004).

Morgan, P. and J. Green. 'Introduction: The Present State of Atlantic History', in J. P. Green and P. D. Morgan (eds), *Atlantic History: A Critical Appraisal* (Oxford and New York: Oxford University Press, 2009), pp. 3–34.

Neils Conzen, K. 'Phantom Landscapes of Colonization: Germans in the Making of a Pluralist America', in F. Trommler and E. Shore (eds), *The German-American Encounter: Conflict and Cooperation between Two Cultures, 1800–2000* (New York and Oxford: Berghahn Books, 2001), pp. 7–21.

Olstein, D. *Thinking History Globally* (New York: Palgrave Macmillan, 2015).

Otterness, P. *Becoming German: The 1709 Palatine Migration to New York* (Ithaca and London: Cornell University Press, 2004).

Palmer, R. R. *The Age of the Democratic Revolution: A Political History of Europe and America, 1760–1800* (Princeton: Princeton University Press, 1959–64).

Paulmann, J. 'Internationaler Vergleich und interkultureller Transfer: Zwei Forschungsansätze zur europäischen Geschichte des 18. bis 20. Jahrhunderts', *Historische Zeitschrift*, 267 (1998), pp. 649–85.

Perry, J. *Christmas in Germany: A Cultural History* (Chapel Hill: University of North Carolina Press, 2010).

Reinhardt, S. and D. Reinhartz (eds), *Transatlantic History* (College Station: Texas A & M University Press, 2006).

Rennella, M. *The Boston Cosmopolitans: International Travel and American Arts and Letters* (New York: Palgrave Macmillan, 2008).

Restad, P. *Christmas in America: A History* (New York and Oxford: Oxford University Press, 1995).

Rodgers, D. T. *Atlantic Crossings: Social Politics in a Progressive Age* (Cambridge, MA and London: The Belknap Press of Harvard University Press, 1998).

Rogers, D. T. 'Exceptionalism', in A. Molho and G. Wood (eds), *Imagined Histories: American Historians Interpret the Past* (Princeton: Princeton University Press, 1998), pp. 21–40.

Saunier, P. *Transnational History* (New York: Palgrave Macmillan, 2013).

Servan-Schreiber, J. *The American Challenge* (New York: Atheneum, 1968).

Tyrrell, I. *Transnational Nation: United States History in Global Perspective since 1789* (New York: Palgrave Macmillan, 2007).

Veblen, T. *The Theory of the Leisure Class: An Economic Study of Institutions* (New York: Modern Library, 1934).

Wallach, A. 'The Birth of the American Art Museum', in S. Beckert and J. Rosenbaum (eds), *The American Bourgeoisie: Distinction and Identity in the Nineteenth Century* (New York: Palgrave Macmillan, 2010), pp. 247–56.

Werner, M. and B. Zimmermann, 'Beyond Comparison: Histoire Croisée and the Challenge of Reflexivity', *History and Theory*, 45 (February 2006), pp. 30–50.

Willett, R. *The Americanization of Germany, 1945–1949* (New York: Routledge, 1989).

Wollons, R. (ed.), *Kindergartens and Cultures: The Global Diffusion of an Idea* (New Haven and London: Yale University Press, 2000).

Index

EU authorised representative for GPSR:
Easy Access System Europe, Mustamäe tee 50,
10621 Tallinn, Estonia
gpsr.requests@easproject.com

www.ingramcontent.com/pod-product-compliance
Lightning Source LLC
Chambersburg PA
CBHW052007270326
41929CB00015B/2822